THE CHAKMAS OF ARUNACHAL PRADESH

HISTORY, CHALLENGES, AND ASPIRATIONS

ARUNJIT KAMBEY CHAKMA

Made with ❤ on the Notion Press Platform

www.notionpress.com

DEDICATION

This book is dedicated to the unsung heroes who paved the way: the first-generation Chakma migrants whose resilience and fortitude laid the foundation for generations to come, and the tireless activists who championed the Chakma rights cause. Their courage is the bedrock upon which this story is built.

CONTENTS

PREFACE

The prevailing narrative concerning the Chakma and Hajong People of Arunachal Pradesh is primarily a political construct imposed upon the populace. Unfortunately, it has now become a widely accepted historical account.

It is imperative to challenge and rewrite this narrative, as it inaccurately portrays the Chakma and Hajong people as threats to indigenous communities, responsible for demographic imbalances, encroachments, and criminal activities. Their history is one of acceptance, brotherhood, and mutual respect. Moreover, it reflects the values of Indian culture, as evidenced by the government's policies for rehabilitating displaced citizens of undivided India.

This narrative lacks a factual foundation; it is a product of the political class's interpretation. These politicians disseminated their propaganda, shaping public perception. Thus, it is crucial to reclaim this history from those who wielded political power and dictated the narrative.

The influence of this narrative was so profound that it gave rise to the "anti-foreigner" movement in the late 1980s, shaping the state's political discourse. Even the victims themselves came to accept this narrative. Credit must be given to the state's political class for creating a political instrument that allowed student leaders to ascend the political hierarchy and political leaders to attain higher positions.

The narrative effectively white-washed the wrongdoings inflicted upon the Chakma people and made them believe a story that was not theirs, nor was it true. This psychological impact led the victims to develop a sense of "Fake Guilt," despite their resettlement in NEFA being a result of a well-defined rehabilitation plan implemented by the Government of India.

The absence of a comprehensive organic historical narrative regarding the Chakmas and Hajongs in Arunachal Pradesh has left a void in scholarly literature and understanding. This gap has allowed a particular narrative, potentially influenced by selective state government documents like the 1996 white paper on Chakma and Hajongs, to gain prominence. As independent scholars and researchers grapple with insufficient sources, their reliance on these limited documents might inadvertently perpetuate a narrative that lacks the depth and nuance necessary to comprehensively understand the organic history, culture, and experiences of these communities within the region.

The reliance on such selective documents poses the risk of shaping a skewed perception of the Chakma and Hajong communities, potentially overlooking crucial aspects of their history and lived experiences. Without a broader range of sources or comprehensive research, there's a danger of perpetuating a narrative that might not accurately reflect the complex reality and diverse perspectives within these communities, leaving their true history and heritage underrepresented or misunderstood.

The portrayal of the Chakma and Hajong communities as outsiders, illegal migrants, refugees, or infiltrators within their own historical narrative imposed a challenging situation upon them. This narrative, perpetuated by several authors, scholars, and writers, essentially framed their story within the context of being perceived as outsiders in the region where they've lived for generations. This skewed portrayal forced the Chakmas and Hajongs into a defensive position, leading them to seek legal recognition of their citizenship in courts, inadvertently validating the narrative propagated by politicians. By engaging in legal battles to establish their citizenship, they unintentionally reinforced the misconception that they were indeed outsiders needing to prove their right to belong.

However, it's essential to recognize a crucial nuance in this scenario. Among the six million individuals who migrated to India from undivided India until 1971, not all pursued or obtained official citizenship certificates. This absence of formal documentation doesn't invalidate their status as Indian citizens. The government's primary focus during that period was on the rehabilitation of these migrants rather than strictly issuing citizenship certificates. The emphasis was on integrating these communities into Indian society, ensuring their resettlement and well-being, rather than solely on the bureaucratic process of documenting their citizenship status. Therefore, the lack of formal certificates does not diminish their rightful status as Indian citizens, as the government's priority lay in their rehabilitation and inclusion rather than the administrative formality of citizenship documentation.

Citizenship formed an integral part of the government's overarching rehabilitation policy, especially within the Ministry of Rehabilitation & Relief (R&R), which was dedicated to executing this policy efficiently. However, the sheer scale of this initiative posed significant logistical hurdles. The task of granting citizenship certificates to the vast number of displaced persons scattered across India proved immensely challenging. As a result, many displaced individuals, despite being considered citizens, ended up living without the formal documentation to validate their citizenship status. The procedural complexities and the overwhelming number of individuals involved made it impractical to ensure that every deserving citizen received the official certification, leading to a scenario where numerous people lived and functioned as citizens without the tangible proof of citizenship in the form of certificates.

The primary focus of the Ministry of Rehabilitation & Relief lay in the comprehensive resettlement and integration of displaced individuals into Indian society rather than the meticulous administration of citizenship documentation. The emphasis was on providing shelter, support, and opportunities for these displaced persons to rebuild their lives within the country. Consequently, while citizenship was an inherent aspect of this rehabilitation effort, the logistical challenges meant that many individuals, despite being considered citizens, navigated life without the formal endorsement of citizenship certificates due to the practical constraints of the certification process.

The decision to settle the Chakma and Hajong people in NEFA (now Arunachal Pradesh) was made following extensive discussions between the Government of India, NEFA administration and its local leaders. This strategic policy decision, prompted by the outcome of the Indo-Sino war of 1962, led to a re-evaluation of NEFA's administrative policies. Similar schemes were also sanctioned for settling ex-servicemen in strategically important areas like Vijaynagar, Seijosa, and Imboliang.

Given that the settlement of the Chakma and Hajongs in NEFA was carried out under the rehabilitation policy of the Government of India, in addition to strategic considerations, and with the Union Government overseeing the area, it is reasonable to conclude that the Chakma and Hajongs were made citizens of the country by default and were exempted from the Bengal Eastern Frontier Regulations Act, 1873, and Chin Hills Regulations Act, 1896.

In support of this view, the Honourable Gauhati High Court made a similar observation in a 2013 case when the All–Arunachal Pradesh Student's Union (AAPSU) challenged the Election Commission of India's special guidelines. The court stated that settling these Chakma refugees in Arunachal Pradesh in consultation with the state authorities made them residents of Arunachal Pradesh, eliminating the need for Inner Line Permits. Furthermore, any other interpretation would undermine the policy decision made by the Government of India in collaboration with the Arunachal Pradesh authorities regarding the settlement of Chakmas in the state.

However, despite their crucial importance, these fundamental aspects are often relegated to the sidelines in the narrative of the Chakmas in Arunachal Pradesh. Hence, the urgent need arises to meticulously document an organic history of the Chakmas. This endeavour becomes pivotal primarily due to the pressing necessity to dispel a myriad of misconceptions and misinterpretations clouding the discourse around the Chakma community.

Moreover, the documentation of this comprehensive historical account serves as a beacon for future generations, offering them a profound insight into their roots and nurturing a strong sense of identity and pride. It stands poised to debunk entrenched misconceptions and stereotypes that have unfairly permeated the narrative surrounding the Chakma people, countering narratives often sculpted by biased sources or political motivations.

Thirdly, there's a profound aspiration that this meticulously crafted organic history will serve as a catalyst, fostering a climate of understanding and empathy among the diverse communities within the state. By illuminating the Chakma people's experiences, trials, and invaluable contributions, it seeks to cultivate empathy and respect, laying the groundwork for enhanced relationships and harmonious coexistence among disparate societal groups.

Furthermore, the significance of this extensively documented history extends to its potential impact on policymakers, scholars, and organisations. It stands poised to offer critical insights into the needs, challenges, and aspirations of the Chakma community. These insights serve as a guiding light, shaping the formulation of more inclusive policies, facilitating judicious resource allocation, and ensuring that their rights and concerns receive the requisite attention and action.

In essence, this organic story of the Chakma people of Arunachal Pradesh isn't just about chronicling the past; it's about affirming their identity, promoting understanding, and ensuring that their story is rightfully acknowledged and respected.

Arunjit Kambey Chakma

ACKNOWLEDGEMENTS

Unravelling the intricate tapestry of the Chakma people's journey – from their migration history, the rehabilitation process initiated by the Government of India, their initial challenges, and into the complexities of contemporary challenges – demanded a comprehensive and meticulous investigation. This endeavour would have been insurmountable without the invaluable contributions of countless individuals.

I am deeply indebted to the hundreds of first-generation Chakma leaders whose firsthand accounts, shared data, and unwavering support formed the bedrock of this research. Their wisdom and generosity have enriched this work immeasurably.

The National Archives of India and the Assam Archives deserve special recognition for their indispensable assistance in providing digitized materials that illuminated the historical dimensions of this study.

I extend my heartfelt thanks to Tufan Chakma, an Indigenous visual artist and storyteller from the Chittagong Hill Tracts, Bangladesh, for allowing me to use one of his poignant art pieces depicting Bor-Porong (The Great Migration). His artwork beautifully complements the theme of this book.

Arunjit Kambey Chakma

PROLOGUE

In 1964, the Chakmas and Hajongs, a collective of 15,000 souls, embarked on a poignant migration to India. This mass exodus from erstwhile East Pakistan was set in motion by the harrowing spectre of large-scale communal violence, which ignited in January of that fateful year. The systematic persecution of minorities had rendered their homeland in the Chittagong Hill Tracts (CHT) for the predominantly Buddhist Chakmas and the Mymensingh District for the Hindu Hajongs in present-day Bangladesh and the surrounding regions, an inhospitable place devoid of peace and dignity.

The Chakmas, who are predominantly followers of Buddhism, had traditionally inhabited the Chittagong Hill Tracts (CHT), while the Hindu Hajongs resided in the Mymensingh District of present-day Bangladesh and the surrounding areas. These territories have since become part of the border states of Mizoram, Assam, Tripura, West Bengal, and Meghalaya on the Indian side. Their historical roots in these regions trace back to time immemorial, underscoring their indigenous connection to these lands.

Understanding their historical context is of paramount importance, particularly considering the unfortunate use of terms such as "outsiders," "migrants," and "refugees" in post-independence narratives concerning the Chakmas. It is worth noting that, except for Arunachal Pradesh, the Chakmas are officially recognized as Scheduled Tribes in the states of Assam, Mizoram, Tripura, Meghalaya, and West Bengal. This recognition acknowledges their indigenous heritage and identity. Furthermore, the Chakmas once ruled their own kingdom and have their own king even to this day.

Relevant historical research sheds light on the Chakmas and their historical presence during the British colonial period. An important scholarly work, "Chakma Resistance to British Domination 1772-1798," authored by Suniti Bhushan Qanungo, a Professor in the Department of History at Chittagong University, delves into this subject. This comprehensive study provides a detailed examination of British policies towards the Chakmas, which ultimately sparked resistance against British imperialism and a struggle for independence, opposing the establishment of colonial rule in the conquered territories.

The period of Chakma resistance, spanning from 1772 to 1798, was characterised by the British government's systematic deprivation of the Chakmas' property rights. What remains relatively obscure in historical accounts is the vigorous resistance mounted by the Chakmas against British colonial rule, resulting in significant loss of lives and property. Instances of revolt and resistance were prevalent, and the author aptly characterises this resistance as “a fight fought by unconquered people in a conquered territory.” Despite the annexation of their territories through the deployment of superior weaponry and the might of colonial forces, the Chakma fighters retained an indomitable spirit that could not be subdued.

The Chakma's unwavering loyalty to India stands out as a remarkable aspect of their political alignment. As demonstrated earlier, this loyalty has deep historical roots, extending back to the British colonial era and the Chakma resistance. Well before the Revolt of 1857 and the initial struggle for independence, the Chakmas, along with other local tribes, engaged in skirmishes, revolts, and rebellions against British rule—events that were previously lesser known. It was a twist of fate and historical circumstance that led to the division of the region they inhabited, resulting in portions falling within both India and Pakistan. Unfortunately, most of their homeland, located in the Chittagong Hill Tracts, ended up under Pakistani jurisdiction, contrary to the fervent desires of the Chakma people, who had always yearned to remain within the Indian Territory.[1]

Partition – A Historical Injustice against the Chakmas

The Chakmas actively participated in the Indian Independence movement. While their specific contributions may not be as widely recognized as some other leaders of the Indian freedom movement, they played a role in various ways and were part of the collective effort that led to India gaining freedom from British colonial rule in 1947. They actively participated in various ways, including joining Mahatma Gandhi's Non-Cooperation Movement in the 1920s, engaging in civil disobedience, raising awareness about colonial injustices, and supporting the Quit India Movement in 1942. Like other indigenous communities, they resisted oppressive British policies affecting their land and resources, contributing to the broader anti-colonial sentiment that ultimately led to India's independence from British rule.

During the volatile period of India's Partition in 1947, the leaders of the Chittagong Hill Tracts, led by the Chakma Raja, Nalinaksha Roy, made significant representations to various authorities. On April 4th, 1947, they approached the Advisor Sub Committee of Excluded & Partially Excluded Areas other than Assam. Their primary plea was to acknowledge the existing Chakma, Mong, and Bohmong "Circles" as constitutional states within the Union of India. They proposed a confederation wherein these states would join hands with neighbouring regions like Tripura, Cooch Behar, Manipur, and Khasi States to form a cohesive unit under the Indian Union.

Later, on April 25th of the same year, these leaders met with Sir Eric Mieville, the Principal Secretary of the Viceroy & Governor General of India, reiterating their reluctance to

---

[1] *Chakma Resistance to British Domination 1772-1798 by Suniti Bhushan Qanungo, Professor, Department of History at Chittagong University*

be part of East Pakistan. Instead, they suggested forming a unified entity with Tripura, Manipur, and the Khasi states, who showed willingness to embrace them.

Again, on June 1st, 1947, the Chakma Raja and other tribal Chiefs petitioned the Prime Minister, Secretary of State for India, Viceroy & Governor General of India, and Governor of Bengal. In this appeal, they acted as emissaries conveying the collective voice and aspirations of the Chakma and other tribal people residing in the Chittagong Hill Tracts. Their overarching request remained consistent: the formal recognition of their "Circles" as constitutional states under the Union of India. These efforts underscored their persistent pursuit of autonomy and a distinct political identity within the framework of a changing geopolitical landscape during the Partition.

During the political turmoil of partition of India, the Chakma Raja and Sneha Kumar Chakma, the leader of the Chakma community, held meetings and submitted petitions to national leaders, including Mahatma Gandhi, Pt. Jawaharlal Nehru, and Sardar Vallabhbhai Patel, requested their intervention for inclusion of their homeland, the Chittagong Hill Tracts (CHT), which had a population primarily consisting of non-Muslims (97%), into India. Despite receiving assurances and support, it was unfortunate that their territory was ultimately included in Pakistan, a decision that contradicted the foundational principles of the two-nation theory. Pandit Nehru himself assured the Chakmas that the Bengal Boundary Commission had no jurisdiction over CHT. Mr. Sneha Kumar Chakma also fervently presented the case for CHT's inclusion in India during the hearings conducted by the Bengal Boundary Commission on July 14th and 19th, 1947.

The partition of India along religious lines meant that the Chittagong Hill Tracts (CHT), with its overwhelmingly non-Muslim population of 97%, predominantly Buddhists, logically should have remained with India.

On August 15, 1947, the Chakmas celebrated Independence Day by raising the Indian flag in Rangamati, the capital of the Chittagong Hill Tracts, in the presence of Col. G.L. Hyde, the Deputy Commissioner of CHT oblivious of the unfortunate fact that the Boundary Commission led by Cyril Redcliff had awarded their homeland to the Pakistan dominion against the will of the Chakmas.

Their shock came on the evening of August 17, 1947, when they learned through a radio broadcast that the CHT had been awarded to Pakistan. The Chakmas strongly opposed this decision and the Chakma Raja (King) resolved not to accept the Radcliffe Award that granted the CHT to Pakistan, vowing to resist it with armed resistance. Sneha Kumar Chakma, a freedom fighter, was immediately sent on a mission to seek arms and support from India while evading arrest.

On August 25, 1947, the Baloch Regiment of the Pakistani Army forcefully removed the Indian flag in the Chittagong Hill Tracts (CHT). At gunpoint, they entered the region and arrested and imprisoned hundreds of Chakmas who had been fighting for the inclusion of the CHT with India. Many prominent leaders who advocated for the CHTs' merger with India were charged with sedition and executed by hanging. To avoid arrest and execution as traitors by the Pakistani Government, hundreds of leaders had to flee the CHT and seek refuge in India.

Sneha Kumar Chakma, accompanied by his aides, approached Sardar Patel to seek support for the merger of the CHTs with India and to request the supply of arms and ammunition to fight against the Pakistani army. The Deputy Prime Minister readily agreed to assist and advised Chakma to also meet with Pandit Nehru regarding this matter. However, it took Chakma 50 days to finally meet Pandit Nehru. Upon hearing the Chakmas' plea, Nehru strongly responded, asking if they intended to subject India to foreign rule once again.

Chakma leaders, such as Sneha Kumar Chakma and Lieutenant Kamini Mohan Dewan, made multiple trips to New Delhi to meet with national leaders, including

Jawaharlal Nehru and Sardar Vallabhbhai Patel, in their efforts to merge the CHT with India.

Despite the formation of a Sub-Committee to consider the demands of the Chakmas and other indigenous peoples of the CHTs, Nehru's dismissive stance on the issue yielded no positive outcome. He refused to assist, fearing that military conflict over the Chittagong Hill Tracts might attract British involvement in India once again.

Nehru's position disheartened the Chakmas, but the Chakma Raja, tribal Rajas, and Chakma leaders continued to petition the Indian Government for the merger of the CHTs with India.

LETTER FROM CHAKMA RAJA TO SARDAR PATEL[2]

Rangamati, Rajbari
HITTAGONG HILL TRACTS
28.8.47

Confidential

D.O. 397

Dear Sir,

I myself and on behalf of the other two Chiefs the Bohomong and Mong and the entire population of the Chittagong Hill Tracts which comprises over 97% non-Muslim inhabitants, were thunderstruck and mortally mortified to hear the announcement of the Boundary Commission on the 18th placing us most unprecedently in Eastern Pakistan. We are at present passing most unhappy days and as a matter of fact feel utterly demoralised and dejected. Our representatives are at New Delhi now and we have given them every instruction to be in touch with your goodselves.

The only ray of hope on our darkened horizon is the intimation in the papers of your goodselves having formed a Sub-Committee to consider the grave issue arising from the incongruous and utterly unlawful and unjust award.

---

[2] *Chittagong Hill Tracts and Boundary Commission Award (National Archives of India)*

So we are now placing ourselves and our ill-fated country at your mercy and earnestly pray for our Hill Tracts to be redeemed from the ill-chosen category of Eastern Pakistan and placed in the Indian Union.

Anxiously awaiting your benign self's support and redress.

With kindest thoughts and regards,

Yours sincerely,

Raja Nalinaksha Roy

To
The Hon'ble Sardar V. Patel
Deputy Prime Minister,
1, Aurangzeb Road, New Delhi

LETTER FROM CHAKMA RAJA TO SARDAR PATEL

Rangamati, Rajbari
HITTAGONG HILL TRACTS
The 12th October, 1947

Confidential

D.O. 463

Dear Sardarji,

I hope you will excuse this intrusion – we the three Chiefs of the Chittagong Hill Tracts and the entire population are passing unhappy and dreamy days in Pakistan pending the final decision of your goodselves regarding the final decision of the Radcliffe award as announced in a Gazette of India Extraordinary.

We now approach you again with the request that when the learned Sub-Committee takes up the question of the Hill Tracts – we the three Chiefs are intimated in time, so that we can present in person ourselves or send some able representatives to put up our case in more details and with stronger grounds if you think it necessary. On looking through various documents, I find I overlooked a very important document regarding a finding by the Judicial Court in Chittagong of our status declaring the Chakma Chief as a Ruling Chief-and a copy of that finding is sent herewith for favour of perusal by your goodself. Ruling Chief has the right to enter into any Dominion he chooses especially when he is supported by his people. I think it can be made a further strong ground in addition to those already put for our joining with the Indian Union.

Hoping to be informed in proper time.

Yours sincerely,

Raja Nalinaksha Roy

To
The Hon'ble Sardar V. Patel
Deputy Prime Minister,
1, Aurangzeb Road, New Delhi

Despite the tireless efforts of Chakma leaders, their aspirations to remain part of the Indian Union were not realised, leading to the Chakma people becoming one of the most affected groups in the aftermath of partition. The independence and partition had a profound impact on the Chakma community as the land they inhabited was divided. With much of the population in the Chittagong Hill Tracts (97%) being non-Muslims, they expressed a preference for being part of India rather than Pakistan. Consequently, after partition, Chakmas residing within the territory of India became Indian citizens, while those in the Chittagong Hills fell under Pakistan's jurisdiction.

Following independence, numerous Chakma nationalist leaders who were pro-India had to flee the Chittagong Hill Tracts due to their loyalty to India. Many Chakmas who remained loyal to India were imprisoned, and some were even executed on charges of treason for supporting the merger of the CHT with India.

Given the Chakmas' demonstration of loyalty to India during the freedom struggle and their ongoing petitions to the Indian government for the merger of the CHT with India, opposing the allocation of the CHT to Pakistan, the Pakistani government viewed the Chakma people with suspicion for their pro-India8 and anti-Pakistani stance. Consequently, the government deliberately implemented discriminatory and cruel policies that resulted in the systematic abuse and misappropriation of land and resources for the Chakmas.

The Pakistan government, in 1963, amended Act XXII of 1860, thereby revoking the special status granted to the Chittagong Hill Tracts as a wholly excluded area. Additionally, they repealed the CHT Frontier Regulation Act of 1881, known as the Hill Tracts Manual, which had provided certain safeguard measures for the indigenous people of the Hill Tracts, including judicial, administrative, and legal provisions.

The Hill Tracts Manual had recognized the Chittagong Hill Tracts as the homeland of the indigenous people, ensuring basic safeguards against the exploitation of the hill people by non-indigenous individuals who might take advantage of their ignorance or lack of business acumen. As a policy, the British administration treated the CHT as an exclusive area for indigenous people, separate from the plains districts, and established a distinct administrative structure for it.

However, following the partition of India, an arbitrary constitutional amendment in 1963 removed the recognition of the Hill Tracts as an indigenous and excluded area. This decision was motivated by the fact that the Chakma people were perceived as being pro-Indian.

During the early 1960s, the Pakistani government constructed the Kaptai Hydel Project on the Karnafuli

River. This project resulted in the submergence of a vast tract of land, including the areas where the Chakmas lived and cultivated their lands.

The construction of the Kaptai Hydro-Electric Dam, which spanned the Karnaphuli River (known as Borgang by the Chakma people), became the catalyst for forced eviction and a mass exodus of approximately 100,000 tribal people from their ancestral lands, predominantly from the Chakma community.

Under the Kaptai Hydroelectric Power project, the Pakistani government built a dam on the Karnaphuli River in Kaptai. Completed in 1963 at a cost of Rs. 4.9 crores, with funding from the US development agency USAID, the dam created a reservoir that submerged an area of 655 square kilometres, leading to the loss of over 40% of the Chakma people's fertile arable land.

In his book "The Departed Melody," the former Chakma Raja, Raja Tridiv Roy, expressed his belief that an important political motive behind the dam's construction was to target and disperse "influential" Chakma families. This sentiment was reinforced by the fact that the Chakma Royal family was pro-India and sought to join the Indian Union during the partition. Additionally, the Chakma Raja's palace, which held significant political influence in the Chittagong Hill Tracts (CHTs), was submerged by the waters of the Karnaphuli River. According to the Chakma Raja, the purpose of the dam was to weaken the politically and economically strong Chakma community. He described the Kaptai dam as the "biggest single calamity" for the Chakmas up to 1960.

While the Kaptai power plant brought electricity to the plain districts, particularly the port city of Chittagong, it swiftly plunged the lives of the Chakma people in the CHTs into darkness. The loss of their primary economic base, coupled with the lack of alternative income-generating opportunities and systematic religious persecution, resulted in around 20,000 Chakmas migrating to various parts of India in 1964. Of which 14,888 individuals were rehabilitated in the NEFA, present-day Arunachal Pradesh, where they continue to endure difficult living conditions to this day due to non-recognition as citizens.[3]

The migration of the Chakmas from the Chittagong Hill Tracts (CHT) to India in 1964 can be understood in a historical context marked by a complex interplay of political, religious, economic, and social factors. These included Partition Legacy, Religious and Political Persecution and Kaptai Dam and Development-Induced Displacement. The Precipitating factor was the large-scale communal riots that erupted in East Pakistan starting in January 1964, specifically targeting minority communities, including the Chakmas. These riots were characterised by religious and ethnic tensions, resulting in violence, discrimination, and property loss. The deteriorating security situation made it increasingly difficult for minority groups like the Chakmas to live in East Pakistan peacefully and with dignity.

This human crisis of displacement from the home and hearth is painfully remembered by the Chakmas as BOR-PORONG meaning the Great Migration.

Indian Independence Act and the Boundary Commission's Award of CHT to Pakistan

B.N. Rau, who was an Indian civil servant, jurist, diplomat and statesman known for his key role in drafting the Constitution of India submitted a note before Jawaharlal Nehru on "The Chittagong Hill Tracts and the Boundary Commission's Award" on August 14, 1947 explaining the legal position of the area.

He writes, *"The Boundary Commission's Award has not yet been declared; but it is said that the Commission has*

---

[3] *Land Rights of the Indigenous Peoples of the Chittagong Hill Tracts, Bangladesh, IWGIA Document No. 99, Copenhagen 2000 by Rajkumari Chandra Kalindi Roy (ISBN: 87-90730-29-1)*

decided to allocate the above Tracts to East Bengal. The following facts are relevant: -

a. *These tracts cover an area of about 5000 sq. mile, with a population (according to the Census of 1941) of about 247,000, only 7300 being Muslims. that is to say, about 97 % of the population is non-Muslim.*
b. *According to the provisional boundaries mentioned in the Indian Independence Act, these Tracts fall in West Bengal and therefore in the Dominion of India.*
c. *These Tracts are an "Excluded Area" under the Act of 1935 and its inhabitants had therefore no representation in the Bengal Legislature and no opportunity of expressing their views on any of the issues connected with the partition of Bengal.*

Therefore, every consideration of natural justice required that before an overwhelmingly non-Muslim area of this character, which had been provisionally included in West Bengal, was finally allocated to East Bengal, its inhabitants should have been fully heard by the deciding authority.

"All persons exercising judicial or quasi-judicial functions must observe the following rules: (1) if the tribunal consists of several members, they must sit and deliberate together and not separately; (2)……, (3) each party must be given an opportunity of stating his case. If these rules of natural justice are not observed, the decision will be voidable, not absolutely void"[Halsbury, Vol. 26, pp. 285-287].[4]

Apparently in the present instance, the Boundary Commission has made an award in contravention of the

---

[4] *Note of B.N. Rau submitted to Jawaharlal Nehru on August 14, 1947, on Chittagong Hill Tracts and Boundary Commission Award (National Archives of India)*

above principles. If so, the question arises, what is the remedy now available. Pakistan will claim these Tracts by virtue of the award and the provisions of S.3 of the Indian Independence Act. India will claim on the other hand, that the Award is vitiated by breach of the principles of natural justice. There will thus be a dispute between the Dominions on a "justiciable" issue. Such a dispute falls to be decided in accordance with the procedure prescribed by the Imperial Conference 1930 for this purpose. That is to say, by an ad hoc arbitral tribunal of 5 members. Each party selects 2 members, one from among States of the Commonwealth that are not parties to the dispute and the other with complete freedom of choice; these four members then choose the Chairman. Assessors may be employed if the parties desire and the expenses are to be equally shared, but each party has to bear the expenses of presenting its case [Halsbury, Vol. XI, p.30]."

Conclusion

These historical facts should be remembered today before the Chakmas are unfairly characterised as outsiders, refugees, and illegal migrants. It is also important to note that just as the British deprived them of their indigenous rights and imposed severe penalties of cotton as taxes, today too the State and private parties vociferously deny the Chakmas their legitimate rights as Indian citizens and as the indigenous people of undivided India.

The interpretation of the story of the Chakmas of Arunachal Pradesh is not merely a historical account; it is a reflection of India's identity, cultural diversity, historical continuity, and commitment to unity in diversity. Any other interpretation of the story of the Chakmas of Arunachal Pradesh would undermine the very idea of India, the Akhand Bharat and its historical and cultural significance.

1
THE GREAT MIGRATION – BOR PORONG

Throughout time, the story of human civilization has often been a chronicle of migrations. Our ancestors, in their quest for better living conditions or in flight from adversities, roamed vast landscapes, shaping history as they moved. The exodus of modern humans from Africa over 60,000 years ago stands testament to this inherent migratory instinct.

In the tapestry of migrations, the tale of the Chakmas from the Chittagong Hills Tracts to Arunachal Pradesh holds a unique thread. On August 15, 1947, Cyril Radcliffe, with a mere stroke of his pen, shifted their homeland from India to Pakistan. However, this wasn't a physical relocation. Overnight, the Chakmas found their national identity and national citizenship altered. They were forcefully put into a foreign and unfamiliar political and cultural geography.

Yet, the wheels of time brought another migration event into their lives. Come 1964, the Chakmas, having been begrudgingly thrust into the Islamic Republic of Pakistan during the tumultuous partition, embarked on a massive movement termed 'Bor-Porong'. For them, this wasn't another dislocation but a poignant 'Ghar-Wapsi' - a homecoming.

This mass migration of Buddhist minorities from East Pakistan began in early 1964, with members of the Chakma tribe crossing over to India in large numbers due to widespread communal riots and the submergence of fertile lands in East Pakistan, a consequence of construction of Kaptai Hydro Power Dam. Between early 1964 and July

1964, approximately 15,000 Chakma Buddhists migrated to the Mizo Hills and Tripura.

The mass migration of Buddhist Chakmas happened for the same reasons that caused millions of minority Hindus and Christians from East Pakistan to move to India before, during, and after the partition, as well as during the same period as the Chakmas. The systematic persecution of minorities created an intolerable environment for them, devoid of peace and dignity. The minority community experienced looting, arson, and plunder of their properties, often with the collaboration of the East Pakistan Rifles and Ansars. These events shattered their trust in the Pakistani authorities.[5]

The journey from the Chittagong Hills Tract to Arunachal Pradesh (NEFA) covered nearly 1200 kilometres, fraught with peril and lasting for months or even years for those living in transit camps, awaiting final rehabilitation. The arduous trek involved travelling by foot, boats, trucks, and trains, but the most challenging part was the 18-day on-foot journey from Demagiri to Aizawl.

Between January and July of 1964, approximately 15,000 Chakmas entered India from East Pakistan, primarily through Tripura and the Mizo Hill District of Assam.

Tragically, many lives were lost during this journey and in the transit camps due to diseases, exhaustion, and food scarcity. Despite enduring immense suffering and desperate attempts to escape ruthless atrocities, fears, and insecurities in East Pakistan, the Chakmas arrived in India with great hope.

A Tragic Incident: On a fine day in May 1964, it was a day etched with horror for the Chakma migrants as they were resting in a transit camp on the bank of Champatoli (Champasuri), at around 4 in the afternoon, the serene skies abruptly transformed as cyclonic winds swept

---

[5] *Press Information Bureau, Government of India, Feature "Foodgrains Airdropped for Buddhist Migrants, Evacuation Posing Big Problem", May 10, 1964*

through the area. It prompted everyone to scramble out desperately and take shelter far from trees. In the midst of this chaos, tragedy struck. A colossal elephant apple tree crashed down upon a temporary resting house where a pregnant woman along with her infant daughter remained trapped inside amidst the frantic rush.

The scene that followed was a harrowing nightmare etched in their memories. The merciless force of the falling tree amidst the cyclonic winds tore apart the fragile house, resulting in an unspeakable horror. The pregnant woman and her infant daughter, unable to escape, faced a gruesome fate. The impact of the tree crushed her, her body and the unborn child's life gruesomely taken. The once-pregnant woman lay sprawled amidst the debris, her intestines and the tiny remnants of the unborn child scattered across the ground, a tragic testament to the merciless force of nature's fury. The haunting image of that distressing loss lingers vividly in the collective memory of the Chakma migrants, a stark reminder of the merciless unpredictability of their circumstances.

1. ENTERING INDIA THROUGH MIZO HILLS

The Chakmas found their way into India via two pivotal land routes – one that snaked through the Mizo Hills District of Assam and the other that journeyed through Tripura. Around 13,000 Chakmas braved the Mizo Hills path, while the Tripura route beckoned approximately 2,000 souls.

The majority of the migrants entered the Mizo Hills District through a land route near the border hamlet of Kalapani. They initially established camps in Champatoli (now Champasuri), located on the banks of the Karnafuli River near the Demagiri reception centre (now Tlabung) in the Lungleh Sub-Division. The Chakmas had to travel along this path for a few days, covering most of the distance on foot.

At Demagiri, Chakma families were systematically grouped into 42 units, each encompassing about 40-60 families. Within these clusters, specific leaders were appointed to maintain discipline and ensure order. These leaders also managed the allocation of rice and other essential provisions to those in their charge.

The other land route used by the Chakma migrants to enter India was through Tripura. They had to embark on an approximately 18-day journey on foot through the Gangaram Reserve Forest (now Central Catchment RF) to reach the Chailengta-Manu transit camp in Tripura.

1.1.EVACUATION OF CHAKMA MIGRANTS

The evacuation of Chakma migrants from the Demagiri transit point in the Mizo Hills has emerged as a formidable challenge for the government. This challenge is exacerbated by the impending monsoon season, which poses a significant obstacle to movement and rules out the feasibility of air dropping ration supplies.

The government is confronted with the urgency of completing the evacuation before the onset of the monsoon, recognizing that the difficult terrain would render transportation impractical during this period. The inability to air-drop essential provisions further compounds the logistical complexities of the operation.

Adding to the complexities are concerns raised by the intelligence bureau, indicating a potential for communal conflict between the Mizos and Chakmas. The intelligence report highlights a growing dissatisfaction among the Mizos in response to the increasing influx of Chakma migrants.[6] This social tension poses an additional layer of complexity to the evacuation efforts.

The plan was to relocate the Chakma migrants from the difficult terrain of the Mizo Hills to the more accessible

---

[6] *Rehabilitation of refugees and others in Assam including hill districts and North East Frontier Agency (MHA File No. 15/12/64(SR)-A, National Archives of India*

Plains of Cachar in Assam, where they would temporarily reside pending their final resettlement. This strategic relocation from Mizo Hills to Cachar aimed to mitigate the challenges posed by the difficult terrain and potential communal tensions, facilitating a smoother and safer evacuation process.

1.2. TRAVERSING TERRAINS: THE 18-DAY TREK FROM DEMAGIRI TO AIZAWL

The lack of a proper all-weather road connecting Demagiri to Aizawl was a major challenge for the authorities. The road was usable by jeeps only during the dry season and became inaccessible during the monsoon. Since the Chakma migrants depended on wet cultivation, the administration relocated them to the plains of Cachar district, where there was potential for their final resettlement.

The difficult land route from Demagiri to Aizawl posed a major challenge for local authorities evacuating the Chakma migrants. They needed to act quickly before the monsoon arrived, but the obstacles were daunting.

Two main evacuation routes were considered. One was a 172-mile stretch from Demagiri to Aijal (now Aizawl), the administrative centre of the Mizo Hills District. However, this road was only suitable for jeeps and became unusable during the monsoon season.

The second route, a more convoluted path, required a combination of foot and boat travel, extending from Demagiri to Marpara and then on to the Cachar district. This journey would span around ten days.

Before the Chakma migrants began their journey on foot from Demagiri, authorities sent reconnaissance teams to find the best route to the plains of the Cachar district. The government set up seventeen transit camps between the Demagiri reception centre and the Aizawl transit camps. The plan was to cover 275 km in 18 days, with each group walking 15 km per day. This schedule aimed to beat the impending monsoons, which would make travel impossible.

The Chakma migrants were divided into 42 groups, with each group consisting of 200 to 400 individuals (equivalent to 40 to 80 families). The group leaders were responsible for distributing rice and other essential supplies.

The Chakma migrants often recount the gruelling 275-km trek from the Demagiri Reception Centre to the transit camps in Aizwal (Tuirial, Chaltlang, and Kante), as the hardest part of the Bor-Porong. The path was full of challenges, and the landscape was treacherous.

Their journey began in stages, with groups of 4 to 6 departing from the Demagiri transit camp around the second week of May 1964. For many, this remains a poignant memory, emblematic of the hardest journey they had ever faced. With loads borne on their heads or backs, they trudged a minimum of 10 hours daily to reach subsequent transit points. A short respite at night was followed by an early morning continuation. The rugged landscape made even the lightest load feel overwhelmingly heavy, and sheer fatigue sometimes made their very limbs feel like weights.

The relentless routine of walking took a toll, both physically and emotionally. Faced with the challenges of the journey, many were forced to abandon treasured belongings to ease their burdens. Despite their quest for a peaceful life in India, the journey claimed the lives of many due to factors like dehydration and disease.

Sukra Mohan Chakma's tearful recollections bear witness to the agonising heartbreaks suffered en route. Many of those who lost their lives along the way were not granted the solemnity of customary funeral rites or traditional observances. Time and circumstances didn't allow for the luxury of mourning or glancing back at those left behind. During this strenuous journey, children and women bore the brunt of the hardships. The government, recognizing the vulnerability of expectant mothers and the ailing, provided jeeps to aid their transportation.

As a beacon of hope and a testament to this journey's gruelling nature, 17 rest camps were set up. Pradeep Kumar Chakma, one of the group leaders, meticulously chronicled this odyssey, listing each transit camp and their respective halt dates, creating a tangible testament to their shared history.

1.3.TRAVERSING TERRAINS: PRADEEP KUMAR CHAKMA'S CHRONICLES

In the mosaic of stories from the Chakma migration, Pradeep Kumar Chakma's records hold a special place. Entrusted with the immense responsibility of overseeing 48 migrant families, he led the second batch of families on their journey. His position was crucial, but what makes his role even more notable was the meticulous journal he maintained throughout their travel. Within its pages, Pradeep noted each of their stops, marking the transit camps and the specific dates of their sojourn.

Here's a snapshot from Pradeep Kumar Chakma's chronicles, detailing the transit camps they traversed and the dates of their stay:

Sl. No. Name of Transit Camps	Date of Stay
1. Demagiri(Chompatuli)	Started 14/05/1964
2.Tuichung (Tuichawng)	15/05/1964
3.Midung Lui	16/05/1964
4.Phairung (Phairuankai)	17/05/1964
5.Pacheng (Pachang) (Panye Bajja)	18/05/1964
6.Lunglei	19/05/1964
7.Zobawk	20/05/1964
8.Mat (Mat Lui)	21/05/1964
9.Daryepeng	23/05/1964
10.Aitur (Aithur Peng)	24/05/1964
11.Thilve	26/05/1964
12.Dapzarkawn	27/05/1964

13.Tarhunkawn	28/05/1964
14.Darnum	29/05/1964
15.Zingal (Pangzawl)	31/05/1964
16.MS	01/06/1964
17.Karkawn	02/06/1964
18.Khante, Tuirial, Chaltlang camps Aizawl	03/06/1964

Pradeep Kumar Chakma migrated to India from Kharekkong village, Post Office Bagchari Bazar, Police Station Rangamati, 59 No. Bandhukbhanga Mouza, Dist. CHT, East Pakistan.

Every entry in his journal wasn't just a name or a date; it was a testament to their perseverance, each camp representing a milestone in their journey towards hope and a better tomorrow.

1.4. ARUN MASTER'S CHRONICLE: JOURNEY THROUGH TRANSIT CAMPS

In the annals of the Chakma migration, few documents are as treasured as the meticulous journal kept by Arun Bikash Chakma, affectionately referred to as "Arun Master". A beacon of knowledge in Sonaram Talukdar's group, he hailed from the serene village of Ulusuri, sheltered within the precincts of Police Station Dhiginala in the Chittagong Hills Tract, East Pakistan.

The narrative of his journey becomes even more captivating when one realises the circumstances of his migration. Through the border at Kalapani (or Harina as some called it), Arun Master set foot on Indian soil, arriving at Demagiri on the marked date of 18th June 1964. A brief sojourn of seven days at the Demagiri Migrants Camp gave him and his companions a brief respite, but by 25th June, they were on the move again, with Aizawl in their sights.

Arun Master's journal gives us a unique window into this arduous trek, mapping out each of the transit camps they navigated:

1. Demagiri (known as Chompatuli or Champasuri)
2. Tuichung (alternatively spelled as Tuichawng)
3. Midung Lui 4. Ridge
5. Ngashi 6. Tharung
7. Mat 8. Daryepang
9. Aithurpan 10. Tilve
11. Sapyor Kaure 12. Arhunkaw
13. Darnum 14. Zinghal
15.[This point seems to be missing] 16. Karkaun
17. Khante, Chantlang - culminating in Aizawl

Each name whispered tales of struggles, hopes, and memories. Through Arun Master's diligent record-keeping, future generations would gain a lens into the past, tracing the footsteps of those who bravely journeyed in search of a better life.

After an intense and challenging 18-day journey on foot, the weary Chakma migrants found solace at the Tuirial, Khante, and Chaltlang Transit camps in Aizawl. Here, in the heart of Aijal, they were given a chance to rest, to gather their strength, and to prepare for the next phase of their lives. Their sojourn in these camps varied widely—some stayed for just a week, while others remained for several months. The duration of their respite was determined by an array of factors, not least of which was the finalisation of settlement schemes and their readiness to embark on the next chapter of their migration story.

1.5. FROM AIZAWL TO ASSAM'S PLAINS

By the conclusion of July 1964, the authorities had diligently relocated all Chakma migrants from Demagiri to transit camps in Aizawl. The main centres for registering them as refugees were the Aizawl transit camps: Khante, Tuirial, and Chaltlang. Migrants typically spent varying durations, from days to months, in these camps before transitioning to the camps in the plains of Cachar and Lakhimpur districts, marking a pit stop before their eventual resettlement.

Upon their arrival in Aizawl, the migrants were systematically categorised into distinct groups and dispatched mainly via trucks to different transit locations in the Cachar district and eventually to the Lakhimpur districts of Assam via special trains. These migrants found temporary refuge in notable camps like Monacherra, Anipur, Bhaga, Silcoorie, Saranarthipur and Dhalai in Cachar District. Their journey culminated in the Ledo Camp, situated in what is now Tinsukia District but was then Lakhimpur, close to the borders of what was formerly the North-East Frontier Agency (NEFA) – their destination for permanent resettlement.

To ensure a smooth transfer from Cachar District, the government commissioned special trains for the Chakma migrants' journey to the Ledo transit camp in Lakhimpur District (now Tinsukia District). Between July and December 1964, about 1,000 Chakma families transitioned from the Cachar camps to Ledo.

From December 1964, when the Chakmas were stationed at the Ledo Transit camp, there was a shift in administrative responsibility. The Assam Government handed over the task of their permanent rehabilitation to the NEFA administration. Following this change, the first batch of around 1000 Chakmas families were methodically moved into NEFA's Noa-Dihing valley of Miao in distinct batches, with this relocation process stretching until around February 1965.

2. ENTERING INDIA THROUGH TRIPURA

In the second week of May 1964, around 2,000 Chakmas journeyed on foot for two weeks through the Gangaram Forest Reserve (Central Catchment RF), departing from East Pakistan. They entered India through Tripura in two distinct batches almost concurrently.

In late May 1964, the first wave of Chakma migrants arrived in Tripura, initially staying at the Majoli Transit Camp in Manu for a brief period of 4-5 days.

Simultaneously, another group also reached Tripura, but they deliberately bypassed the Manu Transit camp, opting instead to head directly to Kumarghat with the intention of settling in Cachar District, Assam.

Upon hearing about the standard practice of re-routing of migrants entering Tripura from East Pakistan, many Chakma families, particularly those with some financial means, chose to leave the camp. They joined the other group travelling independently to Cachar without officially registering as refugees in Manu transit camp of Tripura. Consequently, the former group, which stayed at the Majoli Transit Camp, comprised 106 families, while the latter, known as the Cachar Bound Group, consisted of 52 families.

2.1. THE FIRST BATCH OF CHAKMA MIGRANTS REROUTED TO BIHAR FROM MANU

On June 2, 1964, a contingent of 106 Chakma migrant families residing at the Majoli Transit Camp in Manu were escorted by bus to the Dharmanagar Railway Station. From there, they boarded a train bound for Guwahati, arriving on June 4th.

Subsequently, they set forth from Guwahati by train, eventually reaching the Bettiah Town Railway Junction on June 6th. From this junction, they were shuttled to the West Hazari Transit Camp in Bihar's Champaran District, which was a short two-hour drive away. This camp provided shelter to over a thousand migrant families, a mix that included Hindu refugees from East Pakistan.

Later that month, another batch of 33 Chakma families from the Majoli Transit Camp in Chawmanu were transferred to transit facilities located in Purnea in Bihar.

These groups of Chakma migrants that entered through Tripura were redirected to Bihar due to a particular reason. Post India's Independence, Tripura, then a Union Territory, witnessed a massive wave of migrants from East Pakistan. This surge surpassed the Tripura government's ability to accommodate and rehabilitate them. As a result, by 1964, a strategy was adopted to send these migrants from East Pakistan in Tripura to transit camps in states like Bihar and Madhya Pradesh, where many migrants were already awaiting resettlement.

2.2. THE SECOND BATCH REROUTED TO NEFA BY ASSAM GOVERNMENT

The second batch of Chakma migrants, having deliberately not taken shelter or registered themselves at Majoli, Manu Transit camp at Tripura, found themselves in Kumarghat on June 5, 1964. Not letting this deter them, they journeyed on, targeting the Cachar District of Assam. By June 6, they arrived in Pecharthal and then split into two groups, journeying towards Dharmanagar.

The first group of Chakma migrants encountered challenges for boarding the train without proper tickets or warrants. This led to their arrest by the Railway Police at Karimganj Railway Junction in Assam and subsequent production before the Nowgong (Nogaon) Court. After verification procedures, this group was officially documented as refugees from East Pakistan in Nowgong.

Simultaneously, the other group of migrants was also detained at Karimganj Railway Station on June 7, 1964. The railway authorities turned them over to the Department of Rehabilitation in Assam, where they remained in Karimganj for the next three days.

An event of national significance occurred during their stay in Karimganj. On June 8, 1964, as the nation observed the Terahvin (13th day) following the demise of Prime Minister Jawaharlal Nehru, a countrywide holiday was declared. The Chakma migrants in Karimganj reminisced about that day, remembering how they were provided with special meals and delicacies as part of the traditional feast marking the solemn occasion.

In Karimganj, while women found shelter within the railway station's confines, men were lodged at a nearby

Buddhist temple. The temple's chief abbot, Ven. Jinaratan Bhikkhu, a Baruah Buddhist monk, earned deep respect for his empathy and foresight. He not only offered sanctuary but also accompanied and shepherded the migrants as far as Mergherita, Assam.

During their stay in Karimganj and Nowgong, official procedures were swiftly conducted. By June 9, 1964, all Chakma migrants underwent a screening process, got registered as refugees, and received identification slips. A day later, on June 10, these families began their next phase of the journey, travelling by train from Karimganj to Mergherita through Badarpur and Lumding en route to NEFA.

On the morning of June 12, 1964, these groups of Chakma migrants who entered India through Tripura arrived at Margherita. Upon their arrival, they were generously provided with relief materials by the Base Superintendent of Margherita. For the time being, a local government school became their shelter. Five days later, on June 17, the able-bodied men were dispatched by trucks to the Namphai region near Miao, with the task of constructing shelters for their families. Meanwhile, the women and others continued to stay at the school in Margherita.

By the early days of July 1964, the bamboo-thatch homes had been constructed and stood ready for habitation. The collective efforts of the Chakma migrants culminated in the establishment of these shelters. At this juncture, the Assam Government formally facilitated the transition of all 52 Chakma families, encompassing 488 members, to their new homes. Using trucks, they were relocated to their permanent settlement in the Namphai region under the Miao administrative jurisdiction.

The situation with the second batch of Chakma migrants was distinct from the first. While they also entered India through Tripura, they were not redirected to Bihar like the first batch. This differentiation arose due to a bureaucratic nuance: the Tripura Government did not officially record or acknowledge their entry into the territory, whereas the Assam Government did.

This acknowledgment by the Assam Government became significant due to the prevailing policy in 1964 concerning new migrants. According to this policy, any migrant entering Assam during that period would be the responsibility of the Assam Government when it came to their rehabilitation. If migrants were officially registered upon entering Assam, the onus of providing for their resettlement and well-being shifted to the Assam Government, rather than being a shared or redirected responsibility. Hence, this second batch of Chakma migrants, having been recorded by Assam, had to be rehabilitated by the Assam Government directly, rather than being sent to other states like Bihar.

2.3. RELOCATION: FROM BIHAR TO NEFA (ARUNACHAL PRADESH)

During a meeting in Shillong on June 22, 1965, Mr. Mahavir Tyagi, the Minister of Rehabilitation, Government of India, along with the Rehabilitation Minister, Assam, NEFA Officials and officials from Assam, discussed the matter of Chakma refugees camping in transit camps in Bihar who expressed their desire to be shifted back to Assam.

Following this, on August 2, 1965, Mr. H.S. Butalia, the Liaison Officer of the Ministry of R&R, wrote to Shri K.P. Mathrani, the Secretary of the Government of India's Ministry of R&R, regarding the relocation of Chakma refugee families from Bihar camps to Assam. The case was expected to be finalised in the coming days.

On October 4, 1965, Mr. L.J. Jhonson, ICS, Additional Secretary to the Government of India's Ministry of Rehabilitation, sent a letter (D.O. letter No. 12(6)/65 - Part II) to Shri T.C. Puri, ICS Patna, stating that the Chakmas lodged in Bettiah and Champaran Refugee camps wished to return to Assam due to the lack of cultural affinity and unsuitable climate. The NEFA administration also agreed to their resettlement in NEFA, and it was suggested that these families could be sent there.

Finally, in November 1965, these 133 Chakma families reached NEFA. In November 1965, after a 19-month stay, the 106 Chakma families from West Hazari Transit Camp in Bettiah and the 33 Chakma families from Purnea transit camps in Bihar were transported to NEFA for their final settlement. The camp commander of West Hazari Camp in Bettiah accompanied and supervised this return journey from Bihar to Mergherita, where the NEFA authorities took charge of them and transferred them to NEFA via trucks on the same day.

This feature is one of the earliest news articles on the Chakmas' migration from East Pakistan to India, released by the Press Information Bureau on May 31, 1964:

PRESS INFORMATION BUREAU

GOVERNMENT OF INDIA

****

FOR PUBLICATION ON OR AFTER SUNDAY, MAY 31, 1964 (JYAISTHA 10, 1886)

FEATURE

FOODGRAINS AIRDROPPED FOR BUDDHIST MIGRANTS

EVACUATION POSING BIG PROBLEM

Buddhist minorities in East Pakistan are the latest target of persecution. Over 15,000 of them had crossed over to India for shelter, till the end of April. They all belong to the Chakma tribe of the Chittagong Hill Tract.

The largest number of Buddhist refugees have entered Mizo Hills (Lushai Hills) in Assam and the rest are in Tripura.

They are camping at three places in Mizo Hills - Demagiri in Lungleh Sub-Division, Phuldungsei and Pukzing in Aijal Sub-Division. Manu in Tripura is another point of their entry.

The biggest concentration of Buddhist refugees is in Demagiri - over 12,300, followed by Manu - over 2,000 and Phuldungsei and Pukzing - over 700.

Even now - four months after the first batch of uprooted humanity entered Mizo Hills - migrants are still coming in, on an average of 200 persons daily.

The reason for this mass migration of Buddhists is just the same as that of the Chrisitans who earlier entered Garo Hills in Assam. The systematic persecution of minorities made it "too hot" for them to live there with peace and honour. Loot, arson, and plunder of the properties belonging to the minority community, with the connivance of East Pakistan Rifles and Ansars, shook off their faith in the bonafides of the Pakistan authorities.

Many refugees at Demagiri complained that they did not get any compensation from the authorities for taking over their land for the construction of Karnafuli Dam. Even where compensation was paid, it was far from adequate, they stated.

Some refugees also said that they were asked to embrace the religion of the majority community, if they wanted to stay there.

All these factors contributed to make the condition of the Buddhist minorities 'insecure', resulting in the mass exodus to India.

Purbomohan Chakma of Lawngkawr village of Chittagong Hill Tract, who is now one of the refugee inmates at Demagiri said, a patrol party of the East Pakistan Rifles came to his village and demanded chicken, eggs, rice etc. They took them without paying any price. They also forcibly took away some girls of the village. When the "Karbari" of the village (village headman) protested against this, he was whipped publicly and he was fined Rs. 600.

Thirty-five-year-old India Mohan Chakma of Gulchakhali village, under the police station of Dighinala in the Chittagong Hill Tract, now at Demagiri, described, with tears in his eyes, how his wife was taken away by a local contractor belonging to the majority community. Father of four children, he was not at his house when this unfortunate tragedy occured. Though he went to the police station to record the case, the authorities did not take any action on the matter.

Under such conditions, Indra Mohon and many others like him decided to quit East Pakistan and seek abode in India where they can live without any "fear".

SELF-HELP-SPIRIT

The spirit of self-help exhibited by the refugees impresses anyone visiting the camps. Collecting bamboo and thatch from the nearby jungle, they have constructed their own temporary bamboo huts at Champasuri and Nunsuri, half a mile downstream the Karnafuli river from Demagiri. Even the hut occupied by the Medical Unit at the camp site has been constructed by the refugees.

They have provided voluntary labour, along with local people, in constructing the "dropping zone" for airdropping of foodgrains, as the area is inaccessible. They are also supplying voluntary workers for collecting the rice bags from the dropping zone. Two hundred persons turn up daily at the dropping zone to collect the rice bags and deposit them at the nearby central stores.

To feed the refugees, foodgrains are regularly airdropped. So far more than 2,000 quintals of rice have been airdropped. The authorities are trying to build an adequate buffer stock of foodgrains to meet any eventuality.

The refugees at Demagiri have been divided into forty-two groups. A special Medical Unit has been posted at Demagiri to take precautions against outbreak of any epidemics. Refugees are given inoculation and vaccination against cholera and smallpox.

EVACUATION OF REFUGEES

As an overwhelming majority of the Buddhist refugees are "wet cultivators", plans are now being chalked out to evacuate them to "transit camps"numbering about 17, to be set up in the plains of Cachar district, pending their final resettlement.

Because of the extremely difficult terrain, the evacuation of refugees has posed a very big problem to the local authorities. On the one hand they are racing against time, because the refugees must be moved out before the monsoon and on the other the physical odds are almost baffling.

Two routes for evacuation are being examined. The land route - from Demagiri to Aijal, headquarters of Mizo Hills District, covers a distance of about 172 miles. This jeepable road is unserviceable during the monsoon.

The other route from Demagiri to Marpara and from Marpara to Cachar district would involve part of the journey by boat and part on foot. This would take ten days to reach Cachar.

Reconnaissance parties are being sent to survey the route through which the refugees would be moved out to the plains in Cachar district.

The task of evacuating over 13,000 Buddhist refugees is a challenge the authorities have taken up in earnest.

VFD/RGD/GAU

FOR PUBLICATION ON OR AFTER SUNDAY, MAY 31, 1964 (JYAISTHA 10, 1886)

3. CHAKMA GROUP LEADERS

Amidst the Chakma migrants, the government appointed literate and adept individuals as group leaders responsible for disbursing essential supplies. These leaders served as vital liaisons, connecting the migrants with the government throughout their journey, staying in transit camps, and resettlement in NEFA.

Their role extended far beyond mere logistics; they were the indispensable bridges linking the migrants' needs with governmental provisions. These leaders assumed a multifaceted role, meticulously tending to every facet of the migrants' welfare throughout their journey, tenure in transit camps, and eventual resettlement in NEFA. They were not just distributors of ration; they were the custodians of unity, navigating the intricate tapestry of challenges that encompassed the migrants' voyage, ensuring that every phase, from provision to settlement, was handled with diligence and compassion.

The list of Group Leaders:

1. Kripadhan Karbari
2. Arun Bikash Chakma
3. Bhuban Bihari Chakma
4. Prabhu Ranjan Chakma
5. Ishwar Chandra Chakma
6. Sumoti Ranjan Talukdar
7. Nripendra Lal Chakma
8. Sumendra Lal Chakma
9. Nanda Kumar Chakma
10. Panja Joy Chakma
11. Gyana Ranjan Talukdar
12. Rebati Mohan Chakma
13. Amalendu Chakma
14. Sneha Kumar Chakma
15. Ajit Kumar Chakma
16. Upendra Lal Chakma
17. Pradeep Kumar Chakma
18. Sonaram Talukdar
19. Adi Chandra Talukdar
20. Rajani Kumar Chakma
21. Vishnu Mohan Chakma
22. Rajapya Chakma
23. Saidhan Chakma
24. Jyotirmoy Chakma
25. Mankumar Chakma
26. Sashi Kumar Chakma
27. Tarak Chand Chakma
28. Bhubanya Chakma

29. Rabina Chakma
30. Piri Mohan Chakma
31. Ramani Kumar Chakma
32. Babrubahan Chakma
33. Hiralal Chakma
34. Jagat Mohan Chakma
35. Buddha Lila Chakma
36. Kamesh Kr. Chakma

***** The names of some group leaders could not be compiled.***

4. Discussion on Chakma Migration in Lok Sabha in 1968

The migration of Chakmas came up in a significant parliamentary discussion, specifically in Lok Sabha Starred Question No. 48, initiated by Baburao Patel, the MP from Shajapur, Madhya Pradesh, on February 14, 1968. Patel raised alarming concerns about a state-sponsored gradual genocide targeting Chakmas and other minorities in East Pakistan.

Responding to these grave allegations, Sh. B.R. Bhagat, the Minister of State in the Ministry of External Affairs, presented supplementary information. He detailed the distressing chronology of events surrounding the Buddhist minorities in Pakistan, revealing that the first reports of atrocities emerged in early 1964. This coincided with a significant influx of Chakma tribe members crossing into India amidst escalating turmoil. Bhagat highlighted the harrowing consequences of widespread communal riots in East Pakistan during January and February 1964, which resulted in approximately twenty thousand Chakma Buddhists seeking sanctuary in the Mizo Hills of India. Additionally, thousands more fled into Burma, seeking refuge from the turmoil gripping their homeland.[7]

[7] *MHA File No. P-II/125/2/68, Ministry of External Affairs, Starred Question No. 48 by Shri Babu Rao Patel on 14.2.68 Racial on Genocide in Pakistan (National Archives of India)*

Source: https://en.wikipedia.org/wiki/Mizoram (This map is only for the purpose of representation)

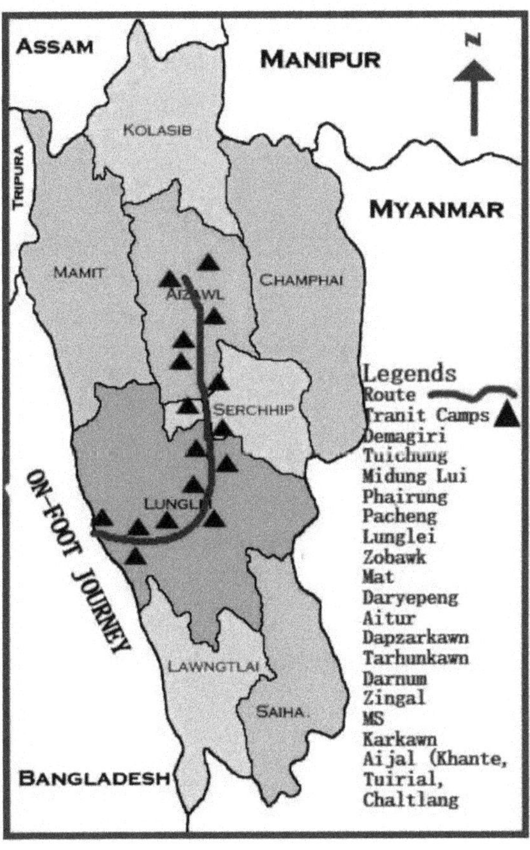

2

INDIA'S MIGRATION & REHABILITATION POLICY

India, a land of ancient wisdom and varied cultures, has been more than just a geographical entity. For millennia, it has extended its arms to those seeking refuge, embodying the true essence of its civilization. From sheltering Persians (Zoroastrians) who fled Persia (modern-day Iran) in the seventh century to escape religious persecution to embracing Polish Jewish children in 1942, India's history is rich with tales of hope and humanity.

Post-1947, after gaining its Independence, India's policies continued to resonate with this legacy. The guiding beacon for the nation's approach towards refugees, displaced individuals, and migrants was the profound Sanskrit tenet: "Vasudhaiva Kutumbakam," translating to "the world is one family." It was not merely a phrase but a deeply ingrained philosophy emphasising compassion, protection, and dignity.

Understanding the magnitude of its responsibilities, the Government of India, in September 1947, instituted the 'Ministry of Relief and Rehabilitation.' Its mandate was clear: Offer a sanctuary and rebuild lives of those who were escaping the shadows of persecution from erstwhile undivided Indian territories. This was not just a policy; it was deemed a national duty.

To delve deeper into the term "rehabilitation" – it stands for reinvigorating the spirit, re-establishing the broken, and reinstating them in societal esteem. This profound meaning was beautifully echoed in the concept of Vasudhaiva Kutumbakam. Acknowledging this depth, in 1949, the government decided to rename the ministry by dropping the term "Relief." The idea was that true rehabilitation went beyond mere immediate assistance; it was about long-term integration and empowerment, not just about financial aid or temporary sustenance.[8]

Embodying this philosophy, the Indian government took upon itself the monumental task of rehabilitating not just the Chakma tribals but also an overwhelming 7.80 lakh souls who sought refuge from East Pakistan in 1964. It was not just about resettlement; it was about ensuring a life of dignity and embracing them in the fold of India's vast tapestry.

The New Influx from East Pakistan: Since the partition of the country, minority communities from East Pakistan have been steadily migrating to the adjacent Indian states of West Bengal, Assam, and Tripura. The primary driving force behind this influx is the pervasive sense of insecurity felt by these minorities in East Pakistan. The fear and insecurity intensified due to widespread and organised riots and targeted attacks on these communities. Economic hardships also contributed to the increasing influx of minority groups.

The initial wave of migration occurred after the riots in 1950, during which a sizable number of people from minority communities in East Pakistan sought refuge in the neighbouring Indian states. This continued until the mid-1952. However, even after this period, a continuous but relatively lower-scale flow of migrants from East Pakistan persisted. By the end of July 1958, it was estimated that the total number of East Pakistani migrants had reached 41.17 lakhs. In March 1958, certain restrictions on immigration from East Pakistan were imposed, but migration continued despite these measures.

In 1962, Rajsahi and other nearby areas of East Pakistan witnessed well-organised riots and attacks targeting minority groups. As a result, around 20-25,000 people were

---

[8] *1947 - The story of Rehabilitation, U. Bhaskar Rao ISBN-9789354091858*

compelled to migrate to India in search of safety and security.

Subsequently, in January and February 1964, a series of riots erupted, surpassing the scale and organisation of the riots in 1950. The exact number of casualties remains unknown, but it is believed to be in the thousands. Consequently, there was a significant surge in immigration from East Pakistan starting in January 1964. Christians and Buddhists, in addition to other minorities, were targeted and harassed, prompting a mass exodus towards India. Alongside the Rajsahi riots in 1962 and the 1964 riots, a considerable number of tribal people also migrated. During their journey across the border, migrants encountered distressing instances of harassment, including assaults on women, robberies, and widespread physical violence.

1. Eligibility for Relief & Rehabilitation in India's Migration Policy:

1.1. Rehabilitation: A Matter of Certification (15.10.1952 - 31.03.1957)

Reports from the Estimates Committee for 1959-60 & 1964-65, specifically the Ninety-Sixth Report (Second Lok Sabha) and the Seventy-First Report (Third Lok Sabha) by the Ministry of Rehabilitation, state that initially, migrants from East Pakistan could enter India by presenting migration certificates issued by the Deputy High Commissioner in Dacca, effective from October 15, 1952. But unrestricted migration continued until the end of 1956. The fluctuating nature of this migration made planning for relief and rehabilitation a challenge. Thus, to regulate the inflow, a priority-based migration certificate system was introduced in 1956.[9]

India experienced an influx of 320,000 migrants in 1956, which saw a stark reduction to 11,000 by 1957. To

[9] *Report of Estimates Committee (1959-60) Ninety-Sixth Report (Second Lok Sabha), Ministry of Rehabilitation, Govt. of India [Eastern Zone]*

tighten migration control, the government ceased rehabilitation aid for those arriving post-March 1958.

1.2. Discontinuation of Rehabilitation Benefits (01.04.1958 - 31.12.1963)

From April 1, 1958, the Indian Government ceased rehabilitation assistance to arrivals from East Pakistan. In return for migration permits, these individuals had to affirm that they wouldn't seek any aid or benefits in India.

Open Migration Period: Rehabilitation Benefits Resume (01.01.1964 - 31.10.1964)[10]

In response to intense communal disturbances, migration rules were relaxed from January 1 to October 31, 1964, allowing migrants unrestricted entry. Recognizing the difficulty distant minorities faced in obtaining migration certificates from Dacca, the need for such certificates was temporarily suspended for humanitarian reasons, permitting border crossings even without travel credentials.

During this period, around 15,000 Chakmas entered India through the Mizo District of Assam and Tripura, qualifying them for the government's relief and rehabilitation programs. The migration process saw further simplifications: migrants no longer had to report to specific police checkpoints, the interview process was streamlined, and a more flexible payment system replaced the fixed postal order fee.

Additionally, cash payments were accepted instead of mandating a postal order fee of Re. 1/- for each migrant.

---

[10] *Report of Estimates Committee (1964-65) Seventy-First Report (Third Lok Sabha) Ministry of Rehabilitation (Reception, Dispersal and Rehabilitation of new Migrants arriving in India from East Pakistan since 1st January, 1964)*

1.3. Revision of free-entry period with effect from 01.11.1964[11]

From November 1, 1964, the government decided to reverse the previously liberalised migration policy that allowed free entry without travel documents. The reason cited for this revised policy was the simplification of the procedure for obtaining migration certificates and the expansion of eligibility categories.

Between January 1, 1964, and mid-October 1964, over 4.27 lakh people had taken advantage of the government's liberalised policy. The government stated that the revised policy, effective from November 1, 1964, would ensure that relief and rehabilitation benefits were granted only to genuine and deserving migrants. It was believed that obtaining migration certificates without difficulty would be possible for genuine migrants. State governments were granted discretion to make exceptions in cases of genuine hardship.

The announcement of the revised policy was made on October 24, 1964, and it came into effect on November 1, 1964. Starting from April 1, 1965, the government imposed a ban on the entry of migrants from East Pakistan, even if they possessed valid documents. This measure was implemented following the Indo-Pakistan war to prevent infiltration of fifth columnists and saboteurs from East Pakistan.

2. The 1964 Migration Wave: A Statistical Overview[12]

From January 1 to December 31, 1964, there was a significant influx of migrants into West Bengal, Assam, and

---

[11] *Report of Estimates Committee (1964-65) Seventy-First Report (Third Lok Sabha) Ministry of Rehabilitation (Reception, Dispersal and Rehabilitation of new Migrants arriving in India from East Pakistan since 1st January, 1964)*

[12] *Report of Estimates Committee (1964-65) Seventy-First Report (Third Lok Sabha) Ministry of Rehabilitation (Reception, Dispersal and Rehabilitation of new Migrants arriving in India from East Pakistan since 1st January, 1964)*

Tripura. This migration comprised predominantly of the Hindu minority from East Pakistan. In addition, certain Tribals, Buddhists, and Christians also formed part of this movement. The data that follows offers a comprehensive understanding of this migration's scale.

The table presented below offers a telling snapshot of the migration patterns in 1964. In the first 10 months of the year, there was a monthly average influx of 77,472 individuals. This number tapered off to an average of 40,641 in the final two months. However, despite this decrease, the steady flow of migrants continued to present formidable challenges to the government. Addressing the immediate needs and long-term rehabilitation of these individuals was no small task, especially given that many entered India in dire circumstances, some teetering on the brink of destitution.

Breaking down the data further, of the 8.56 lakh immigrants who sought refuge in India that year:

- 4.42 lakhs (or 51.6%) entered without any passport.
- 2.50 lakhs (or 29.2%) presented Migration Certificates issued by the Deputy High Commissioner for India in Dacca.
- 1.64 lakhs (or 19.2%) possessed standard passports granted by the Government of Pakistan.

Period	West Bengal	Assam	Tripura	Total	Monthly Avg.
01.01.64	509332	170713	94670	774715	77471
to 31.10.64	65.74%	22.04%	12.22%		
01.11.64	69106	6505	5670	81281	40,640
to	85.02%	8%	6.98%		

31.12.64					
Grand Total	578438	177218	100340	855996	

Here's a more detailed distribution of these migrants, categorised by their entry into West Bengal, Assam, and Tripura:

Travel Documents	Period	West Bengal	Assam	Tripura	Total
With Migration Certificate	01.01.64 to 31.10.64	214738 (96.98%)	6458 (2.92%)	230 (.10%)	221426
With Migration Certificate	01.11.64 to 31.12.64	26474 (92.89%)	1899 (6.67%)	125 (.44%)	28498
Travel Documents	Period	West Bengal	Assam	Tripura	Total
With Pakistani Passport	01.01.64 to 31.10.64	137401 (98.19%)	2268 (1.62%)	271 (.19%)	139940
With Pakistani	01.11.64 to	22604 (94.96%)	1168 (4.91%)	30 (.13%)	23802

Passport	31.12.64				

Without Travel Documents	Period	West Bengal	Assam	Tripura	Total
Without Travel Documents	01.01.64 to 31.10.64	157193 38.03%	161987 39.19%	94169 22.78%	413349
Without Travel Documents	01.11.64 to 31.12.64	20028 69.14%	3438 11.86%	5515 19%	28981

3. Reception/Interception Centres: An Overview of the Relief Measures[13]

To cater to the influx of immigrants from East Pakistan, the Ministry of Rehabilitation proactively set up Reception/Interception Centres at strategic locations along the border. These centres were designed to streamline the arrival process by:

- Welcoming the migrants as they crossed the border.
- Providing temporary accommodation and meals.
- Checking and verifying documents.
- Conducting necessary interviews.

---

[13] *Report of Estimates Committee (1964-65) Seventy-First Report (Third Lok Sabha) Ministry of Rehabilitation (Reception, Dispersal and Rehabilitation of new Migrants arriving in India from East Pakistan since 1st January, 1964)*

- Administering essential vaccinations.

3.1. Provisions at the Reception Centres for 1964 Arrivals: For those who landed in India on or after January 1, 1964, and qualified for the relief and rehabilitation benefits, the centres were equipped to provide:

- A daily allowance of 0.50 paise per individual.
- Basic clothing: Adult men received shirts and dhotis; women were given saris; boys got shirts and shorts; and girls received pants and frocks. The financial cap was set at Rs. 16 for individuals aged 8 and above, and Rs. 8 for those below 8 years.
- Essential commodities: Each family could receive up to three woollen blankets, with one per adult. Utensils, such as mats, mugs, karais, plates, buckets, and glasses, were allotted based on two items per adult.
- Monetary provisions for travel: Before setting off, migrants were handed a dry meal and a cash allowance, with expenses capped at Rs. 2.00 for adults and Rs. 1.30 for minors. Moreover, an advance of 10 days' allowance was given to assist in their onward journey. All were eligible for third-class railway warrants for transit.
- Food rations: Adults were provided with a diet that included rice or a rice-atta mix, dal, salt, chira, gur, and a small cash amount of 06 paise. Children under 8 received half the adult portion.

3.2. From Reception to Resettlement:

Upon entering India, migrants typically spent 1 to 3 days in the Reception Centres. From there, they transitioned to Relief Camps and, over time, moved to more permanent rehabilitation sites. Here, they received:

- Land allocation or industrial employment opportunities.

- Loan facilities to kickstart trades, businesses, or professional ventures.
- Support in house construction and allocation of homestead land equipped with basic infrastructure like roads, water, and drainage systems.
- Access to essential education and medical facilities.

4. Migrant Screening for Relief and Rehabilitation[14]

The influx of migrants arriving in India post-1st January 1964 necessitated a structured approach to understand their backgrounds and assess their needs. A systematic procedure was developed to glean insights into these new arrivals' personal histories and circumstances.

Data Collection:

A comprehensive process was designed to accumulate critical data from migrant families. This encompassed:

- Their former occupations in Pakistan.
- Family size and composition.
- Educational credentials of each family member.
- Details about their former residence in Pakistan.
- Any other significant information shedding light on their personal and familial histories.

Objective: The primary goal of this information gathering was twofold:

- To affirm the veracity of migrants arriving without official travel documents.

[14] *Report of Estimates Committee (1964-65) Seventy-First Report (Third Lok Sabha) Ministry of Rehabilitation (Reception, Dispersal and Rehabilitation of new Migrants arriving in India from East Pakistan since 1st January 1964)*

- To assist State Governments in formally recognizing them as genuine migrants from East Pakistan since the stipulated date of 1st January 1964.

Screening and Verification Process: Once the initial data was recorded on the Relief Eligibility Certificate, a deeper dive into each migrant's history was initiated, barring minors. This detailed inquiry covered:

- Their specific migration pathways.
- Any notable incidents or challenges they faced during their journey.
- Other related circumstances that could validate their migrant status.

The outcome of these inquiries was pivotal in determining their authenticity as migrants post-1st January 1964 and evaluating their genuine need for government support.

Towards Rehabilitation:

To ensure that the rehabilitation process was tailored to the migrants' skills and past experiences, additional data was extracted concerning their qualifications and vocational histories. For a streamlined approach, a standardised "Screening Report" form was instituted to capture these specifics.

5. Land Resettlement Initiatives for New Migrants

As migration from East Pakistan increased starting in January 1964, the Indian government quickly recognized it as a national priority. This urgent situation led them to rethink and reorganise their existing plans to help the new migrants.

On February 8, 1964, New Delhi played host to a pivotal 'Conference on Rehabilitation of Migrants.' The primary goal was to holistically address the intricate challenges posed by the inflow of refugees fleeing the disturbances in East Pakistan. Key policymakers, including Cabinet ministers and Chief Ministers from various states, gathered to deliberate and devise responsive strategies.

A collective responsibility was envisaged, with the central government earnestly seeking state-level collaboration. The states were solicited to participate in this national endeavour by allocating vacant lands within their territories for resettling the new migrants.

By December 1, 1964, the proactive response from the state governments was evident. Twelve states, inclusive of the Andamans and NEFA (bar Tripura), pledged approximately 1.86 lakh acres of land, aiming to resettle an estimated 75,600 migrant families. NEFA, taking the initiative, offered lands enough to accommodate 1,000 families, spanning 3,000 acres.[15]

However, a significant challenge emerged. Much of the proposed land, while expansive, comprised largely of forest tracts. Before facilitating resettlement, these areas would require substantial and mechanised reclamation efforts. Recognizing the need for systematic groundwork, many state governments undertook soil surveys to assess and prepare the land's viability.

By February 1, 1965, the commitment towards rehabilitation manifested in tangible outcomes. A total of 50 schemes, both agricultural (34) and non-agricultural/industrial (16), received official sanctions across multiple states. These schemes were poised to benefit 23,296 migrant families, with 22,040 earmarked for agricultural resettlement and 1,256 for industrial and other sectors. The overall financial outlay for these initiatives, including the NEFA scheme, was projected at Rs. 776.79 lakhs.

6. The Chakma Rehabilitation Endeavor

In 1964, there was a large-scale migration of Buddhist Chakmas from East Pakistan to India. Their objective was to find resettlement in the neighbouring states of Assam

---

[15] *Rehabilitation of Displaced Persons and Repatriates, Facts and Figures at a Glance, 1967, Committee of Review of Rehabilitation Work in West Bengal, Ministry of Labour, Employment and Rehabilitation, New Delhi*

(including the Mizo District) and Tripura (a Union Territory). However, the rehabilitation policy and standard operating procedure in place during that time dictated that migrants entering through Tripura should be transported to transit camps in Bihar, Madhya Pradesh, and other states until their final rehabilitation. Consequently, except for a group of 488 people, the Chakmas who entered India through Tripura were taken to Purnea and Bettiah transit camps. It is important to note that these 139 Chakma families were ultimately rehabilitated in NEFA (North-East Frontier Agency) in 1966.

Although both Tripura and Assam experienced a significant influx of migrants from East Pakistan after India's independence, the Tripura government faced challenges in providing rehabilitation to migrants within the state. Assam, on the other hand, had more land and resources available for this purpose. During the screening process in 1964, migrants who sought relief and rehabilitation were required to declare their willingness to settle outside of West Bengal and Tripura.[16]

As for Assam, the policy for migrants entering the state from East Pakistan was to offer rehabilitation within Assam itself. The Ministry of Rehabilitation, Government of India, would bear 75% of the expenses, while the state government would contribute the remaining 25%. Although the expenditure would eventually be reimbursed by the Government of India, the initial costs had to be covered by the state budget.

A letter dated 5th July 1964 offers a deeper insight into this unfolding narrative. Penned by Mr. R. Natarajan, the Deputy Commissioner of Cachar District, it was addressed to Mr. B.S. Sarao, the Secretary to the Government of Assam. In it, Natarajan discussed the fate of the Chakma migrants who had, by then, settled in a camp near

[16] *Report of Estimates Committee (1964-65) Seventy-First Report (Third Lok Sabha) Ministry of Rehabilitation (Reception, Dispersal and Rehabilitation of new Migrants arriving in India from East Pakistan since 1st January 1964)*

Hailakandi. His proposition was clear: Cachar District could be their potential home. Yet, challenges awaited; their farming practices needed modernization. The solution, as Natarajan saw it, was to integrate them into existing forest villages.

There was another, rather intriguing, facet to the Chakma community: their impeccable bamboo craftsmanship. Their talent in weaving mats and baskets had caught Natarajan's eye. With an ever-present demand in the local tea estates, he envisioned a symbiotic relationship: Chakmas could supply the estates with bamboo goods. This arrangement promised dual benefits — a steady income for the Chakmas and quality products for the estates.[17]

The 1965-66 General Administration Report on Relief & Rehabilitation sheds light on Assam's commitment to the refugee crisis. Compiled by Mr. S. Baruah, Under Secretary of the Relief & Rehabilitation Department of Assam, it underlines the state's pledge to rehabilitate around 75,000 refugees, equating to 15,000 families. Of these, the North Eastern Frontier Agency (NEFA) was earmarked to welcome 3,000 families.[18]

Originally, NEFA had generously set aside 3,000 acres for 1,000 families. Yet, the central government's urging for Assam to expand its rehabilitation ambit led to a rethink. Consequently, an additional 2,000 Chakma families were greenlit for settlement in NEFA.

This decision crystalized during a pivotal meeting on 22nd June 1965, held at Raj Bhavan in Shillong. Attendees included the rehabilitation minister from both the Government of India and Assam, along with key officials of Assam and NEFA. By the end of this assembly, the

[17] *Assam Archive File: Land for rehabilitation of refugees in Cachar District, Assam 1964*

[18] *Assam Archive File: General Administration Reports on Relief and Rehabilitation activities for the year 1965-66.*

collective consensus saw NEFA's Chakma resettlement quota increase to 3,000 families.

The Estimates Committee's Seventy-First Report (from the Third Lok Sabha) for the Ministry of Rehabilitation delves into the "Reception, Dispersal, and Rehabilitation of migrants arriving from East Pakistan post-1st January 1964." The report underlines the importance of preserving the identity and culture of tribal migrant families, especially the Chakmas. To this end, the committee suggests considering the resettlement of the Buddhist Chakmas from the Chittagong Hill Districts in NEFA, Tripura, and Assam, ensuring they inhabit compact areas.[19]

The resettlement of Chakma families in NEFA was carried out through an Agricultural Scheme implemented by the NEFA government as part of its development program. The government's approach aimed to achieve complete and permanent rehabilitation of the migrants by promoting their independence and self-sufficiency, rather than relying on monetary aid and humanitarian assistance. Consequently, two primary rehabilitation programs were established, focusing on the occupations of the refugees: rural and urban settlement.

Within the rural policies, two distinct categories were identified. Firstly, agriculturist migrants, who required both homestead land and a significant amount of cultivable land to support themselves and their families. Secondly, non-agriculturist migrants, who needed homestead land as well as various types of loans to establish themselves.

The government designed a well-defined rehabilitation policy for Chakmas and Hajongs, who were primarily agriculturists, and settled them in NEFA. Each family was allocated 5 acres of land, along with rehabilitation

[19] *Report of Estimates Committee (1964-65) Seventy-First Report (Third Lok Sabha) Ministry of Rehabilitation (Reception, Dispersal and Rehabilitation of new Migrants arriving in India from East Pakistan since 1st January 1964)*

assistance in the form of cash, cattle, tools and implements, and potential government employment opportunities.

Recognizing that rehabilitation necessitates a permanent status as a citizen of the nation, as well as other associated rights and privileges, the government's policy included de facto Indian citizenship for the Chakma migrants, ensuring their entitlements and privileges as citizens.

In accordance with a prudent government policy, the Ministry of Relief and Rehabilitation underwent a name change to the Ministry of Rehabilitation, eliminating the term "relief." This decision stemmed from the understanding that the mere provision of relief, which includes short-term assistance such as cash handouts and support for immediate survival, is insufficient to fully restore the shattered lives of displaced individuals.

During the period between 1964 and 1970, over 8,50,000 Hindu, Christian, and Buddhist refugees from East Pakistan migrated to India and were successfully rehabilitated in various states such as West Bengal, Meghalaya, Assam, Bihar, Delhi, Madhya Pradesh, Maharashtra, among others.

Ironically, apart from in Assam and Arunachal Pradesh, these migrants faced no issues with their citizenship status and were seamlessly integrated into society.

However, the story took a twist in Arunachal Pradesh. While the initial phases of rehabilitation for Chakmas and Hajongs seemed promising, a slow roll-back by the state government led to a de-rehabilitation phase, depriving these communities of their earlier granted privileges.

3

THE INCEPTION OF CHAKMA SETTLEMENTS IN ARUNACHAL PRADESH

The area now called Arunachal Pradesh was previously known as the North East Frontier Tract (NEFT) and then the North East Frontier Agency (NEFA). It shared similarities with the Chittagong Hill Tracts (CHT), where the Chakma migrants came from. The British had deemed both areas as "excluded areas." This label arose not out of British disinterest in these regions but rather from a pragmatic perspective: the wild and challenging landscapes didn't offer them enough incentive to engage in direct administration.

However, while the British were hesitant to dive deep into direct governance, they were also wary of unchecked British entrepreneurial advances. They aimed to safeguard their future economic aspirations in these areas, leading to the formulation and execution of the Bengal Eastern Frontier Regulation Act in 1873 (BEFR Act, 1873). This act fortified the British's exclusionary policy, barring both "British subjects and foreign citizens." This decision decisively isolated the region, severing its ties and interactions with the rest of the nation.

Upon India's tryst with independence, the administrative policies of NEFA saw only minimal modifications. Prime Minister Nehru, diverging slightly from the absolute non-interference doctrine of the British, advocated a policy of minimum interference. This approach was profoundly influenced by anthropologist Dr. Verrier Elwin's manifesto, "A Philosophy for NEFA." The core tenet of this philosophy was to maintain a delicate equilibrium: honouring the region's distinct cultural nuances and traditions while sanctioning limited interventions when indispensable.

Nehru once said, ***"I am not at all sure which is better way of living, the tribal or our own. In some respects, I am quite certain there is better. Therefore, it is grossly presumptuous on our part to approach them with an air of superiority to tell them how to behave or what to do or not to do. There is no point in trying to make them a second copy of ourselves".*** [i20]

Until 1972, NEFA was constitutionally a part of the Assam state and was directly administered by the governor of Assam as an agent of the President of India. On 21 January 1972, the North-East Frontier Agency became the Union Territory of Arunachal Pradesh and was placed under the charge of a Chief Commissioner.

Redefining NEFA: From Isolation to Integration

The doctrine of "minimum interference" was crafted as a judicious balance, ensuring the tribal people of NEFA weren't kept in isolation, yet preventing their abrupt assimilation into the broader Indian landscape with due regard to their cultural uniqueness. In essence, NEFA, for a significant duration, was perceived more as an administrative term rather than a vibrant region pulsating with its own cultural heartbeat.

The 1962 Chinese incursion served as a wake-up call for India. Beyond the immediate territorial concerns, it shook the bedrock of India's administrative stance toward NEFA. The inadequacies of the "minimum interference" policy came under the scanner, with opposition parties

---

[20] *The Indian Frontier Administrative Service: Romanticism and Hostile Borders by Claude Apri* *https://claudearpi.blogspot.com/2014/12/romanticism-and-hostile-borders.html*

condemning it as a mere "Museum of Specimen Approach." They argued that such a hands-off approach impeded NEFA's seamless integration with mainland India, inadvertently setting the stage for the calamitous aftermath of the Sino-Indian conflict.[21]

Facing mounting criticism, Nehru's government recalibrated its stance on NEFA, veering away from its earlier isolationist methodology.

A slew of administrative reforms was promptly rolled out, aiming to knit NEFA closer to India's administrative fabric. The territory was transitioned from the purview of the Ministry of External Affairs to the Ministry of Home Affairs. Concurrently, the officers from the Indian Frontier Administrative Service (IFAS) were amalgamated into the broader frameworks of the Indian Administrative Service (IAS) and the Indian Police Service (IPS). This structural overhaul was complemented by a rapid expansion of the bureaucratic machinery within NEFA.

Political empowerment was deemed as the linchpin to truly integrating the people of NEFA. In acknowledgment, the North East Frontier Agency Panchayat Raj Regulation was promulgated in 1967, underscoring the importance of grassroots political participation.

The demographic thinness of NEFA was another pressing concern. The sparse populace was perceived as a strategic Achilles heel. To bolster the population and, by extension, fortify the region against external aggressions, the government sanctioned the influx of settlers from outside NEFA. This strategic migration aimed to populate and consolidate the region, reducing border skirmishes and repelling incursion attempts from neighbouring areas.

---

[21] *NEFA-An Introduction: R.N. Haldipur*

1. Scheme to Colonise Vijaynagar/Miao area[22]

A review of archival records unveils a letter numbered A.VIII/1-62/83, dated April 2, 1962, exchanged between the Inspector General of Assam Rifles and the Adviser to the Governor of Assam in Shillong. These correspondence sheds light on a proposed initiative known as the "Colonisation of Noa Dihing Valley by Ex-Servicemen of Assam Rifles." The scheme aimed to settle former Assam Rifles personnel in the unexplored territories of the Noa Dihing Valley.

The document presented highlighted the strategic and economic significance of the scheme in this region, emphasising its proximity to sympathetic territories of Communist China in Burma. It sought approval for the settlement plan, underscoring the area's importance for strategic considerations and economic development.

On October 8, 1963, R. Yusuf Ali, Deputy Secretary at the Ministry of External Affairs, corresponded with the Ministry of Food and Agriculture (vide U.O. No. 210/11/63/) seeking advice on a scheme's technical validity. The aim was to determine if the scheme met the necessary technical criteria before seeking financial approval from the relevant ministry.

Following this, on October 16, 1963, a news article appeared in The Statesman, attributed to their Amritsar Correspondent and titled "Ex-Servicemen to be Settled in NEFA." This publication confirmed the official announcement that ex-servicemen would indeed be resettled in specific parts of NEFA. It read "There is sufficient land available in that region for cultivation. The Central Government is anxious the area should be developed in every possible manner".

On December 10, 1963, R. Yusuf Ali, Deputy Secretary at the Ministry of External Affairs, corresponded with P.N.

---

[22] *MHA File No. 210(11)/63-NI (Agricultural Settlement in NEFA Model Schemes for settlement corresponding regarding Vijaynagar/Preetnagar Settlements) National Archives of India*

Luthra, Advisor to the Governor of Assam, discussing the preparedness of a particular scheme and seeking the Governor's guidance as the ultimate authority in NEFA. He mentioned that following discussions with relevant officials, there was consensus to initiate the scheme in the vicinity of the Miao Bordumsa area, close to the road-head.

In another letter dated December 18, 1963, R. Yusuf Ali, Deputy Secretary at the Ministry of External Affairs, wrote again to P.N. Luthra, Advisor to the Governor of Assam, confirming further modifications to the scheme after discussions. It was agreed upon to raise the land ceiling and include additional categories of beneficiaries such as ex-Army personnel, former NEFA employees, ex-ALC members, and individuals recommended by the DIB.

Ultimately, on January 22, 1964, the Ministry of External Affairs communicated the Government of India's endorsement of the scheme for an air-maintained settlement in Vijay Nagar via letter No. 210(11)/63_NI addressed to the Adviser to the Governor of Assam.

2. Scheme for settlement of agrarian communities in Miao-Vijoynagar area

On January 22, 1964, W.S. Rynjah, Secretary (General Administration) of NEFA, vide No. For 44/63 sent some correspondence to all Political Officers, Department Heads, and Deputy Directors of Supply & Transport within NEFA. This communication forwarded an approved scheme regarding the resettlement of agrarian communities in the Miao-Vijoynagar Area, situated within the Tirap Frontier Division of NEFA.

Simultaneously, on January 25, 1964, W.S. Rynjah, Secretary (General Administration) of NEFA, corresponded with R. Yusuf Ali, Deputy Secretary at the Ministry of External Affairs (No. FOR.44/64,1226). The letter outlined that while the implementation of the ex-servicemen resettlement scheme in NEFA was pending, an alternative modest scheme was being initiated. This new scheme aimed to resettle a diverse agricultural community in the available vacant land bordering the region. In essence, the plan entailed the allocation of homesteads and cultivable land to 200 families in Vijaynagar and 1000 families in Miao.

The NEFA administration's rationale for these agrarian community settlement schemes is, in fact, a reflection of the lessons gleaned from the experience of the 1962 war with China.

Post the 1962 skirmish with China, the thinly populated NEFA, with its tribal inhabitants, was seen as a vulnerable target for potential aggression from the neighbouring countries. Initially, there was a strong push to relocate 100,000 sturdy farmers from Punjab and Haryana to NEFA. This initiative intended to promote cohesion between the tribal communities and the broader Indian populace while fortifying the region against any subsequent Chinese advances.

Subsequently, to counter the region's low population density, a key strategic policy was taken. The plan was to populate the region with settled communities, which would serve as a deterrent against infiltration from across the border and diminish the likelihood of border disputes.

Following this, various strategies were developed to tackle the population vacuum in NEFA and multiple resettlement schemes were created. The advantages of these schemes, as highlighted in the Public Accounts Committee's 1977-78 report, are as follows:

(a) The North East Frontier Agency, now known as Arunachal Pradesh, is characterised by a relatively low population density, with an average of approximately 11 individuals per square mile.

(b) The absence of a significant population near the border increases the risk of hostile neighbouring countries exploiting the situation to their advantage.

(c) Establishing a settled community along the border serves as a positive deterrent against potential infiltration from neighbouring territories.

(d) The presence of a settled community along the border significantly diminishes the potential for any border disputes.

(e) The existence of a progressive community fosters a sense of motivation and enthusiasm among the local inhabitants, thereby promoting accelerated economic development.

(f) The settlement of individuals from diverse backgrounds in NEFA contributes to the emotional integration of the local population with the rest of the country.[23]

3. Inception of settlement schemes in NEFA in Historical Perspective

It is evident that following the conclusion of the 1962 Sino-India war, India experienced a pivotal policy transformation, especially concerning the North-East Frontier Agency (NEFA). This evolution can be traced back to several factors, but one that stands out prominently is the region's low population density.

In the aftermath of the 1962 conflict, it became evident that the thin population spread in NEFA presented a strategic vulnerability. The Central Government of India, recognizing the criticality of this, instigated a policy shift. The primary objective was two-fold: to address population scarcity and to reinforce the region's strategic defence capabilities. By advocating for the establishment of mixed communities and optimising the use of unoccupied lands, the government aspired to not only enhance NEFA's

[23] *Public Accounts Committee (1977-78) Sixth Lok Sabha, Twenty-First Report on Resettlement of Ex-Servicemen Near Seijosa, Ministry of Home Affairs*

demographic profile but also to rectify the strategic shortcomings spotlighted during the war.

This renewed approach signified a momentous shift in India's stance towards NEFA, underscoring the region's significance in the broader narrative of national security and development.

In 1963, reflecting a renewed strategic vision for NEFA, the NEFA Development Commissioner took a decisive step by constituting a committee to oversee the resettlement of families in the Noa-Dihing valley. The initial plan was to settle a diverse group of individuals, including Biharis, ex-servicemen, and former Assam Rifle personnel, in this area to call this valley their home.

File No. FOR.44/63 (later renumbered as DRS/35/69) gives us further insight into this initiative that to ensure the success of this initiative, the committee's composition was deliberately made interdisciplinary. The committee, comprising key officials such as NEFA's Director of Forest (P.B. Kar), Director of Agriculture and Community Development (B.R. Raisinghani), Superintending Engineer (J.C. Chakravarty), Executive Engineer in Margherita (Kulwant Singh), and Base Superintendent in Vijaynagar (L. Mansar), worked together to devise a comprehensive resettlement plan.

In March 1963, the area was inspected by representatives from Health Services, the Architect of NEFA Administration, and the Agriculture Department. Subsequently, the District Agriculture Officer of Tirap District compiled a consolidated report, which was then submitted to the NEFA administration.[24]

In late 1963, P.N. Luthra, in his esteemed capacity as the Adviser to the Governor of Assam and the chief administrative overseer for NEFA, convened a crucial meeting. This assembly brought together the heads of

---

[24] *Report of the Committee to study Refugee Settlements in Arunachal Pradesh constituted by the Govt. of Arunachal Pradesh vide Memo No. POL.236/72, dated 08.12.1976*

various departments in NEFA. The central agenda of this meeting was to deliberate on the settlement of three distinct groups of individuals into the NEFA landscape.

The envisioned settlement plan included the following groups:

(a) **Ex-Servicemen:** These veterans were to be channelled into the region under the aegis of the Director of Settlement.

(b) **Assam Rifles Personnel:** The responsibility for their resettlement fell to the Inspector General of Assam Rifles (IGAR).

(c) **Landless people** from the neighbouring districts of Assam.

This deliberation was the inception of a detailed blueprint, eventually leading to the settlement of communities such as the Deoris, Ahoms, Chakmas, and Hajongs within NEFA.

As NEFA administration sought prospective settlers from adjoining districts of Assam's landless populace, January 1964 witnessed the migration's first wave, with landless settlers primarily from the Deori and Ahom ethnicities settling in the Miao area. The area chosen for this pioneering settlement was M'Pen, an old established village that had become uninhabited. The Divisional Forest Officer of Changlang Forest Division received explicit directives from the Director of Forests regarding the M'Pen settlement plan.[25]

During this period, the Miao administrative unit was established, and Mr. Sunil Chowdhury was appointed as the Base Superintendent. On January 20, 1964, Mr. P.B. Kar, the Director of Forests in NEFA, was designated as the Ex-officio Settlement Officer to oversee the implementation of the Miao-Vijaynagar Settlement Scheme. Several positions,

[25] *Report of the Committee to study Refugee Settlements in Arunachal Pradesh constituted by the Govt. of Arunachal Pradesh vide Memo No. POL.236/72, dated 08.12.1976*

including Land Record Officers, were created, and Mr. Sunil Chowdhury, the Base Superintendent of Miao, was placed under his authority.[26]

As these administrative reforms were being rolled out, another crucial development transpired on January 24, 1964. The Director of Forests in NEFA approved an agricultural community settlement scheme for the Vijaynagar region. This plan was also reviewed and endorsed by the Inspector General of Assam Rifles (IGAR)[27]

4. The 1964 Migrant Crisis and India's Rehabilitation Response

Simultaneously, a national emergency emerged with the sudden influx of migrants from East Pakistan, starting in January 1964. Consequently, a "Conference on the Rehabilitation of Migrants" was held in New Delhi on February 8, 1964, to address the situation.[28]

The 'Conference on Migrant Rehabilitation' held discussions and reached an agreement in line with India's policy to make every effort to rehabilitate individuals who had arrived in India due to the ongoing insecurity in East Pakistan, affecting their lives and properties. The conference was attended by several Indian Cabinet ministers, select Chief Ministers, and NEFA administrators.

During the conference, the central government urged state governments to contribute to the national responsibility of rehabilitating the new migrants by

---

[26] *Press India Bureau, Weekly Digest of News, Vol.IX. No. 15 dated April 11 1965*

[27] *Report of the Committee to study Refugee Settlements in Arunachal Pradesh constituted by the Govt. of Arunachal Pradesh vide Memo No. POL.236/72, dated 08.12.1976*

[28] *Report of Estimates Committee (1964-65) Seventy-First Report (Third Lok Sabha) Ministry of Rehabilitation (Reception, Dispersal and Rehabilitation of new Migrants arriving in India from East Pakistan since 1st January 1964)*

resettling them on available vacant lands. In this context, the NEFA administration initially offered 3,000 acres of land to accommodate around 1,000 families for rehabilitation purposes.

On February 13, 1964, the Secretary of Planning & Development in NEFA instructed Mr. P.B. Kar, the Settlement Officer, to screen a lengthy list of Garos, Kochs, Barmans, and Hajong families for potential rehabilitation in the Miao-Vijaynagar area. These families were residing in various camps in Assam and Garo Hills (Now Meghalaya) at that time.

Extract from D.O. No. F-3/64 dated March 16, 1964, from the Governor of Assam to President of India confirms that the NEFA administration had sanctioned a sum of Rs. 15 Lakhs for the settlement in Tirap Frontier Division of about 1000 families of ex-Servicemen, ex-Assam Rifles personnel, ex-NEFA employees and certain other landless persons from the adjoining areas of Assam. It sheds light on the various initiatives undertaken by the NEFA administration to provide land in the NEFA division for tribal refugees who have been recently driven out of East Pakistan into the Garo Hills.[29]

Subsequently, on March 19, 1964, a high-level meeting took place between the NEFA administration and the Ministry of Rehabilitation, Government of India. The meeting aimed to discuss the rehabilitation of displaced persons from East Pakistan in the Tirap Frontier Division. Representatives from the NEFA administration, including P.N. Luthra (Adviser to the Governor of Assam), L.B. Thanga (Development Commissioner), P.B. Kar (Director of Forest & Resettlement Officer), and J.C. Chakraborty (Superintendent Engineer), attended the meeting along with officials from the Ministry of Rehabilitation, Government of India that included Bhagwant Singh,

---

[29] *MHA File No. 210(11)/63-NI (Agricultural Settlement in NEFA Model Schemes for settlement corresponding regarding Vijaynagar/Preetnagar Settlements) National Archives of India*

Officer on Special Duty, N.V. Ventakataraman, Dy. Secretary (Finance) and K.B. Mathur, Under Secretary.[30]

As a result of the meeting, a decision was made to settle one thousand families in the Miao-Vijaynagar area of the Noa-Dihing valley in the Tirap Frontier Division for the purpose of rehabilitation.

Another meeting was held on the same subject on March 20, 1964, among the highest officials of NEFA that included P.N. Luthra, Adviser to the Governor of Assam, R.M. Agarwal, Financial Adviser, P.B. Kar, Director of Forest & Resettlement Officer, P.N. Nag, Joint Director of Agriculture & Shri L.B. Thanga, Development Commissioner. In this meeting it was decided that P.B. Kar, Director of Forest, NEFA would function as Ex-officio Resettlement Officer for complete execution of the settlement scheme. For the implementation of the resettlement scheme, a separate set of staff was to be provided at the disposal of the Resettlement Officer.

On April 10, 1964, Mr. Vishnu Sahay, Governor of Assam, wrote a letter vide No. GA-71/64 to Mr. B.P Chaliha, Chief Minister of Assam and, recommended that the displaced Chakma community from East Pakistan, who were camping in the Mizo District of Assam, would be quite suitable people to settle into Tirap Division, NEFA where unoccupied land was plentifully found. He writes *"The Chakmas would be quite suitable people to go into the Tirap Division of NEFA where there is easily found vacant land in the area about which you and I have often spoken".* [31]

On April 11, 1964, a note was endorsed to the Director of Forests (Resettlement Officer), advising that allotment of 5 acres of land per family should be considered adequate for the purpose of settlement of refugees.

---

[30] *Report of the Committee to study Refugee Settlements in Arunachal Pradesh constituted by the Govt. of Arunachal Pradesh vide Memo No. POL.236/72, dated 08.12.1976*

[31] *White Paper on Chakma and Hajong Refugee Issue, Govt. of Arunachal Pradesh, 1996*

Subsequently, Mr. B.P Chaliha, Chief Minister of Assam and Mr. Vishnu Sahay, Governor of Assam had a discussion on April 16, 1964, regarding easing the burden of rehabilitation of East Pakistan refugees into Assam. NEFA administration was urged by the Government of Assam to accommodate 12,000 migrant families into the empty pockets of NEFA.

With regards to the suggestion to settle Chakmas in NEFA, made by the Governor of Assam in a letter dated April 10, 1964, to the Chief Minister of Assam, the Chief Secretary of Assam, Mr. A.N Kidwai, on April 27, 1964, vide letter No. No. RHM-24/64/10 requested P.N. Luthra, Adviser to the Governor, Assam, to make necessary arrangements for the rehabilitation of 10,000 East Pakistan displaced persons in Tirap Division, NEFA.

With reference to the discussion between the Governor and Chief Minister of Assam on April 16, 1964, P.N Luthra, Advisor to the Governor of Assam, wrote to A.N Kidwai, Chief Secretary, Government of Assam, on May 6, 1964 expressing their inability to accommodate 12000 migrant families into NEFA and only 3000 Chakma families from Assam's Mizo District might be rehabilitated in the area available in Tirap Division.

5. Chakma Resettlement in Arunachal Pradesh: A Journey from Displacement to New Beginnings

On April 10, 1964, a significant development unfolded when Governor Shri Vishnu Sahay of Assam corresponded with Chief Minister Shri B.P. Chaliha of Assam. In his letter, Governor Sahay proposed a thoughtful initiative, suggesting that the Chakma community, who had been displaced from East Pakistan and were presently residing in the Mizo District of Assam, could find a suitable resettlement in the Tirap Division of the North-East Frontier Agency (NEFA). This proposal was grounded in the availability of abundant unoccupied land in the Tirap Division.

Archival sources reveal that the NEFA administration swiftly swung into action. They consented to host 500 Chakma families who had entered India via Tripura and were not housed in refugee camps. The mantle of executing this monumental task fell on the shoulders of Utankamoni Chakma, the astute Political Officer based in Pasighat

By May 26, 1964, Utankamoni Chakma, leveraging his role as the Political Officer, unveiled a robust blueprint of the Miao-Vijaynagar valley settlement scheme. This document bore witness to his meticulous negotiations with local chieftains. Intriguingly, these local figureheads exhibited an enthusiastic attitude, displaying their genuine intent to accommodate the Buddhist Chakma community within their dominions. Their message was clear – they were keen on the immediate arrival of the Chakma migrants.

This historical account underscores the initiative-taking role played by Utankamoni Chakma in facilitating communication with local leaders and gauging their readiness to welcome the Chakma migrants. It also highlights the positive response from the local communities in the North-East Frontier Agency (NEFA) towards the settlement of Buddhist Chakma families in their respective regions.

Fast forward to July 1964, the initial group of 488 Chakmas, consisting of fifty-two families, were brought to the Namphai area of Miao. These Chakma migrants had travelled from Tripura, where they had undergone screening and registration as refugees in Karimganj, located in the Cachar District, and Nowgong (now Nogaon) in Assam.

On August 1, 1964, Mr. Tarapada Bhattacharji, MLA from Silchar, Assam, addressed a letter to the Prime Minister of India, Mr. Lal Bahadur Shastri. In the letter, he enclosed a map along with a note highlighting the NEFA region's vast area, approximately four thousand square miles, which presented significant opportunities for development. Mr. Bhattacharji emphasised that this development could contribute to achieving three primary objectives:

(i) Ensuring defence and security,

(ii) Increasing food production, and

(iii) Facilitating the resettlement of ex-servicemen, local NEFA residents, and refugees.

On August 6, 1964, under D.O. No.GA-195/64, Mr. Vishnu Sahay, the Governor of Assam, wrote to Mr. Mahavir Tyagi, Minister of Rehabilitation, Government of India. In the letter, he suggested that the one thousand families intended for resettlement in the Miao-Vijaynagar valley of NEFA should be distributed among the Chakmas, the Garos, and the plains tribal people from Assam.

Later, on August 24, 1964, Mr. Sahay conveyed that the Chief Minister of Assam, however, insisted that the existing proposal for resettling one thousand Chakma families should remain unchanged. The reason provided was that since these refugees had already moved close to NEFA, the Assam State preferred not to divert them at this stage.

He went on to clarify that this decision would not contradict the policy of settling a mixed population in the NEFA border areas. Mr. Sahay explained that, in addition to the proposed one thousand Chakmas, plans were underway to resettle more people from various communities in the same region.[32]

On September 25, 1964, Mr. G.L. Nanda, the Home Minister of India, addressed Mr. B.P. Chaliha, the Chief Minister of Assam, through D.O. No. 15/12/64-SR(R)-A. The communication outlined those following communal disturbances in East Pakistan, approximately 80,000 Garos, Hajongs, and Dolus (primarily Christians), along with

---

[32] *Rehabilitation of refugees and others in Assam including hill districts and North East Frontier Agency. MHA File No. 15/12/64-SR/R-A (National Archives of India)*

about 15,000 Chakmas (mostly Buddhists), had migrated to Assam by August 31, 1964. While it was reported that the influx of tribal population had not posed any challenges, there were indications of resistance in the rehabilitation of Bengali Hindus.[33]

5.1. The Chakma Resettlement: Initial Challenges, Controversies, and Consensus

Correspondence records from that era bring to light some internal frictions in the resettlement initiative. Specifically, P.B. Kar, who held dual responsibilities as the Director of Forest and the Ex-Officio Settlement Officer, expressed reservations about the actions of Utankamoni Chakma, the Political Officer in Pasighat. It seemed that overlapping roles and responsibilities led to differing opinions on the resettlement process.

Reacting to these disagreements, P.N. Luthra, Adviser to the Governor of Assam, wrote to U. Chakma, Political Officer, Pasigha on July 17, 1964 (bearing reference number P.O -70/64/115), specifying that no new settlements should be initiated near existing villages unless the explicit and written consent of the villagers themselves was obtained.

Soon after, on July 29, 1964, S.D. Lahakar, the Deputy Secretary for Planning and Development in NEFA, issued a more restrictive directive. In this letter (No. PC. 70/64/ 132), he communicated to the Advisor to the Assam Governor that the Political Officer in Pasighat had been instructed not to accept any additional Chakma migrant families, except for the 490 individuals who had already arrived in NEFA via Tripura, for the purpose of rehabilitation.[34]

---

[33] *Rehabilitation of refugees and others in Assam including hill districts and North East Frontier Agency. MHA File No. 15/12/64-SR/R-A (National Archives of India)*

[34] *White Paper on Chakma and Hajong Refugee Issue, Govt. of Arunachal Pradesh, 1996*

These details shed light on the challenges and disagreements that arose during the settlement process of the Chakma community in the Namphai area of Miao. The involvement of different officials and the concerns raised regarding settlement locations highlight the complexities and administrative considerations involved in the resettlement efforts during that time.

In a sequence of events, on August 12, 1964, Sunil Chaudhury, the Base Superintendent in Miao, forwarded a letter (No. STL/62/2/26) to the Director of Forest, NEFA, Shillong. This correspondence detailed a list of 490 Chakma migrants from the first group that had recently settled in the Namphai area and arrived via Tripura.

Just a few weeks later, on August 25, 1964, there was a notable dissent from the local leadership. The village chiefs and elders from Namphai area, voiced their reservations. They penned a letter directed to the Advisor to the Assam Governor, P.N Luthra, expressing their objections to the permanent settlement of Chakmas specifically in Namphai area. Their plea was clear: they wished for the Chakmas to be settled in regions extending beyond the Namphai area.

As a result of the controversy and objections raised by the local Singpho and Tangsa Communities regarding the settlement of Chakmas near Namphai village in Miao, Utankamoni Chakma, the Political Officer stationed in Pasighat, chose to avoid interfering with the affairs of their settlement in the area. This indicates a shift in approach to address the concerns raised and maintain harmony between the Chakma community and the local inhabitants.

In a change of direction from the Namphai controversy, on October 10, 1964, P.N. Luthra, the Advisor to the Governor of Assam vide his file noting wrote that "*We should get on with resettlement of Chakma refugees (up to one thousand families) from Assam to Miao area*" on the file No. PCT-71/63 containing the Assam Governor's order to resettle 1000 Chakma families. The same was forwarded to the concerned authorities by S.D. Lahakar, Deputy Secretary, Planning & Development, NEFA on October 17,

1964. This marks the beginning of the operation of settlement schemes for settlement of Chakmas in Arunachal Pradesh.

On December 03, 1964, S.D. Lahakar, Deputy Secretary, Planning & Development, NEFA vide his letter No. 18/64 wrote to the Political Officer, Khonsa to ensure non-controversial settlement of Chakma migrants by settling them far from the vicinity of existing villages. He also advised to obtain a written consent wherever people are being settled in the vicinity of the existing villages.[35]

5.2. Efforts to Rehabilitate Chakma Migrants: Challenges, Coordination, and Commitment

The tumultuous journey of Chakma migrants from East Pakistan saw them finding an initial refuge in the Mizo Hills and Cachar Districts of Assam. By July's end in 1964, a formidable task lay ahead: transporting roughly a thousand Chakma families to their next transit location in Ledo. This was seen as a strategic stopover, given Ledo's proximity to their future homes in Arunachal Pradesh.

The logistical feat of moving such a substantial number from the Cachar and Mizo Districts to Ledo was monumental. It demanded rigorous coordination. The Assam government, through its Relief and Rehabilitation Department, rose to the occasion by partnering with the Railways. Special train provisions facilitated a smooth transition, ensuring the Chakmas reached Ledo's transit camps efficiently.

A pivotal report, presented by the Ministry of Rehabilitation, titled "Reception, Dispersal, and Rehabilitation of New Migrants arriving in India from East Pakistan since January 1, 1964," offered a roadmap for these migrants' future. Recognizing the Chakmas' unique cultural identity, the report underscored the necessity to house

[35] *White Paper on Chakma and Hajong Refugee Issue, Govt. of Arunachal Pradesh, 1996*

them in consolidated areas. With a specific emphasis on the Chakmas, there was a proposal to explore resettlement opportunities in the areas of NEFA, Tripura, and Assam.[36]

By early December 1964, the NEFA administration took the mantle of responsibility for the first wave of Chakma migrants from Assam. Totaling 1,070 families, or 5,558 individuals, the Chakmas began their transition to the Miao region in batches, spanning December 1964 to February 1965. Together with an earlier batch from Tripura, the collective number swelled to 6,048 individuals across 1,122 families.

The resettlement of these migrants was not without its challenges. Faced with land constraints, Mr. L.J. Johnson, ICS, Additional Secretary to the Government of India, Ministry of Rehabilitation, New Delhi, along with prominent officials from the Assam government and NEFA Administration, undertook a visit to the Miao area in January 1965. They sought suitable regions to continue the resettlement process for more migrants.

According to a report published by the Press Information Bureau on April 11, 1965, development efforts were intensified in NEFA (North-East Frontier Agency). It was proposed that approximately 7,000 East Pakistan Chakma refugees would be settled in the Miao-Vijaynagar area of the Tirap Frontier Division. At that point, 488 individuals had already arrived, and the settlement process was underway.[37]

Beyond the 1,122 Chakma families already settled in the Miao region, the NEFA administration anticipated the influx of more refugees, especially as the country grappled with a massive migration wave from East Pakistan and Burma. On April 21, 1965, under reference No. RR 17/64,

---

[36] *The Seventy-First Report of the Estimates Committee (Third Lok Sabha)*

[37] *https://archive.pib.gov.in/archive/ArchiveSecondPhase/EXTERNAL%20AFFAIRS/1965-APRIL-MAY-VOL-2-EXTERNAL-AFFAIRS/PDF/EXT-1965-04-04_036.pdf*

P.N. Luthra, the Adviser to the Governor of Assam, addressed letters to all the Political Officers and their Additional counterparts in NEFA. He sought detailed proposals outlining available land in their jurisdictions suitable for refugee resettlement, specifying the precise location, potential family count, and the feasibility of irrigation.[38]

He further highlighted that relocating people to NEFA would aid in the advancement of areas presently unutilized and uninhabited by the local community. Moreover, having extensive stretches of undeveloped territory along the frontier is strategically disadvantageous, as demonstrated by the 1962 Chinese incursion. Populating these vacant border regions would enhance and fortify our national boundaries.

He also issued specific guidelines to be ensured before proposing settlement schemes which included avoidance of arousing people's suspicions, unnecessary controversy and misplaced agitation or misunderstanding. He also preferred voluntary donation of land, consultation.

A few months later, in the Tour Note dated June 15, 1965, Mr. L.J. Johnson, ICS, Additional Secretary of the Ministry of Rehabilitation, Government of India, documented his visit to Assam from June 8, 1965, to June 13, 1965. He reported that plans were underway to relocate an additional 1000 Chakma families to the Miao-NoaDihing area and another 1000 families to the Lohit Frontier Division. During his visit, he had discussions with Mr. P.B. Kar, the Director of Forests in NEFA, informed him that a survey of the areas further up the Valley towards Vijaynagar revealed limited availability of land with light soil. This meant that enough land would have to be allocated to allow for a jhuming (shifting cultivation) cycle of 5 to 6 years, at a rate of 3 to 4 acres per year. The NEFA Administration was exploring the possibility of identifying

---

[38] *White Paper on Chakma and Hajong Refugee Issue, Govt. of Arunachal Pradesh, 1996*

other areas for resettlement, but it was too early to determine whether these efforts would be successful.[39]

With the surging influx of refugees from East Pakistan, the Assam Government faced increasing strain to accommodate more displaced people. Consequently, a group of local technical officials, spearheaded by the Divisional Forest Officer of the Working Plan Division in NEFA, was formed. Their mandate was to evaluate land availability for displaced migrants' resettlement in the area beyond Noa-Dihing Valley.

By June 15, 1965, the committee presented a report detailing land distribution across 9 segments. It is crucial to mention that these calculations were tentative and approximate. Their research suggested that around 1,500 more families could be accommodated in the Noa-Dihing valley. This estimation was based on the premise that five acres of Wet Rice Cultivation (WRC) or 20 acres of Jhum land would suffice for a family of two adults, one adolescent, and two younger children. The resettlement blueprint aimed to allocate 500 of these families to the WRC region, with the residual 1,000 earmarked for the Jhum region.[40]

On June 22, 1965, a significant development occurred in the resettlement effort. A crucial meeting at Raj Bhavan in Shillong included Mahavir Tyagi, the Minister of Rehabilitation for the Government of India, along with the rehabilitation minister, Chief Secretary, and other Assam government officials. During this meeting, the NEFA Administration agreed to accommodate 2000 more Chakma families. This increased the total number of

---

[39] *Tour Note of Mr. L.J Johnson, ICS, Additional Secretary, Ministry of Rehabilitation, Govt. of India on his visit to Assam between 08.06.65 and 13.06.65*

[40] *Record note of discussion by Minister of Rehabilitation, Government of India, with the Rehabilitation Minister, Assam, Chief Secretary, Assam, Rehabilitation Secretary, Assam and other officers of the State Government dated 22.06.1965*

families slated for resettlement in the Miao region to 3000.[41]

Moreover, the meeting also addressed the plight of Chakma migrants languishing in Bihar's transit camps. These refugees harboured aspirations of returning to Assam. The Minister of Rehabilitation brought this significant concern to the forefront, ensuring it was deliberated upon. This meeting wasn't just about numbers and logistics; it reflected the government's earnest endeavours to comprehend and alleviate the Chakma community's challenges, reaffirming its dedication to the refugee cause.

In a report detailing his travels to Goalpara, Garo Hills Districts, and Tripura, Mr. H.S. Butalia, the Liaison Officer from the Ministry of Rehabilitation, Government of India, shared insights on various progressions. In a tour note from July 19, 1965, he highlighted that the Adviser to the Governor of Assam had proposed land in the Yangsang Tso valley, close to Tuting in the Siang Frontier Division of NEFA, to resettle an estimated 400-500 Chakma families. This valley is nestled along the Indo-Tibetan frontier.

Further amplifying the efforts, the NEFA administration was crafting a comprehensive strategy to house an additional 2,000 Chakma migrant families. Their relocation was slated for October of the same year, and the comprehensive plans were due to reach the Ministry soon.[42]

Fast forward to August 2, 1965, and Mr. Butalia, Liaison Officer, Ministry of Rehabilitation, penned another

---

[41] *Record note of discussion by Minister of Rehabilitation, Government of India, with the Rehabilitation Minister, Assam, Chief Secretary, Assam, Rehabilitation Secretary, Assam and other officers of the State Government dated 22.06.1965*

[42] *Tour Note of H.S Butalia, Liaison Officer, Ministry of Rehabilitation, Govt. of India vide No. 13(23)/65-RH. I dated 19th July, 1965 regarding his visit to Goalpara and Garo Hills District and Tripura*

significant letter, this time to Shri K.P. Mathrani, the Secretary of the Ministry of Relief & Rehabilitation. The letter discussed the upcoming transfer of Chakma refugee families from camps in Bihar to Assam. It hinted that these arrangements were nearing completion.

In a correspondence marked D.O. No. RR.65/65 dated September 3, 1965, P.N. Luthra, Adviser to the Governor of Assam, communicated to A.D. Pandey, Joint Secretary at MHA, apprising him about the administration's resettlement of civilians in NEFA. This resettlement scheme mirrored the one designed for ex-servicemen in the border regions of NEFA. Additionally, he furnished detailed figures and locations as outlined in Appendix 'B'.[43]

APPENDIX - B

LOCATIONS WHERE CIVILIANS HAVE BEEN RESETTLED

Sl.	Division	Location	No. of Families Settled	Remarks
1	Tirap Frontier Division	Khagam Area	52 Families (319+84=403)	Chakmas who came directly via Tripura
		Miao Area	419 families 2229+415=2644	1st batch of Chakmas from Ledo camp
		Deban, M'Pen Khagam & Kharsang areas	581 families 2632+372=3004	1st batch of Chakmas from Ledo camp

[43] *Development & Resettlement of of ex-services Sectors of the Indo Pakistan border and NEFA (217/16/65-NEFA) National Archives of India*

2	Lohit Frontier Division	Chowkham -Wakro Area	1000 families	1000 East Pakistan Chakma families to be rehabilitated from next month
3	Tirap Frontier Division	Between Bordumsa and Vijaynagar	1000 families	1000 East Pakistan Hajong families to be rehabilitated from next month

A subsequent update emerged on September 7, 1965. Once again, Mr. Butalia, Liaison Officer, Ministry of Rehabilitation, corresponded with Mr. Mathrani, sharing vital information. NEFA's administration had extended its invitation to 150 more Chakma families from Bihar's camps, adding to the already agreed-upon 2,000 refugees. These families were set to commence their journey to NEFA post-October 15.

Mr. Butalia elucidated further on the grand plan: the combined 3,000 Chakma families, which included the initially resettled 1,000, were poised for relocation from Assam's camps by mid-October 1965. In this intricate manoeuvre, the NEFA authorities had requested sanction for the proposals they had submitted regarding the rehabilitation of new migrations in Lohit and Tirap, as stated in their communications numbered No. FOR/RR/170/65/10667-71 and No. FOR/RR/172 /65/ 10662-65, both dated July 16, 1965.

In a D.O. letter numbered No. 12(6)/65 - Part II, dated October 4, 1965, Mr. L.J. Jhonson, ICS, Additional Secretary to the Government of India, Ministry of Rehabilitation, New Delhi, corresponded with Shri T.C. Puri, ICS Patna, regarding the Chakmas residing in Bettiah and Champaran

Refugee camps who expressed a desire to return to Assam due to a lack of cultural affinity and unsuitable climate. Mr. Jhonson informed that the NEFA administration had also agreed to their resettlement in NEFA and suggested that these families could be sent there.[44]

The 139 Chakma families who were initially relocated from the Majoli Camp Chawmanu in Tripura to Bihar in May 1964, these families had endured a stay spanning 19 months. Their relocation journey concluded in November 1965 when they were handed over to the NEFA administration. Ensuring their safe transit, the camp commander from the West Hazari Camp Bettiah supervised their relocation from Bihar, first to Margherita, and then their eventual resettlement in the Miao area.

Mr. Hari Sharma, Secretary (UT) at MHA, conducted a visit to the Namchik, Miao, and Khagam Settlement area on December 20 and 21, 1965. During his visit to the Khagam Settlement area, he observed that approximately 18 months had elapsed since the Chakmas had settled there and appeared to be actively striving to ensure the settlement's success and self-sufficiency. Notably, the agricultural produce, particularly vegetables, already exceeded local demands. Overall, this settlement appeared to be a thriving endeavour, with expectations for an increased influx of Chakmas. Requests were made for the establishment of a school and a dispensary. While the area faced poor connectivity, efforts were underway to construct a road on the opposite side, which would facilitate the transportation of the settlement's produce.

During the visit to Miao village, Sharma encountered the Hajongs residing in transit camps. It appeared that the Hajongs were hesitant to settle in the valley. Nevertheless,

[44] *White Paper on Chakma and Hajong Refugee Issue, Govt. of Arunachal Pradesh, 1996*

administrative officials were actively encouraging them to follow the Chakmas' example and consider settling down.[45]

However, as resettlement efforts continued, challenges arose. A telegram, sent by Ramesh Chandra, Secretary of Relief & Rehabilitation, Government of Assam, to L.J. Johnson on January 13, 1966, offered insights into these obstacles. The first group of 412 Hajong families, relocated to Miao in NEFA, experienced divisions. A majority, 370 families, rejected the allocated lands and expressed their intention to return to Ledo. Only 40 families chose to stay, accepting the land grants in NEFA.

Despite these setbacks, relentless efforts were made to encourage the resettlement of other families. Efforts were underway to persuade another 588 families from the Ledo camp to consider Miao as their new home. Stringent guidelines were set; the Ledo Camp commandant received instructions to deny any amenities or rehabilitation benefits to the Hajong families that decided to abandon the resettlement process.[46]

On November 30, 1967, M.R. Yardi, Additional Secretary to the Government of India, compiled the minutes of the Meeting of MHA's Internal Affairs Committee of Secretaries vide F.No.217(16)/65-NI, conducted in June 1967, addressing the resettlement of ex-servicemen, ex-Assam Rifles personnel, agrarian families, including East Pakistan refugees, in NEFA. In the document, he emphasised the objectives behind formulating such initiatives: augmenting NEFA's population density to fill the demographic gaps near the border, establishing a stable community to deter hostile border infiltration, and bolstering the morale of local

---

[45] *Influx/Removal of Tibetan refugees in NEFA (File No. File No. NI/102/1/65) Extract from Secy (UT)'s Note dated 8.1.1966 on his tour to NEFA from 14.12.1965 to 22.12.1965 (National Archives of India)*

[46] *Assam Archive File: Movement of Second Group of Chakma Refugees from Cachar & Mizo District to NEFA (File No. RHMC-6/66)*

inhabitants. Yardi also stressed the potential benefits, such as diversifying the area's economy and fostering emotional integration of the local populace with the wider nation. He acknowledged the challenges in settling populations in NEFA. However, despite these obstacles, approximately 2000 Chakma families from East Pakistan were successfully rehabilitated in Khagam, Miao, and other areas of the Tirap District. Additionally, over 200 Chakma families were resettled in the Chowkham area of Lohit District.[47]

6. Movement & Resettlement of Second Group of Chakmas migrants from Cachar & Mizo Districts to NEFA

In a decisive move to aid the relocation of the second batch of Chakma migrants from Cachar and Mizo Districts to the Ledo transit camp, the Relief and Rehabilitation Department of the Assam government allied with the Railway authorities. This alliance aimed at ensuring a smooth transition for the migrating Chakmas. Here is a detailed timeline encapsulating the series of events leading up to the resettlement of these Chakma migrants:

February 28, 1966:

The Deputy Secretary of the Relief Rehabilitation Department in the Government of Assam contacted Mr. Kranti Kumar, who was serving as the Officer on Special Duty (OSD) in the Transportation Department. They asked for Mr. Kumar's help in arranging special train services. The goal was to transport 2,000 Chakmas from Monacherra to the Ledo transit camp by March 10, 1966. This group included 250 Chakma migrants who were earlier living in camps in the Mizo Hill District.

March 1, 1966:

---

[47] *Development Resettlement of of ex-services Sectors of the Indo Pakistan border and NEFA (217/16/65-NEFA) National Archives of India*

An official memo, identified as No. RHMC.6/66/2, was dispatched via WT Message. The sender: The Sub-Divisional Officer of the Rehabilitation Department stationed in Hailakandi. The recipients: Rehabilitation Departments located in Silchar, Aijal, and Margherita APO. This memo appraised them of the government's resolution to shift 2,000 Chakma refugees, inclusive of the 250 from Mizo Hills, from Monacherra to Ledo. This was a part of the grand scheme to rehabilitate them in NEFA. The memo was clear in its directives. It called upon the Mizo District authorities to liaise with the Communication Department in Silchar. The objective was clear-cut: Ensure all Chakmas in the Mizo Hills District Camps make their way to Monacherra before the stipulated deadline of March 10, 1966. Further, the Deputy Commissioner of Cachar was entrusted with the responsibility of setting up interim housing facilities at the Monacherra camp for these migrants until their onward journey. Lastly, the Margherita APO was tasked with overseeing the welcoming and housing of the arriving Chakma migrants at Ledo.

March 2, 1966:

The Department of Relief and Rehabilitation, Assam, dispatched a letter to the Officer on Special Duty (Railways) within the Transport Department. This communique specifically sought the organisation of a special train journey connecting Monacherra Railway Station to Ledo Railway Station. Set for March 10, 1966, the objective was the relocation of 2,000 Chakma refugees. In a proactive move, an upfront fare of Rs. 1000/- was credited to the Railway's primary account, streamlining the planning process.[48]

Simultaneously, in another letter bearing the same date (DO No. 12(14)/65-RL. II), Mr. Pyare Lal Gupta, Deputy Secretary of the Ministry of Relief & Rehabilitation under the Central Government, initiated a dialogue with Mr.

---

[48] *Assam Archive File: Movement of Second Group of Chakma Refugees from Cachar & Mizo District to NEFA (File No. RHMC-6/66)*

Ramesh Chandra, the Relief & Rehabilitation Secretary of Assam's state government. This discourse was centred around the Hajong Families who had opted to leave the Miao camp located in NEFA. While Mr. Ingty was undertaking efforts to persuade their relocation to NEFA territories, their hesitance was palpable. The Hajong's unfamiliarity with hill-based agriculture brewed apprehensions about the potential success of their rehabilitation in the hilly NEFA. In contrast, the Chakma families, who had settled in NEFA during 1964-65, conveyed a narrative of contentment and prosperity in their new habitats. Their positive recounts kindled enthusiasm among other Chakma clans in Cachar. After thorough deliberation, a consensus was reached to channelize the Chakma families settled across various Assam camps towards resettlement in NEFA.

March 5, 1966: A letter, catalogued as No. RHMC.6/66/7, was penned by Mr. P.C. Deb, ACS, the Deputy Relief & Rehabilitation Commissioner of Assam stationed in Shillong. Addressed to the Director of Forest in NEFA, also based in Shillong, the letter served to notify about the impending transfer of approximately 2,000 Chakma refugees. With their departure from camps in Cachar slated for a journey to Ledo and subsequent rehabilitation in NEFA, a special train was earmarked for March 10, 1966. Furthermore, Mr. Deb emphasised the necessity for prearranged logistics to ensure a seamless transition of the refugees from Ledo to NEFA, with the process commencing upon their arrival in Ledo.

Through this series of orchestrated correspondences and strategic planning, the government authorities aimed to ensure the systematic and efficient resettlement of the Chakma migrants, underlining their commitment to the cause.

March 8, 1966:

Mr. P.C Deb, ACS, Dy. Relief & Rehabilitation Commissioner, based in Shillong, wrote a letter (designated No. RHMC.6/66/7) addressed to the IGP of Shillong. The letter explicitly sought a police escort to accompany the special train designated to relocate Chakma refugees from the Cachar camp to Ledo, targeting their eventual rehabilitation in NEFA. It was further revealed that the DC Cachar was incapacitated from offering police support, largely attributed to heightened tensions in the Mizo district.

March 9, 1966: Two significant communications took place:

A WT message (bearing No. RHMC.6/66/13A) was relayed by the Relief & Rehabilitation Commissioner, Assam, to its Silchar counterpart. The communiqué intimated a slight change in plans: Some Chakma families, initially scheduled to proceed to Ledo on March 10, were now earmarked for rehabilitation in Lohit. It further urged that Chakma representatives, previously deputed to Lohit to facilitate discussions with local tribal chiefs, be incorporated within this train relocation batch.

A U.O Note (identified as No. TRY.44/65) was issued by the OSD (Railways) of the Transport Department, which detailed the logistical arrangements for two special train services. These trains, each fitted with 10 compartments, were slated to relocate Chakmas from Hailakandi to Ledo on March 11 and March 14. To expedite the process, a sum of Rs. 5000/- was sought as a deposit for each train service.[49]

March 16, 1966:

Mr. P.C Deb received a formal acknowledgment from ADC, Silchar, detailing the recent transfer metrics of Chakma refugees to Ledo. The data highlighted the transportation of 172 families (1,028 individuals) on March 11, while the March 14 transit accounted for 160 families (972 individuals).

---

[49] *Assam Archive File: Movement of Second Group of Chakma Refugees from Cachar & Mizo District to NEFA (File No. RHMC-6/66)*

March 25, 1966:

In a comprehensive letter (catalogued as No. CR/24/66858-60), Mr. L.N Das, Commandant of the Ledo Refugee Camp, conveyed to the Circle Officer of Miao, Tirap District, about the fresh relocation of Chakma refugees to the Miao Camp. This communication also encapsulated a meticulous list enumerating the Chakma migrants.[50]

6.1. Dynamics of Rehabilitation and the Changing Goals

May 19, 1966:

Mr. P.B Kar, Director of Forests for NEFA, conveyed concerns to Mr. S.D. Lahakar, Deputy Secretary (Planning & Development), via letter No. FOR/RR/172/65. The correspondence depicted a burgeoning challenge: the incapacity to provide settlement to more Chakma families within Lohit District. This challenge emerged due to significant opposition from the Khamtis, Mishmis, and Singphos residing in Lohit District.

Despite initial plans by the NEFA administration to settle around 1000 Chakma families in Chowkham within Lohit District, local opposition led to a stark reduction. Only 214 families were successfully resettled between the Bareng and Kamlang rivers. However, in an alternative arrangement, 250 Chakma families found a new home in the Subansiri District, currently recognized as Papumpare, specifically within the domains of Hollongi & Dirgha area.

June 24, 1966:

Mr. S.D. Lahakar, the Deputy Secretary (Planning & Development) of NEFA, wrote a letter (No. RR.38/65) to the Liaison Officer of the Ministry of Labour, Employment and Rehabilitation in Shillong. The purpose of the letter was

---

[50] *Assam Archive File: Movement of Second Group of Chakma Refugees from Cachar & Mizo District to NEFA (File No. RHMC-6/66)*

to inform the Liaison Officer about the revised settlement plans in Lohit Division. Initially, there were intentions to settle 1000 families there, but due to opposition from the Khamtis, Singphos, and Mishmis, the progress had to be slowed down. The letter also mentions the revised target of rehabilitating 2253 families by the end of 1966-67, as opposed to the original goal of 3000 families.[51]

February 22, 1967:

In a comprehensive analysis, the Committee of Review of Rehabilitation Work in West Bengal, under the aegis of the Ministry of Labour Employment and Rehabilitation, New Delhi, spotlighted an intriguing proposition. The report highlighted the benevolent offer by the NEFA administration, willing to extend a hand of assistance to the national cause. They proposed to furnish resettlement avenues for an additional 3000 migrants originating from East Pakistan. This gesture aimed to ease the burgeoning pressures linked to refugee rehabilitation on the national front. [52]

6.2. Chronicles of Rehabilitation Efforts

April 13, 1967:

In the General Administration Report on Relief & Rehabilitation activities for the year 1965-66, S. Baruah, the Under Secretary of R&R in Assam, detailed the magnitude of rehabilitation efforts to the Under Secretary of the Government of Assam, General Administration Department, Rehabilitation vide (No. RHE.25/66/16). He highlighted that the state Government of Assam had consented to the rehabilitation of approximately 75,000

---

[51] *White Paper on Chakma and Hajong Refugee Issue, Govt. of Arunachal Pradesh, 1996*

[52] *Committee of Review of Rehabilitation Work in West Bengal, Ministry of Labour Employment and Rehabilitation, New Delhi dated 22nd February 1967. Legislation, Survey Reports and Statistics/Compilation No. I (Fact and Figures at a Glance)*

refugees or 15,000 families. This figure includes 3,000 families who are slated to be resettled in NEFA.[53]

July 1967: A consequential survey, named "REHABILITATION OF DISPLACED PERSONS AND REPATRIATES: Facts and Figures at a Glance", emphasised NEFA's offer to rehabilitate 3000 migrant families within its borders.

1967-68:

According to the 8th Report of the Estimates Committee in the Fourth Lok Sabha, the Ministry of Employment & Rehabilitation in 1967-68 acknowledged and approved the recommendation of resettling Chakma Buddhist migrants from the Chittagong Hill Districts. The government aimed to relocate them to suitable and compact areas in NEFA (North-East Frontier Agency). Additionally, the Ministry of Employment & Rehabilitation stated their intent to explore the feasibility of establishing forest-based and small-scale industries in the NEFA region, in collaboration with the NEFA Administration. This information is documented in the Ministry of Rehabilitation's Office Memorandum No. 3 (3) 165-RH-I, dated 12-10-1965.[54]

July 5, 1968: J.M. Syiem, the Under Secretary (R&W) at the NEFA Secretariat in Shillong, communicated with the Deputy Commissioner of Lohit about allocating land to the Chakmas. The letter indicated the administration's intention to lease the land to the Chakmas for an initial five-year term, with potential extensions later. The communication also underscored the need for a swift survey of areas presently inhabited by the Chakmas. Moreover, any Chakma-occupied territories within

---

[53] *Assam Archive File: General Administration Reports File No. RHE.35/66*

[54] *Estimates Committee, 8th Report, Fourth Lok Sabha, Ministry of Employment & Rehabilitation, 1967-68*

reserved forests were suggested to be de-reserved for efficient resolution. [55]

December 12, 1968: Under the notification No. RR-12/68 issued by the NEFA Administration, the Directorate of Rehabilitation and Resettlement was established. This newly formed directorate operates within the framework of the Planning and Development Department.[56]

April 10, 1969: In a D.O. letter, P.N. Luthra, Adviser to the Governor of Assam, communicated to Mr. M.R. Yardi, Additional Secretary at the Ministry of Home Affairs in New Delhi. The letter informed that the final group of 207 Chakma families from East Pakistan had been successfully relocated to the Deban-Namdapha region, marking the completion of settling a total of 2,899 East Pakistan migrants in NEFA thus far. It was further mentioned that there would be no further intake of East Pakistan migrants from this point onwards. It is noteworthy that the NEFA Administration had previously agreed to accommodate approximately 3,000 Chakma families a few years ago.[57]

7. Reuniting separated Chakma Families

As thousands of Chakma families were during migration and temporarily residing in transit camps within Assam, a significant number of these families experienced the unfortunate and distressing circumstances leading to separation from their loved ones. This separation occurred for a multitude of reasons and under various circumstances.

The migration process itself was marked by challenges and uncertainties. In the chaos of migration, individuals

---

[55] *White Paper on Chakma and Hajong Refugee Issue, Govt. of Arunachal Pradesh, 1996*

[56] *Report of the Committee to study Refugee Settlements in Arunachal Pradesh constituted by the Govt. of Arunachal Pradesh under Memo No. POL.236/72, dated 08.12.1976*

[57] *Letter of Mr. P.N. Luthra, Adviser to the Governor of Assam vide No. D.O.R.R.14/69 dated 10th April 1969 to M.R. Yardi, Additional Secretary, Ministry of Home Affairs, New Delhi*

within these Chakma families become separated from one another due to the sheer magnitude of the movement, overcrowded transit camps, and the difficulty of keeping track of all family members.

Furthermore, the tumultuous nature of the migration journey, which often involved long, and arduous travels caused them to become separated from their families. These circumstances included accidents, illnesses, maternity related issues or even instances where family members were unintentionally left behind at various transit points.

The result of these factors was that many Chakma families faced the heart-wrenching reality of being torn apart during their migration and their stay in transit camps in Assam. This not only added to the challenges they were already confronting but also created a profound emotional toll as families sought to reunite with their missing members during an uncertain and challenging period in their lives.

July 22, 1966, and July 27, 1966:

The ripple effects of the letter penned by Mr. P.B. Kar, the Director of Forests for NEFA, combined with subsequent communication from the Liaison Officer of the Ministry of Relief and Rehabilitation, intensified inter-departmental engagements. These series of dialogues specifically aimed at ensuring the seamless transport and reunion of separated family units within the Chakma community—members of which had earlier embarked on rehabilitation journeys in NEFA. Reports suggested that these separated relatives could be traced back to the Monacherra camp.

October 7, 1966:

Culminating these intensive discussions, J. Chakrabarty, Camp Commandant of Silcoorie New Migrants' Camp, Cachar, drafted a letter (denoted as No. SC-B/23/65/125). This letter, directed at the Circle Officer in Miao, confirmed the successful transition of separated Chakma family members into NEFA territories.

The government embarked on specific endeavours to bring together those who had been separated from their families. Analysis of official communications indicates that distinct efforts were undertaken to reunify the following families who had experienced separation:

(i) Chokya Chakma: From the Transit camp in Assam, he was sent to work as a casual worker and from the work site he was sent to Ledo for settlement in NEFA. His father, Kistolal Kamal Chakma with five others were staying in Manachera camp.

(ii) Mukunda Chakma: He was also sent to work as a casual worker and from the work site he was sent to Ledo for settlement in NEFA. His father, Kalagulu Chakma with five others were staying in Manachera camp.[58]

(iii) Harimala Chakma, the wife of the late Madhajoy Chakma, along with her son Mayadhan Chakma, aged 10, faced separation from their extended family following her husband's passing at Monacherra Camp. Eventually, she was successfully reunited with Akshoy Moni Chakma, her late husband's brother, along with his family.[59]

(iv) Mana Chakma got settlement in Chowkham while his family members, including Hegera Chakma (father), Rajangini Chakma (mother), and his sisters Nidhur Kala Chakma and Panyamala Chakma, continued to stay at Manacherra Camp in Cachar. Eventually, they were successfully reunited.[60]

---

[58] *Letter of P.B Kar, Director of Forests, NEFA to Liaison Officer, Ministry of Rehabilitation, Shillong vide No. FOR/RR/128/66/10380 dated July 22, 1966*

[59] *Letter of Camp Commandant, Saranarthipur Migrants Camp, Monacherra to SDO, Hailandi vide No. SCE9/66/1033 dated 29.07.1966*

[60] *Letter of Under Secretary, Govt. of Assam to the R&R Commissioner, Assam, Shillong dated August 30, 1966*

(v) Matilal Chakma who got separated from his family and camped at Silcoorie New Migrants Camp, Cachar was eventually reunited with his family members (Ranga Choka Chakma) in NEFA.[61]

8. Rehabilitating Chakmas and Hajongs: Settlement Schemes in Arunachal Pradesh

In the rehabilitation journey of the Chakmas and Hajongs, the Indian Government implemented five key settlement schemes in what was previously known as NEFA, now Arunachal Pradesh.

SCHEME-I: Recognizing the need for settlement in Chowkham, nestled between the Bareng and Kamlang rivers in the erstwhile Lohit district (now Namsai district), a financial sanction of Rs. 8,83,800/- was allocated. This was meant to accommodate 214 Chakma families. The green signal came through official communiqués on 07.03.1968 and 14.10.1968, bearing the reference 27(10)/67-RH-II(i).

SCHEME-II: In an important revision, Rs. 43,69,512/- was earmarked for the resettlement of 150 Hajong families alongside 855 Chakma families. These families found their homes in the Pakan, Deban, and Namdapha regions of Nao-Dihing Valley, part of the former Tirap District (now Changlang district). This revised fund allocation, which surpassed the original budget of Rs. 19,88,000/-, was officially approved on 07/03/1968 and 14/10/1968, referenced as 27(10)/67-RH-II(i) and 27(10)/67-RH-(ii).

SCHEME-III: For a sizable group of 1122 Chakma families, a funding of Rs. 24,64,356.47/- was allotted. Upon review by the Government of India's Screening Team, these families were later reorganised into 1286

---

[61] *Letter of Camp Commandant, Silcoorie New Migrants Camp, Cachar to CO, Miao, Tirap vide No. RR/SC-B/23/65/125 dated October 7, 1966*

natural family units. Miao, Khagam, Manthi, and M'Pen in the Noa-Dihing Valley of Tirap District became their designated settlement zones. The scheme was formalised via communications on 26.02.1966 and 10.10.1968, referenced under 27(2)/65-RH-II(i) and 27(10)/67-RH-II respectively.

SCHEME-IV: Carving a niche for 350 Chakma families in the Namdapha region of Noa-Dihing valley in Tirap District, Rs. 26,72,870/- was set aside. A significant highlight of this scheme was the proposed construction of a 30-mile road. Official endorsement for this plan was received on 14.01.1969, under the reference 27(11)67-RH(i).

SCHEME-V: With an allocation of Rs. 12,36,530/-, the scheme aimed to establish a new home for 250 Chakma families in the Hollongi and Dirgha zones of the erstwhile Subansiri district (now part of Papumpare). The government's nod was recorded on 14.01.1969, referencing 27(11)67-RH-II(i).[62]

8.1. Overview of the Family Distribution Across Settlement Schemes [63]

Settlement Scheme	Families	Location
Scheme-I	214	Chowkham, Lohit District (Now Namsai)
Scheme-II	1005	Deban-Namdapha, Tirap Dist

[62] *A Comprehensive Note on Chakma Settlers in Changlang District by Mr. Arun Goyal, IAS, Deputy Commissioner, Changlang enclosed in his letter No. CA-108/89 dated Changlang the 8th September, 1990 to the Home Secretary, Govt. of Arunachal Pradesh.*

[63] *Report of the Committee to study Refugee Settlements in Arunachal Pradesh constituted by the Govt. of Arunachal Pradesh under Memo No. POL.236/72, dated 08.12.1976*

		(Now Changlang)
Scheme-III	1122	Khagam, Miao, Manthi, Mpen, Tirap District (Now Changlang)
Scheme-IV	350	Namdapha (Firm base), Tirap Tirap District (Now Changlang)
Scheme-V	250	Hollongi-Dirgha areas in Subansiri District (Papumpare)

Total Families: 2941

From the years 1964 to 1969, within the backdrop of the Northeast Frontier Agency (NEFA), which is today's Arunachal Pradesh, the Indian Government sanctioned an aggregate sum of Rs. 11,626,268.00. This substantial investment was directed towards the rehabilitation and resettlement of an estimated 2,899 Chakma and Hajong families across three distinct districts. This reiterates the government's commitment to ensuring the seamless integration and welfare of these communities in the northeastern region of the country.

8.1. Overview of Scheme-wise items sanctioned by the Govt. of India for settlement of Chakmas[64]

Details of the items	1st Scheme (214 families)	2nd Scheme (1000 families)	3rd Scheme (1286 families)	4th Scheme (350 families)	5th Scheme (250 families)	Total
(i) Camp Barracks	26660	114214	104582	70620	124980	441056

[64] *Archive of India, File No. 13024/5/73AP (Settlement of Chakma Refugees in Arunachal Pradesh)*

(ii) Staff Quarters, Ration Godown	-	-	-	-	-	30285
(iii) Ration	656505	274129 7	247910 3	113022 0	8073 00	7814425
(iv) Establish ment	50172	141500	132760	130400	1151 00	569932
(v) Agri. tools and implemen ts / seeds, pesticide etc.	28564	133000	134242	42860	3925 0	377916
(vi) Transport & maintenan ce of vehicles	91083	571570	87554	436270	9782 0	1284297
(vii) Other facilities e.g. marriage grant, sradh grant etc.	33564	128000	499		3298 0	194143
(viii) Boats and maintenan ce	5158	19148	5759	13950		44012

(ix) Office equipment, furniture & misc. items		3900	2648			6548
(x) Water supply arrangement	2500	16886		10000	10000	39386
(xi) Cotton clothing			62911			62911
(xii) Internal roads / approach roads	10000		935	460000	10000	486935
(xiii) Irrigation facilities				151000		151000
(xiv) Land Development	107000	500000	643000	175000	118500	1543500
	1012206	4369512	3684279	2620320	135530	13040346
Or say	1012200	4369500	3684000	2620000	135500	13041000

9. Selection of Chakmas for settlement in Arunachal Pradesh

The 1962 war demonstrated the strategic significance of the NEFA region, prompting the government to swiftly adjust its administration policies. It shifted the policy from non-interference to minimal interference. The administration of NEFA was likewise moved from the Ministry of External Affairs to the Ministry of Home Affairs.

As a result, one of the most pondered and discussed policy matters for the central government and the administrators of NEFA was the selection of persons from outside for rehabilitation into NEFA because population vacuum in the region was strategically undesirable.[65]

The selection of ex-servicemen personnel of Assam Rifles who were made to settle in Vijaynagar area of Tirap District (now Changlang District) and ex-servicemen from Punjab and Haryana in Seijosa in Kameng District (now East Kameng District) was to fill in the population vacuum and to use them as positive deterrent in the event of emergency like the one in 1962.

Similarly, the Chakmas were also selected from among other numbers of tribes who migrated from East Pakistan during the same time to be rehabilitated at a strategically significant NEFA after the Central government made a well-considered policy decision.

On April 10, 1964, Shri Vishnu Sahay, Governor of Assam, wrote a letter to Shri B.P Chaliha, Chief Minister of Assam, recommending that the displaced Chakma community from East Pakistan, who were camping in the Mizo District of Assam, would be quite suitable people settle into Tirap Division, NEFA where unoccupied land is plentifully found.

As per the Ministry of Home Affairs letter to the Lt. Governor of Arunachal Pradesh vide letter No. 13024/5/83-AP on October 15, 1981, before settlement of

---

[65] *Internal Displacement, Migration, and Policy in Northeastern India Author(s): Uddipana Goswami East-West Center (2007) http://www.jstor.com/stable/resrep06479*

Chakma in NEFA, these families were selected after they were screened by the SIB, Shillong.

Chakmas were found to be most suitable people for rehabilitation into NEFA due to the following important factors, i.e. Ethno-cultural Link with India, Tribal Character of Chakmas and Sense of undoing of the injustice of partition.

The Estimates Committee (1964-65) Seventy-First Report (Third Lok Sabha) Ministry of Rehabilitation (Reception, Dispersal and Rehabilitation of new migrants arriving in India from East Pakistan since 1st January 1964) also suggested that while drawing up plans for rehabilitation of migrant tribal families (Chakmas), every effort should be made to put them in compact areas so as to enable them to retain their identity and culture.

In this contcxt, thc Committee also suggested that the question of resettling Buddhist migrants (Chakma) from the Chittagong Hill Districts in suitable and compact areas, preferably in NEFA, Tripura and Assam may be considered.[66]

9.1. ***Ethno-cultural Affiliation with India:*** The Chakmas, from an anthropological perspective, are part of the Tibeto-Burman subset of the Mongolian race and their language is rooted in the Indo-Aryan linguistic family. They bear a resemblance to the Tibeto-Burman Mongolian racial traits and their dialect is closely aligned with Assamese. Predominantly Buddhists, they follow Theravada Buddhism, enriched with aspects of Hinduism and other religious traditions.

The chosen location for their integration in NEFA, specifically the Noa-Dihing valley in the erstwhile Tirap District (now Changlang), was also home to the Singphos and Thikhaks. Even though these communities were

---

[66] *Recommendation of Estimates Committee Seventy-First Report (Third Lok Sabha) Ministry of Rehabilitation (Reception, Dispersal, and Rehabilitation of new migrants arriving in India from East Pakistan since 1st January 1964)*

numerically smaller (less than 800 at the time), they too followed Theravada Buddhism and belonged to the Tibeto-Burman Mongolian racial group. This ethno-cultural compatibility between the Chakmas and the region's original inhabitants was a pivotal factor in the decision to introduce external populations into NEFA.[67]

9.2. ***Chakmas' Intrinsic Tribal Attributes:*** Given NEFA's tribal nature, the strategic intent was to populate less inhabited zones without compromising the region's inherent tribal character. The integration of Chakmas into NEFA was seen as non-threatening to the native tribes, given the Chakmas' own tribal heritage. Their unique social customs, folklore, ecology, and spiritual beliefs mirrored those of the NEFA tribes.

9.3. ***Rectifying Partition's Injustice:*** The bifurcation of India, rooted in religious differences, resulted in the Chittagong Hill Tracts (CHT) — where 97% of the population was non-Muslim, predominantly Buddhist — being handed to Pakistan rather than India. Given that the CHT bordered Assam more than East Bengal and the Chakmas' inclination to join the Indian Union (without a chance for a referendum), their opposition to this decision was palpable yet unsuccessful.

With a sentiment to redress this historical injustice during the country's partition, the Indian government actively opted to resettle the displaced Chakmas from CHT into NEFA.

10. Settlement Schemes for Ex-Servicemen in NEFA

Prior to the policy decision to settle Chakmas and Hajongs in NEFA, the NEFA administration planned settlement schemes to rehabilitate Ex-Servicemen, Ex-

[67] *Chittagong Hills Tract and the Boundary Commission's Award, File No. 7/6/6, Ministry of Home Affairs*

Assam Rifles, and Landless people from Assam's neighbouring districts.

Due to the sudden influx of millions of refugees from East Pakistan that began from January 1964, the NEFA administration put those settlement schemes on back burner except for Vijayanagar settlement Scheme to work on the permanent rehabilitation work of Chakma-Hajong migrants. With the coming of the last batch of Chakmas migrants, 207 families in the early part of 1969 completed the promise made by NEFA to rehabilitate 3000 Chakma-Hajong migrants.

The NEFA administration authorities were simultaneously working to resettle Ex-Assam Rifles Personnel and Ex-Servicemen in the strategically important Vijaynagar valley. A scheme for settlement of ex-Assam Rifles at Vijoynagar in NEFA was submitted to the Ministry under the Administration's letter No. RR. 29/66 dated 19.10.67. This scheme was framed for a total of 200 families. Based on this scheme, the Government of India communicated their sanction vide their order No. 9(4)/67 NEFA dated 27.05.68. Thereafter a scheme for 25 Ex-Assam Rifles personnel was sanctioned vide No. RR.29/66 dated 17.8.68. In continuation of the same, another scheme for 52 Ex-Assam Rifles personnel was sanctioned by the local administration vide order No. DRS.173/69 dated 26.6.69.

The first batch of 23 Ex-Assam Rifles families was settled in Vijaynagar in 1967, the 2nd batch consisting of 25 families in 1968 and 3rd batch consisting of 52 families in 1969. In total, 200 families of Ex. Servicemen were sent to Vijaynagar by the government for settlement.[68]

Another settlement scheme for the settlement of 115 families of Ex-servicemen at Seijosa in Kameng District during 1969-70 was also sanctioned under the

---

[68] *Scheme for settlement of ex-servicemen families in Seijosa and another scheme for settlement of ex-servicemen families in Namdapha region of Miao-Vijaynagar. File No. 11(9)/1969 NEFA*

Administration's order No. DRS.170/69 dated 02.07.1969 at the cost of Rs. 14,03, 160/-.

In March 1969, the first group of 70 ex-servicemen and their families arrived at Seijosa and were assigned to sector 'A.' Eighty-six further families were inducted in April and May 1970, as well as one family in July 1973, and were stationed in the Jolly and Dibru sectors.[69]

In pattern with Seijosa settlement scheme, the NEFA administration also sanctioned a settlement scheme for settlement of 75 families of ex-servicemen in Imboliang area of Noa-Dihing valley in Tirap District under powers delegated to the Governor of Assam as the expenditure involved is less than 50 lakhs vide order No. DRS.169/69 dated 6th November, 1970. However, the scheme for settlement of ex-servicemen in Amboliang area of Noa-Dihing valley in Tirap District was never implemented after it was approved by the Home Ministry, Government of India in 1970 for reasons best known to the administration.[70]

From the various records, it is also evident that the government contemplated settlement of ex-servicemen through special development incentives for sparsely populated border areas along the Indo-Bhutan-Tibet border as late as 1988. In this connection, meetings of the Committee of Secretaries (COS) were held on numerous occasions from 1985 till 1988.

In these meetings of COS, various points emerged including feasibility of regular human settlement on the international borders in the North-Eastern sector, to encourage ex-servicemen or other groups of people to move to and settle on the border areas in the interest of

---

[69] *Public Accounts Committee Report 1977-78, Sixth Lok Sabha, 21st Report, RESETTLEMENT OF EX-SERVICEMEN NEAR SEIJOSA*

[70] *Settlement of ex-servicemen in Amboliang area of Noa-Dihing valley in Tirap District. File No. 11/31/70-NEFA, Ministry of Home Affairs*

national security and for maintaining constant vigilance on the border.

To achieve the desired goal, a proper scheme was suggested to be framed after conducting necessary surveys of the areas to identify the places where human settlement is possible. Further, the COS consulted the state Governments of Arunachal Pradesh and Sikkim and finally the state Governments decided against it.[71]

11. Rehabilitation Plans for Chakma Migrants in Cachar District

As the Chakma community embarked on their exodus from East Pakistan (present-day Bangladesh) in 1964, they were fuelled by a collective hope: to rejuvenate their lives amidst the verdant landscapes of the Cachar district in Assam. Their trajectory through Mizoram and Tripura towards India was charged with this vision.

Yet, what they did not anticipate was the government's plan for their final rehabilitation, which would ultimately take them to the North-East Frontier Agency (NEFA), now known as Arunachal Pradesh. This decision by the government came as a surprise to the Chakma migrants, as they had little to no prior knowledge or expectation of being relocated to NEFA.

A perusal of historical archives reveals earnest governmental dialogues regarding the potential resettlement of the Chakmas in the Cachar District. These conversations imply that while there was genuine consideration of housing the Chakmas in Cachar, the final decision tilted in favour of NEFA.

In a communication dated 05.07.1964, Mr. R. Natarajan, the Deputy Commissioner of Cachar District, corresponded with Mr. B.S. Sarao, the Secretary to the Government of

---

[71] *Special Development incentives for sparsely populated Border Areas and settlement of ex-servicemen-Settlement along the Indo-Bhutan-Tibet Border-Ref from Cabinet Sectt. MHA, NOTES/CORRESPONDENCE File No. 1/5/87-AP*

Assam, Relief and Rehabilitation, Shillong, discussing the potential rehabilitation options for newly arrived Chakma migrants. Mr. Natarajan mentioned that Chakma migrants initially located in the Mizo district had been temporarily settled near Hailakandi but suggested that settling them in Cachar District might be necessary in the long term.

He emphasised the need for a separate rehabilitation scheme, particularly in existing forest villages, as it would take time for the Chakma refugees to adapt to new farming techniques. Mr. Natarajan also highlighted the valuable bamboo work skills possessed by the Chakma refugees at the Monacherra camp, including mat and basket making, which were in high demand in nearby tea gardens. He proposed utilising their talents to supply baskets to the Tea Estates, which would not only help them generate income but also be economically beneficial.[72]

Fast forward to April 10, 1967, the Chakma community, who had taken shelter in Migrant Camps within Cachar, presented a heartfelt plea to the Commissioner of Relief and Rehabilitation, Government of Assam. They beseeched for a permanent home on fertile land that would accommodate their traditional jhum cultivation, pinpointing the Tilla Land region of the district as their preferred destination.[73]

12. **Chakma Resettlement in NEFA: Through Consultation with Local People**

The rehabilitation and resettlement of Chakmas in NEFA, now Arunachal Pradesh, started because of a policy decision made by the Government of India in concurrence with the NEFA administration and the Arunachal Pradesh indigenous people.

---

[72] *Movement of Second Group of Chakma Refugees from Cachar and Mizo District to NEFA, File No. RHMC-6/66*

[73] *Land for rehabilitation of refugees in Cachar District, Assam 1964, File No. RHH/35/1964*

The government had been considering settlement proposals to populate the vacant pockets of NEFA for strategic and developmental reasons after 1962 Chinese aggression and prior to the decision to resettle the Chakmas and Hajongs.

One crucial aspect to underline here is the government's sensitive approach. For the rehabilitation and resettlement of Chakma and Hajong migrants, the government did not acquire or take away land from any of the state's Indigenous people. The architect of NEFA had a specific policy in mind with regard to the land that would be made available for settlement proposals. In this regard, P.N. Luthra, Adviser to the Government of Assam, articulated the policy in his letter to the NEFA Political Officers, No. RR. 17/64, dated April 21, 1965, which comprised the following points:

"While progressing any settlement schemes the following important points may kindly be borne in mind:"-

(a) Land should be voluntarily given by the people to whom an emotional approach has to be made. Such an approach should be made by the Political Officer himself and he should consult the leaders in the areas to ensure that our resettlement proposal does not lead to misplaced agitation or misunderstandings.

(b) Land should as per as possible not belong to anyone and this point should be fully cleared herein its utilisation for settlement. There are areas where full rights are not likely to be affected by settlement of people in NEFA".

11.1. Testament of Consultation:

(a) **May 1966 Parliamentary Delegation:** A parliamentary delegation, including Dr. Daying Ering (then a Parliamentary Secretary) alongside 15 Members of Parliament and the Deputy Speaker of the Lok Sabha, visited NEFA (now Arunachal Pradesh) in May 1966. Dr. Ering, in the subsequent delegation report (Item No. XVI), proposed the need for prior consultation and consent from local residents before resettling outsider communities like the Chakmas from East Pakistan, particularly in areas like Nao-Dihing and near Chowkham.

The government responded to Dr. Daying Ering's recommendation, stating that, before initiating Chakma rehabilitation schemes in the Noa-Dihing and Chowkham regions, the Deputy Commissioners of respective Districts consulted local people, especially villagers claiming ancestral land rights in proposed settlement areas. Concerning the Nao-Dihing area, the entire area was part of the proposed Diyun Reserved Forest, and a Gazette notification inviting objections and claims was issued as early as 1951-52. This designated the area as Government Reserve Forest land, precluding villagers from asserting hereditary rights over it.

Regarding the resettlement area in Chowkham, the initiative to rehabilitate East Pakistan refugees commenced only after the local Khampti-Singpho Tribal Council consented to allocate this land for the purpose. Notably, although the Khampti-Singpho Tribal Council initially agreed to accommodate up to 1000 families in the area, their subsequent suggestion to limit it to 200 families led to a revision of the rehabilitation scheme. As per the council's request, the scheme was revised to accommodate only 200 families.

On September 22, 1966, the Deputy Secretary (Pol) NEFA conveyed the following comment to the Deputy Secretary of MHA (vide No. PLA.94/66) on Dr. Daying Ering's recommendation.

"In the interest of security and emotional integration the Govt of India approved the schemes of resettling ex-servicemen and other progressive farmers including the Chakmas and Hajongs in the vacant unclaimed land in NEFA".

"Prior to undertaking these rehabilitation schemes the local people were consulted for their agreement. Also only

unclaimed land or land as the people could spare on payment (or otherwise) was used for the foregoing schemes."

"There are some areas still under consideration for resettlement. As suggested by the Parliamentary Secretary these are mostly situated in far-flung places in the Agency".[74]

(b) 1980 Union Home Minister's Letter: Further, On July 19, 1980, Mr. Zail Singh, then serving as the Home Minister of India, corresponded with Mr. Gegong Apang, the Chief Minister of Arunachal Pradesh, via D.O. No.13024/5/73-AP. II. In his communication, Mr. Singh explicitly stated that "the Government of India had decided to settle Chakma migrants after due consultation with the Arunachal Pradesh Administration who in turn had consulted the local people before deciding the settlement site".[75]

(c) 1982 Central Team Visit to Arunachal Pradesh: The significance of consultation in the decision-making process was underscored in the explanation of Shri B.P. Mishra, Deputy Secretary of the Ministry of Home Affairs in a meeting held on February 16, 1982, at the Chief Minister's residential office in Arunachal Pradesh. During this meeting, the Chief Minister urged the Central team to provide a summary of their impressions of the rehabilitation areas they had visited. He also sought clarification on the Government of India's policy concerning the Chakmas.

In response, Shri B.P. Mishra, Deputy Secretary of the Ministry of Home Affairs, emphasised that the situation of Chakmas in Arunachal Pradesh differed from the issue of infiltration in Assam. He highlighted that the Chakmas

---

[74] *Visit of Members of Parliament to NEFA in May, 1966 (File No. NI/463/2/66) National Archives of India*

[75] *MHA File No. 13024/5/73-AP. II (Development and Regulatory Measures, Security Matters - Settlement of Chakma Refugees in Arunachal Pradesh) - National Archives of India*

were registered refugees who arrived in 1964 and were settled by the Government of India in consultation with the Arunachal Pradesh Administration at that time. Mishra asserted that there was no infiltration involved, and the Chakmas had been settled conclusively by the government.

(d) 1992 Home Ministry's Reply: On September 23, 1992, Mr. M.M. Jacob, Minister of State for Home and Parliamentary Affairs, addressed a query from Lok Sabha MP Laeta Umbrey regarding the Chakmas of Arunachal Pradesh. He emphasised that the Chakma settlement in Arunachal Pradesh was not a random decision but rather the result of a carefully devised plan implemented in collaboration with the State Administration through extensive consultation.

(e) Letter of K.G. Singpho to L.K. Advani in 2000: A letter dated December 20, 2000, from Mr. K.G. Singpho, a former MLA of Arunachal Pradesh, to Mr. L.K. Advani, the then Home Minister of India, highlighted a key meeting in 1964. During this meeting, Mr. Sunil Chowdhury, Circle Officer cum Base Superintendent in Miao, 11 Gaon Buras from the Khagam Area, and Shri Pisila Singpho, a political interpreter, agreed on the settlement of Chakmas and Hajongs. They decided these groups would be settled in areas of the Noa-Dihing valley that were not occupied by local tribes. The local Indigenous Gaonburahs approved this plan from the Ministry of Rehabilitation. This detail was clearly communicated in the letter to Mr. Advani.

Drawing from the meticulous account of K.G. Singpho, a list of key stakeholders from various villages emerges, all of whom have appended their approval for the settlement of Chakma and Hajong communities in the scenic Noa-Dihing Valley of Tirap District:

1. *Sh. Kunkula Singpho, Gaonburah, Khagam Village*
2. *Sh. Pupong Singho, Gaonburah, Phup Village*
3. *Sh. Sinengthung Singph, Gaonburah, Lewang Village*
4. *Shri Pisidukum Singpho, Gaonburah, Khamuk Village*

5. Shri Pisiduja Singpho, Gaonburah, Pisi Village

6. Shri Lagainong Singpho, Gaonburah, Namphai Village

7. Sh. Sikaonong Singpho, Gaonburah, Sikao Village

8. Sh. Lagainong Singpho, Gaonburah, Miao Village

9. Sh. Ningrang Gam Singpho, Gaonburah, Chief of the Ningrang Singpho

10. Sh. Kamlu Tikhak, Gaonburah, Khachang Village

11. Sh. Nongkhen Tikhak, Gaonburah, Maithong Village

These historical facts serve as compelling evidence that refutes the claims made by certain individuals who oppose the settlement of Chakma and Hajong communities in Arunachal Pradesh (formerly NEFA). Specifically, their contention that the administration at that time failed to consider or consult with the Indigenous people before the Chakma and Hajong settlement is proven to be incorrect.

The historical records available provide substantial evidence of extensive consultations and meetings that occurred prior to the settlement of Chakmas and Hajongs in the region. These records highlight that the decision to settle these communities was not made hastily but was instead a well-considered policy decision. Multiple government entities were involved in the process, including the Ministry of Rehabilitation, Ministry of Home Affairs, Ministry of External Affairs, the Government of Assam, NEFA administration, and local leadership. Through a series of meetings and correspondences, these entities collaborated to ensure thorough discussions and careful planning.

Among the participants in these meetings were key officials from NEFA, as well as Goan Buras representing the Khagam Area under the Miao circle. Their involvement demonstrates the importance placed on gathering input from various stakeholders, including local leaders who have direct knowledge and understanding of the region and its communities. Furthermore, the presence of Shri Pisila Singpho, a political interpreter (Kotoki), in these discussions emphasises the inclusive nature of the deliberations.

The inclusion of multiple government ministries and the engagement of local leaders and interpreters in these consultations highlight the comprehensive approach taken to address the settlement of Chakmas and Hajongs. The aim was to ensure that all relevant perspectives were considered and that decisions were made in a manner that respected the interests and concerns of all parties involved.

Furthermore, it is important to note that the settlement plans were approved and accepted by the local Indigenous Gaonburahs during these meetings. The consensus reached during these discussions solidified the Ministry of Rehabilitation's proposal to settle the Chakmas and Hajongs in Singpho areas. It is crucial to emphasise that the settlement areas chosen were confirmed to be non-occupied by the local tribal populations, thus dispelling any notions of unlawful settlement.

By shedding light on these historical facts, it becomes evident that the claims suggesting a lack of consideration or consultation with the Indigenous people and the alleged unlawful nature of the Chakma and Hajong settlement in Arunachal Pradesh hold no merit. The records establish a robust foundation of consultation, consensus, and adherence to appropriate protocols during the settlement process.

Thus, in retracing these historical steps, we unearth a tale far removed from the misconceptions about the Chakma and Hajong settlements. Instead of unilateral decisions, the narrative is one of consensus, collaboration, and a genuine quest for an inclusive solution. This chapter, through its historical exposition, emphasises the importance of revisiting records to understand the truth, which in this case, testifies to the thoughtful planning and unanimous agreement that underpinned the settlements.

4

A JOURNEY FROM TRANSIT TO PERMANENT RESETTLEMENT

Between April and June of 1964, around 15,000 Chakmas, fleeing the communal violence in East Pakistan, set foot on Indian soil. Their initial destination was to settle in the Cachar District of Assam. The transit camps of Cachar district, albeit temporary, served as the initial refuge for the weary travellers and laid the groundwork for a definite plan of rehabilitation.

Once the blueprint for their resettlement was etched out, the baton of responsibility transitioned from the Government of Assam to the NEFA administration. To ensure a seamless migration, the Chakmas were strategically moved in batches, taking them step by step closer to their would-be permanent homes in NEFA.

The phased transportation of the Chakmas ensured a systematic and organised approach to their resettlement process. This approach allowed for the efficient allocation of resources and facilitated the smooth integration of the Chakma community into their new surroundings. By carefully coordinating the transportation of the Chakmas in separate phases, the authorities could effectively manage the logistical aspects of the resettlement, such as housing, infrastructure, and support services.

The transfer of responsibility from the Government of Assam to the NEFA administration marked a crucial milestone in the Chakmas' journey towards their final rehabilitation. It signalled a shift from temporary arrangements in transit camps to more permanent settlement areas where the Chakmas could establish their homes and rebuild their lives.

The first week of June 1964 saw the inaugural batch of Chakmas making their way to NEFA, transiting through the scenic landscape of Tripura. Comprising 52 families, a sum of 488 souls, their first stop was Namphai, close to Miao. However, destiny beckoned them further to the lush Khagam region.

By December 1964, the NEFA administration took over the responsibility of the Chakma migrants who had been kept at the transit camp in Ledo, Assam. These migrants were brought into NEFA in successive batches until around February 1965. The first batch consisted of 52 families, and subsequently, an additional 1,070 families were brought in. Thus, the total number of families accommodated in NEFA through the first and subsequent batches amounted to approximately 1,122 families. In total, these families comprised around 6,048 individuals.[76]

In May 1964, a group of 139 Chakma families entered India through Tripura. They were initially directed to the West Hazari camp located in Bettiah, Champaran District, and Purnea, Bihar. These families resided in these camps temporarily while their long-term rehabilitation plans were being formulated.

Fast forward to December 1965, a pivotal moment in the Chakmas' resettlement saga unfurled. The NEFA administration stepped in, taking the reins of responsibility from the Bihar Government. This wasn't merely a bureaucratic shift but a profound move, signalling NEFA's unwavering commitment to the welfare and resettlement of these Chakma families.

In parallel, other batches of Chakma families who had been housed in transit camps within the Cachar District and Mizo District of Assam were also relocated to the Ledo Camp. These families were transported to the Ledo Camp via special trains, enabling efficient and organised

---

[76] *Report of the Committee to study Refugee Settlements in Arunachal Pradesh constituted by the Govt. of Arunachal Pradesh under Memo No. POL.236/72, dated 08.12.1976*

movement. From the Ledo Camp, they were subsequently assigned to various regions within NEFA for their final rehabilitation.

The relocation and induction of Chakma families from different transit camps to the Ledo Camp and their subsequent dispersal across NEFA demonstrated the concerted efforts made by the authorities to ensure the smooth transition and successful resettlement of the Chakma community. It involved careful coordination and logistics management to accommodate the needs of the families and facilitate their integration into their new homes and communities.

Fast forward again, in the years 1968-69, the final group of 207 Chakma families who had migrated from East Pakistan was officially incorporated into the Deban-Namdapha region of the Noa-Dihing valley. This marked the culmination of the resettlement process for a total of 2,899 East Pakistan migrants who had been successfully accommodated in NEFA (now Arunachal Pradesh) up until that point.

It is important to note that a few years earlier, an agreement had been reached to help and shelter to approximately 3,000 Chakma refugees from East Pakistan. However, with the inclusion of the last batch of 207 families, the total number of settled migrants fell slightly below the initial target.

1. Land Allocation and the Odyssey of Chakma Settlements

Initially, the Director of Forests, who also served as the settlement officer, provided a general directive stating that each Chakma family should be allocated 5 acres of land for cultivation purposes, along with an additional 2 acres for building their homestead and establishing a kitchen garden. This would amount to a total allocation of 7 acres per family. However, it was observed that this prescribed allocation was not strictly adhered to.

Instead, the Chakma families were guided to settle in specific areas as designated by the responsible authorities overseeing the settlement process. Interestingly, there was no formal demarcation or individual plot allocation carried out during this period. The families were settled in groups in the designated areas without the precise delineation of boundaries for each family's land.[77]

(a) Khagam Scheme: A New Dawn in Settlement

Under Settlement Scheme No. III, a significant allocation of Rs. 24,64,356.47/- was sanctioned through Letter No. 27(2)/65-RH-II(i) on 26.02.1966 and No. 27(10)/67-RH-II on 10.10.1968. This funding aimed to facilitate the settlement of 1122 Chakma families in the areas of Miao, Khagam, Manthi, and M'Pen. However, because of the Screening Team's assessment conducted by the Government of India, these families were later reconstituted into 1286 natural families.

Significantly, during the first quarter of 1964, the Miao administrative unit was established under the Ministry of External Affairs, Government of India, despite having limited resources at its disposal. Around the same time, the initial wave of Chakma migrants, totaling 1001 families, arrived in Assam via the Mizo District. These families were initially sheltered in the Ledo area and were later transferred from the Assam Government's jurisdiction to the NEFA (North East Frontier Agency) administration.

From the chilly days of December 1964 to the early blossoms of February 1965, the NEFA administration gradually relocated these Chakma families to the Miao region in several organised groups in a phased manner. Subsequent batches of Chakma migrants arrived in 1966-67, further adding to their numbers. Initially, upon their induction into NEFA, the families were temporarily accommodated in barracks within Miao for a period of 7 to

---

[77] *Report of the Committee to study Refugee Settlements in Arunachal Pradesh constituted by the Govt. of Arunachal Pradesh under Memo No. POL.236/72, dated 08.12.1976*

15 days. However, they were subsequently instructed to move to the designated resettlement sites located in the Deban and Khagam area, where their permanent resettlement took place.

In the historical annals, it's discernible that the initial intention was to rehabilitate close to 1000 Chakma families in the embrace of the Deban area. Notably, the group leaders of these pioneering batches were even escorted to explore the terrains of Deban, envisaging a future where their communities would flourish. Yet, as is often the case, nature and foresight had other plans. Deban, with its unyielding terrain, rudimentary road networks, and general unpreparedness, seemed less of a haven and more of a challenge.

Given these hurdles, the administration, in its wisdom, pivoted. They directed their gaze and the hopes of the Chakma families to the inviting landscapes of Khagam. Here, the plains whispered of promise, the terrain seemed forgiving, beckoning the settlers to put down roots. The shift was not merely geographical but also about seeking better, more viable horizons. The terrain of Khagam seemed primed for the ambitious vision of building homes and communities, in stark contrast to the rugged challenges posed by Deban.

This vast expanse, the Khagam settlement scheme, encompassed the regions of M'pen, Manthi, portions of Miao, and extended to six more blocks, stretching its fingers from Manabhum to Diyun along the serene Noa-Dihing river's right bank. Recognizing its potential, this pivotal region, termed the Khagam area, underwent rapid development. An administrative circle emerged in Deban, and an array of SP Type buildings began dotting the landscape, each a testament to the commitment towards settling the Chakma and Hajong communities.

Yet, Khagam, despite its allure, had its own trials. Its forests were dense, the tree canopy so thick that sunlight played hide and seek with the ground beneath. Nestled within the Noa-Dihing valley, this region held the promise of wet rice cultivation, thanks to its basin-like geography. In contrast, Deban's elevated lands whispered tales of Jhum cultivation, a dance of shifting agriculture.

Navigating these intricacies, a substantial 1286 Chakma migrant families eventually found their sanctuary within the Khagam settlement scheme. Leading them were resolute group leaders, each entrusted with guiding and overseeing the resettlement of between 40 to 80 families. They became the linchpins of this monumental endeavour, ensuring that each family transitioned smoothly into their new homes and lives.

(b) The Unfolding Tale of the Deban & Namdapha Settlements

In January of 1965, L.J. Johnson, Additional Secretary of the Ministry of Rehabilitation, Government of India, along with key officials from the Government of Assam and NEFA administration, visited the Deban and Namdapha areas in Miao. The purpose of their visit was to identify more suitable areas for the resettlement of additional Chakma migrant families.

In response to the Government of Assam's request to accommodate more refugees from East Pakistan, a team of local technical officers was assembled. This team, led by the Divisional Forest Officer of the Working Plan Division in NEFA, was tasked with assessing the availability of land for refugee settlement in the trans Noa-Dihing area. On June 15, 1965, the committee submitted a report summarising the land availability in nine blocks as follows:[78]

BLOCK	WRC	JHUM
	(Figure in sq. miles)	
1	2.48	Nil
2	Nil	12.80

[78] *Report of the Committee to study Refugee Settlements in Arunachal Pradesh constituted by the Govt. of Arunachal Pradesh under Memo No. POL.236/72, dated 08.12.1976*

3 & 4	Nil	9.13
5	Nil	6.45
6	1.50	Nil
7	Nil	3.60
8	1.00	Nil
9	0.13	Nil
Total	**5.11**	**31.98**

The study team emphasised that the provided figures should be considered as tentative and approximate. According to their findings, approximately 1500 additional families could potentially be settled in the Noa-Dihing valley. The team used a standard guideline wherein a family consisting of two adults, one grown-up child, and two minor children would require either five acres of Wet Rice Cultivation (WRC) land or 20 acres of Jhum land to sustain their livelihood. Out of the estimated 1500 families, it was determined that 500 families should be settled in the WRC area, while the remaining 1000 families should be settled in the Jhum area.

An adjusted amount of Rs. 43,69,512/- was sanctioned for the resettlement of 150 Hajong families and 855 Chakma families in the Pakan, Deban, and Namdapha areas located in the Nao-Dihing Valley of the Tirap District (now Changlang district). This revised allocation replaced the original amount of Rs. 19,88,000/- and was officially approved through two letters dated 07/03/1968 and 14/10/1968, with reference numbers 27(10)/67-RH-II(i) and 27(10)/67-RH-(ii) respectively.

A total of 1006 Chakma and Hajong families were subsequently inducted into the Deban-Namdapha area for their resettlement. This scheme encompassed the Pakan, Deban, and Namdapha areas within the Noa-Dihing valley, situated in the Tirap district.

Below is the breakdown of the households included in Scheme No III, which is widely recognized as the Deban

Settlement Scheme, implemented in the Trans Noa-Dihing Valley within the Deban-Namdapha region.[79]

1.	Dec '1965	39 families of Hajong
2.	Dec '1965	59 families of Hajong
3.	Jan '1966	139 families of Chakmas from Bihar
4.	Jan '1966	59 families of Hajong
5.	Feb '1966	22 families of Hajong
6.	Mar '1966	12 families of Hajong
7.	Apr '1966	165 Chakma families from Monacherra
8.	Apr '1966	8 families of Hajong
9.	1966-67	473 families of Chakmas from Monacherra and Anipur TransitCamps
10.	Nov '1967	53 families of Chakmas
	Total	**1006 Chakma & Hajong Families**

As the months turned and the landscape of the Deban-Namdapha region evolved, villages sprouted, each with its own distinct identity. Here is a snapshot of the villages established starting in the year 1965:[80]

[79] *Number of Families inducted into Noa Dihing Valley under Scheme II*

[80] *Census of India 1971, Series No. 24, Arunachal Pradesh, Part X, District Census Handbook Tirap District*

Sl.	Village Name	Tribe	Location(RiverBank)
1.	Bodhisatta	Chakma	Deban & Pakhan (Noa-Dihing)
2.	Anandapur	Chakma	Deban & Pakhan (Noa-Dihing)
3.	Kamalapuri	Chakma	Deban & Pakhan (Noa-Dihing)
4.	Nandakanan	Chakma	Deban & Pakhan (Noa-Dihing)
5.	Debapuri	Chakma	Deban & Pakhan (Noa-Dihing)
6.	Brajapur	Chakma	Deban & Pakhan (Pakhan river)
7.	Punyabhumi	Chakma	Deban & Pakhan (Noa-Dihing)
8.	Shivatala	Hajong	Tapun (Deban river Bank)
9.	Sumangal	Chakma	Tapun (Deban river Bank)
10.	Monmohini	Chakma	Tapun (Deban river Bank)
11.	Sundarpur	Chakma	Tapun (Deban river Bank)
12.	Jagatjyoti	Chakma	Tapun (Deban river Bank)

(c) The Namdapha Firm Base Area Scheme

In the years 1965-66, under the fourth settlement scheme, the Namdapha Firm Base area in Tirap District (currently known as Changlang) saw the induction of 350 Chakma families. Nestled in the Namdapha valley, this settlement lay gracefully between two vital rivers: the Noa-Dihing and the Deban, converging at a point named Deban.

During 1965-66, 350 Chakma families were inducted in the Namdapha (Firm base) area, Tirap Dist (now Changlang) under settlement scheme No. 4. This settlement site is situated in the Namdapha valley between the two rivers viz. Noa-Dihing and Deban River and the point of their confluence at Deban.

The settlement burgeoned into three vibrant villages: Buddha Bhakti, Ramrajpur, and Udaynagar. However, time unveiled that commitment to this new land was not unanimous. A considerable number from these villages sought solace elsewhere, vacating the newly settled villages in just a few years after their establishment.

To facilitate this massive resettlement, an allocation of Rs. 26,72,870/- was set aside for the rehabilitation of the Chakma families in the Namdapha Firm Base area. Beyond housing and infrastructure, the vision for this new settlement was grander. A 30-mile road network was envisioned and integrated into the scheme, acting as the lifeline for this budding community. The stamp of approval for this endeavour was officially inked on 14.01.1969, evidenced by the letter with reference number 27(11)67-RH(i).

(d) The Chowkham Settlement Scheme

Historical documents reveal that NEFA's blueprint initially aimed to establish a home for 1,000 Chakma families in Chowkham, located in the Lohit District. However, due to opposition from the Khamptis and Mishmis, only 214 families were eventually rehabilitated. These families were resettled between the rivers Bareng and Kamlang, comprising a total population of 1254 individuals.

Their resettlement took place in two separate batches. While March and April of 1966 saw the resettlement of 164 families, December added another 50 families to the Chowkham tapestry. Despite the challenges, the region offered fertile ground, with each family being allocated 5 acres of sandy loam soil. With a spirit of self-reliance, families took to the earth, reclaiming it with diligent hands. The government, acknowledging their determination, pitched in with subsidies, most notably a pair of bullocks per family. By 1971, these combined efforts bore fruit, with 1,000 acres of once dormant land now teeming with life.

Over the years, migration patterns saw shifts. Many Chakma families have since relocated to various areas within the Tirap District, where they initially settled in the Chowkham region. Conversely, some families from the Tirap District have also relocated to the Chowkham area.

However, it is notable that the number of people moving out of the Chowkham region exceeds those moving in.

A total of Rs. 8,83,800/- was sanctioned for 214 Chakma families in Chowkham, located between the Bareng and Kamlang rivers in the former Lohit district (now Namsai district). This approval was granted through letters dated 07.03.1968 and 14.10.1968, with reference numbers 27(10)/67-RH-II(i).

(e) The Kokila-Hollongi Settlement in Subansiri

Between the months of January and March in 1968, 250 Chakma migrant families from East Pakistan were inducted into Balijan-Kokila area of Subansiri district (now Papumpare) and have been settled in ten Blocks. In total, a sum of Rs. 11,07,589.50 was spent by the Government of India for settlement of these families.

Initially, 6 acres of land were given to each household for settlement (5 acres WRC and 1 acre house site). Allotted land has been determined to be sufficient if used appropriately for all the households. Because of the sandy nature of the soil in blocks 5 and 6, the administration tried to move a few families from there to block No. 4, where the land was better suited, and the irrigation facilities were more than adequate. However, settlers did not like to move to any other areas from their existing block, so the idea was abandoned.

In a bid to eliminate ambiguities, the boundaries of the Chakma settlements in Hollongi-Kokila were explicitly demarcated on the 16th of August 1978 vide No. FOR.223/71. This decision was publicised in the Arunachal Pradesh Extraordinary Gazette on July 28, 1979. By this delineation, the Chakma settlement spanned from Chengmara to the Magoni river, encapsulating a flat terrain nestled between the inner line and the foothills, while notably excluding the existing plantation area demarcated, approx. area 14 Sq. Km

Despite such clear demarcations and the absence of land disputes in the Hollongi-Kokila regions, population dynamics witnessed shifts. A considerable number of individuals migrated to the Tirap District. This trend has persisted, with Chakma families continuously transitioning from Hollongi-Dirgha areas to various regions within the Tirap District.

5

AD-HOC ARRANGEMENTS MARK THE BEGINNING OF CHAKMA SETTLEMENTS IN NEFA

From the outset, the administrative approach to the resettlement of Chakmas and Hajongs in NEFA (North East Frontier Agency) was characterised by pragmatic decision-making and improvised arrangements based on the prevailing circumstances.

As the Miao administrative unit was newly established, it was impractical to accommodate over a thousand Chakma migrant families in temporary barracks at Miao for an extended period before the official approval of schemes by the Central government. Consequently, it was necessary to expedite the administrative procedures, such as the de-reservation of forest areas, cadastral surveys of potential settlement sites, and land allotment processes. To facilitate their ultimate rehabilitation, the Chakmas and Hajongs were directed to move to the new settlement areas in Khagam and Deban-Namdapha regions.

This approach allowed for the swift transition of the displaced communities, bypassing the prolonged stay in temporary barracks, and enabling them to settle in the designated areas before the completion of administrative procedures required for formal resettlement.

The settlement area at that time was full of thick jungles, crisscrossed by several streams and rivers and infested by wild elephants and other beasts. As such a few variations in the original plan had to be made during this period to mitigate the hardship and difficulties and other problems faced by the Chakma families. Some people had to shift from allotted areas as well.

The administration's approach to land settlement and reclamation can be summarised as follows:

- The administration presented the migrants with an area, namely the Khagam area and Deban area (now part of Diyun Circle and Deban-Namdapha), which had undefined boundaries. The migrants were tasked with clearing the forest and transforming the forest land into cultivable land suitable for agricultural-based settlement.

- To support the migrants in their agricultural endeavours, the administration provided them with necessary tools, implements, a pair of oxen, as well as seeds and plants. These resources were intended to facilitate the initiation of agricultural practices on the reclaimed forest land.
- The administration encouraged the migrants to develop the agricultural land to its maximum potential, with the goal of achieving self-sufficiency in food production. This involved implementing sustainable farming methods and optimising the productivity of the cultivated land.
- As part of the land settlement policy, the administration aimed to allocate a sufficient amount of land measuring 7 acres for the permanent rehabilitation of the migrants. This allocation was intended to provide them with a secure and stable basis for their resettlement and livelihoods.

(1) Administrative Pragmatism and Ad-Hoc Arrangements

(a) Settlement Initiated Without Cadastral and Soil Surveys:

Prior to the resettlement of the Chakma and Hajong communities in the Noa-Dihing valley, there was a notable absence of thorough cadastral and soil surveys. Insufficient efforts were made to conduct these surveys beforehand, resulting in a lack of accurate information regarding the settlement sites and the suitability of the land.

A comprehensive cadastral survey would have been instrumental in establishing precise boundaries, enabling more accurate planning of the settlements, and effectively mapping the landscapes of the designated areas. Unfortunately, due to the absence of such surveys, the settlement boundaries for the Chakmas and Hajongs were not clearly defined. Consequently, numerous unresolved issues arose during the later stages of the settlement process, leading to complications such as land abandonment and disputes.

The absence of cadastral and soil surveys hindered the ability to make informed decisions about land allocation and utilisation, which further contributed to the emergence of vexing land settlement problems. The lack of accurate boundary demarcation and inadequate knowledge of the soil's suitability for cultivation created challenges that needed to be addressed post-settlement, resulting in additional complexities and unresolved issues for the communities involved.

Had proper cadastral and soil surveys been conducted prior to the settlement, a more systematic and well-informed approach could have been adopted, reducing the likelihood of subsequent complications, and promoting a smoother and more sustainable resettlement process.

(b) Absence of Clearly Defined Settlement Boundaries:

During the resettlement of the Chakma and Hajong communities in the upper reaches of the Noa-Dihing river, specifically in the Deban and Pakan areas, there was a lack of clearly defined demarcation lines to establish the boundaries of the settlement areas. Instead, the settlers were provided with verbal explanations of the boundary lines beyond which they were not supposed to venture.

To facilitate the allotment of land to the Chakma and Hajong migrants, the entire area was divided into four sectors: Sector-I, Sector-II, Sector-III, and Sector-IV. The forest department marked a demarcation line between the reserve forest and the Noa-Dihing river on the right bank, running along the foothills opposite the Miao Administrative unit. The settlers intended to occupy the area between this demarcation line and the Noa-Dihing river. Additionally, some migrants were allowed to settle in the M'Pen area on the left bank of the river.[81]

However, instead of providing individual land allotments, the administration assigned each group leader, responsible for 40 to 100 families, a designated area where they could settle. The leaders then guided their respective groups to these areas, and cultivation activities commenced.

Due to the lack of clear boundary demarcation specifically for the reclamation of forest land, when the migrants moved from their transit camps in Miao in search of suitable land for cultivation, they began clearing the thick and dense forests in the Khagam area. This area was found to have relatively easier terrain compared to Deban and was well-suited for wet cultivation. Similarly, in the upper reaches of the Deban settlement area, numerous families practised jhumming (slash-and-burn agriculture) up to the Tapun area along the Lohit-Tirap boundary.

As a result, forest lands were reclaimed, and settlements were established beyond the designated areas. This led to a situation where villages had to be subsequently evicted as they encroached upon areas not originally designated for settlement. The absence of clearly defined boundaries and inadequate enforcement of settlement limits contributed to the need for eviction and the emergence of complex land settlement issues in the region.

---

[81] *Report of the Committee to study Refugee Settlements in Arunachal Pradesh constituted by the Govt. of Arunachal Pradesh under Memo No. POL.236/72, dated 08.12.1976*

(c) Jhum based Settlement overlooked:

It was proposed to bring a specific number of Chakma families to the Miao area, assuming that some of them would engage in jhumming, which was their traditional farming practice in their original state. However, this aspect was overlooked during their settlement. The Jhum-based settlement plan was disregarded despite previous indications.

According to an expert committee report submitted on 15.06.1965, it was estimated that approximately 1500 families could be settled in the Noa-Dihing valley. The report suggested that five acres of WRC land or 20 acres of Jhum land would be sufficient to sustain a family consisting of two adults, one grown-up child, and two minor children. Out of these 1500 families, 500 were meant to be settled in the WRC area, while 1000 were intended for the Jhum area.[82]

Right from the initiation of the Deban and Namdapha settlement scheme, a crucial aspect was disregarded: the implementation of jhum-based land settlement for Chakma migrants. The administration failed to pursue this approach, despite its significance. This oversight was highlighted to the authorities by U. Chakma, the Political Officer in Pasighat, through a letter (D.O. No. Cap-110/64 dated 02.05.1964). In the letter, U. Chakma explicitly mentioned that most of the settlers likely engaged in jhum cultivation, while some might also possess knowledge of wet rice cultivation.

Because of this negligence, Chakma migrants, who traditionally practised jhum cultivation, were compelled to seek WRC land in the lower areas of the Noa-Dihing valley.

---

[82] *Report of the Committee to study Refugee Settlements in Arunachal Pradesh constituted by the Govt. of Arunachal Pradesh under Memo No. POL.236/72, dated 08.12.1976*

(d) Allotment of land in lump-sum:

Initially, the authorities did not make individual family-wise land allotments, but allotment of land was made in lump-sum to a group of families ranging from 40 to 80 families. This had encouraged the group leaders and members of the group to call their kins from different groups and even from trans-settlement scheme areas to join them resulting in deserting of original settlement areas.

This situation created significant challenges in managing the movement of Chakma migrant families and preventing the desertion of the original settlement areas. The collective land allotment system fueled a natural desire to settle near their kin, intensifying the difficulties in regulating population distribution and preventing the scattering of settlements.

(e) Introduction of Land Record Maintenance Neglected:

From the outset, the system of settling land and maintaining land records was not implemented. The crucial aspect of following the standard revenue procedure, which involves allocating a specific amount of land to individual families, was overlooked during the initial settlement of the Chakma migrants.

It is important to acknowledge that during the settlement of Chakma and Hajong migrants in the Miao Sub-Division, the administrative unit was in its initial stages and not adequately equipped with manpower and infrastructure to handle such a large-scale influx of people.

These administrative oversights, combined with a pragmatic and ad-hoc approach, resulted in various complex land settlement issues that persist to this day, particularly within the settlement areas of the present-day Changlang District.

(f) Unregulated migration from highland settlement areas of Deban-Namdapha:

As mentioned earlier, a considerable number of families made the decision to abandon their settlement areas in the higher regions of Deban and Namdapha and instead settled in the lower lying areas of the Khagam settlement area. Unfortunately, there was no established mechanism in place to regulate or monitor such extensive migration from one settlement area to another. This unregulated movement further complicated the already challenging process of settling the Chakma-Hajong migrants.

The administration loosely permitted hundreds of families, along with their group leaders, to move out from the temporary barracks in Miao, where they had been initially housed for a few days upon their arrival. These families were granted permission to relocate to the Khagam Settlement Scheme area. Among this group of migrants were 139 families who were transferred from the Bihar Government in January 1966.

This uncontrolled migration not only added to the complexity of the settlement process but also highlighted the lack of effective oversight and coordination in managing the movement of Chakma-Hajong migrants during that period.

By 1975, the Chakma and Hajong migrants had abandoned a total of eight settlement villages in the Deban-Namdapha area. These deserted villages consisted of Sundarpur, Sumangal, Shivatola, Monmohini, and Jagatjyoti in the Deban Settlement scheme area, as well as Ramrajpur, Budhha Bhakti, and Udoypuri in the Namdapha Firm Base Settlement scheme area.

(g) Forest de-reservation did not precede the settlement of Chakmas

The forest land in the Noa-Dihing valley, where the Chakmas and Hajongs began settling with government encouragement, was never officially denotified after reclamation.

As mentioned earlier, several villages were established by the Chakmas and Hajongs as part of the Khagam and Deban Settlement schemes. While the government acknowledged the existence of these villages, the areas were never officially denotified or removed from the reserved forest land. This process of denotification is a required procedure that should have taken place before the settlement occurred.

Except for the Chakma villages located in the Hollongi-Dirgha area, none of the Chakma and Hajong villages in the Changlang and Namsai districts have been officially declared as non-forest land. This situation has given rise to numerous additional problems.

Interestingly, the Committee's Report on Resettlement in Miao Sub-Division in 1979, led by Deputy Commissioner J.M Syiem, acknowledged the problem and recommended denotification of the villages; however, they were not formally de-notified as non-forest land. These villages specifically include Ratnapur, Milanpur, Gulokpur (present-day Kharsang circle), and Dharmapur in the Dweep area.

Likewise, in the Khagam settlement area, the villages of Kamakhyapur, Jyotsnapur, and Rajnagar were recognized as Chakma resettlement villages, but the proper procedure of de-notifying them as non-forest land was not followed.[83]

---

[83] *Report of the Committee about Resettlement in Miao Sub-Division, 1979 (J.M Syiem Committee, Deputy Commissioner, Changlang District)*

6

LANDLESSNESS: RISE OF LAND SETTLEMENT ISSUES AND SOCIO-ECONOMIC CONFLICTS

Historical Context

From the outset of Arunachal Pradesh's settlement history, a considerable number of Chakma families found themselves marginalised, missing out on land allotments amidst their quest for rehabilitation. This oversight wasn't merely a consequence of administrative inefficiencies; it bore roots in ad-hoc decision-making and a lack of foresight. Moreover, many Chakmas allocated to Namdapha and Deban highland settlement schemes found themselves compelled to abandon their assigned regions. This migration pattern, characterised by Chakmas shifting from their original settlement zones, brewed a storm of multifaceted challenges tied to their genuine rehabilitation.

This continuous exodus of Chakma migrants, from designated settlement areas to newer territories, did not merely challenge administrative norms. It brewed socio-economic tensions between the migrating Chakmas and the Indigenous Singphos and Tangsas.

Driving the Exodus

The crux of the Chakma migration from the highland regions of Namdapha and Deban lies in the unsuitability of these lands for sustenance. Harsh topographical features made their traditional livelihoods unsustainable. Consequently, their descent to the more fertile lowlands became not just an option, but a desperate necessity for survival.

The consequence of this lateral movement had rendered the government or administration unable to accommodate hundreds of Chakma families for their land settlement. This has given rise to a range of pressing problems concerning the proper rehabilitation of these displaced families. The challenges include ensuring access to basic amenities, securing adequate housing and infrastructure, and addressing the socio-economic impacts of their resettlement.

As landless Chakma families looked for places to settle, they moved into Singpho areas in Bordumsa and Diyun. They made various agreements with the local Singpho tribe members to use land for wet rice cultivation. This led to many conflicts of interest between the Chakmas and the Singpho in their daily lives. Additionally, when hundreds of Chakma families encroached on the Namphuk and Diyun Reserve forests, they came into direct conflict with the government.

The scarcity of available land for settlement compelled the Chakmas to encroach upon forest areas, leading to heightened tensions and conflicts with both the Singpho tribesmen and the local administration. These conflicts, which initially arose from the encroachment of land, gradually intensified over time and emerged as one of the most contentious issues in the state. The overlapping interests and disputes between the Singpho community, the Chakma settlers, and the government have become overly complex and challenging to resolve.

The emergence of complex land settlement and socio-economic conflict can be attributed to several underlying factors. The NEFA administration's pragmatic and ad-hoc approach, while attempting to address immediate needs, may have neglected the long-term implications of these factors, exacerbating the complexity of the issues at hand.

1. Landlessness: emergence of complex land settlement issues

(a) An Inception Marked by Land Scarcity

From the earliest days of rehabilitation, the scarcity of land cast a shadow over the resettlement efforts for the Chakma migrants. Over a thousand families found themselves bereft of agricultural or shifting cultivation land (commonly referred to as "jhum land").

In response to the emerging crisis, an assessment committee was formed to survey the available land suitable for resettling the Chakma refugees in the trans Noa-Dihing Deban-Namdapha region. On June 15, 1965, they revealed that only about 1500 families could be reasonably settled within the confines of the Deban & Namdapha valley. Following a set norm, each family – two adults, a grown-up child, and two minors – would require either five acres of WRC or 20 acres of Jhum land. While 500 families were slated to occupy the WRC land, the plan was for the remaining 1000 to inhabit the Jhum land.

However, reality veered away from this plan. Out of the 1210 Chakma families that made their way to the Deban valley and the Namdapha Firm Base area, a mere 425 found solace in land allotment. The remaining 785 families confronted the stark reality of landlessness from the get-go. The primary oversight was on the part of the administration, which did not consider the potential of Jhum-based settlements and did not guide the migrants to the available Jhum lands.[84]

To add to the complexities, the Noa-Dihing river's erosive nature wreaked havoc. The river's extensive erosion and silting led to a staggering 184 families losing their settlements in the villages of Shantipur, Jyotipur, Madhupur, and Haripur, located in the Khagam settlement. This meant that around 1000 families now grappled with the dilemma of displacement.

Historical data sheds more light on the issue. A total of 2496 Chakma and Hajong families were earmarked for

---

[84] *Report of the Committee to study Refugee Settlements in Arunachal Pradesh constituted by the Govt. of Arunachal Pradesh under Memo No. POL.236/72, dated 08.12.1976*

resettlement across various sites, namely Scheme No.II (Khagam), III (Deban), and IV (Namdapha Firm Base) situated in the Noa-Dihing valley of Tirap district. But the pressing land constraints meant that the NEFA administration could only successfully allocate land to 1689 of these families. The breakdown saw 1220 families settled under the Khagam scheme, 44 in the Mpen area, and 425 in the Deban Settlement Scheme. This left an unsettling figure of 807 families without any land allocation, underscoring the gravity of the land settlement challenges.[85]

(b) Desertion from Deban and Namdapha Settlement Areas

Between 1965 and 1967, the Namdapha area in Tirap District (now known as Changlang) welcomed 204 Chakma families under the settlement scheme No. IV. Meanwhile, 1006 Chakma families found a new home in the Deban area as part of scheme No. II.

However, by the late 1960s, many families began leaving these areas. A note from T.N. Dwivedi, a District Agricultural Officer from Khonsa, highlighted this migration in December 1968. By 1971, out of the families that initially settled in the Namdapha area, only 100 remained across three villages: Ramrajpur (59 families), Udaynagar (12 families), and Buddhabhakti (29 families). In the Deban area, about 650 families still resided across 12 villages viz. Anandpur, Brajapur, Buddhisatta, Devapuri, Jagatjyoti, Kamalapuri, Monmohini, Nandankanon, Punyabhumi, Sivtola, Sumangal, Sundarpur.[86]

By 1973, the Namdapha area was entirely abandoned by Chakma families, despite the initial investment in the settlement which included a 30-mile road construction project funded at Rs. 26,72,870 vide reference number 27(11)67-RH(i).

---

[85] *Report of the Committee about Resettlement in Miao Sub-Division, 1979 under the Chairmanship of J.M. Syiem, Deputy Commission, Tirap District*

[86] *CENSUS OF INDIA 1971, ARUNACHAL PRADESH*

The exodus from the Deban settlement persisted, and by 1981, only 383 Chakma families remained in eight villages like Bodhisatta (88), Anandpur I (32), Anandpur-II (26), Kamalpuri (31), Devapuri (65), Nandan Kanan (29), Punya Bhumi (64) and Brajapur (18). The reasons for this significant migration remain complex and multi-faceted.

(2) Shifting Settlements caused multiple challenges

Many Chakma families began abandoning their highland settlement areas in the Deban and Namdapha areas in the late 1960s. This shifting from original settlement areas further complicated the rehabilitation process of Chakmas. Soon hundreds of Chakma families spread themselves out into the plain areas under Reserved Forests and in the river, islands formed by trifurcation of the Noa-Dihing river below the Miao administrative headquarters, which is locally known as "Dweep" area. In the quest for better land, a constant stream of Chakma families from the Deban and Namdapha area also entered the Dweep area, Khagam area and Singpho areas in Bordumsa and Diyun. In a brief period, roughly 5–6 years, many ancillary problems with the settlement of Chakmas and Hajongs emerged for a variety of causes.

(a) Land Abandonment and New Settlements:

Abandonment of highland areas combined with people who did not get land allotment resulted in encroachment in the so-called Dweep area and Namphuk Reserve Forest area and Diyun Reserve Forest and establishment of a number of new villages.

- **Dweep & Namphuk Reserve Forest Area Settlements:** Due to abandonment of highland areas and unallotted land, encroachments led to the establishment of Dharmapur, Milanpur, Gulokpur, and Ratnapur.
- **Khagam-Diyun Area Settlements:** Villages sprouted near the original 6 settlement blocks: Moitripur, Gautampur, Shantipur, Jyotipur,

Avoipur, and Dumpani. New villages included Kamakhyapur, Jyotsnapur, and Rajnagar.

(b) Land Agreements and Settlements in Singpho areas:

Land Transactions with Singpho Tribesmen: Landless Chakmas entered into several types of agreements with the Singpho tribesmen for purchase of land. These consisted of cash transactions and cases of promise for bonded labour for an agreed period in lieu of land as gift. For this purpose, in most cases, the Chakma migrants documented the agreements they arrived at.

- New Villages Established:
  - **Diyun Area:** Dumpather, Udaipur, Mudoidweep, Joypur, Balupather, Chandrapur, Shakyapur, and Navajyotipur.
  - **Bordumsa Area:** Bijoypur.
- Eviction Challenges: Many of these settlement villages faced eviction due to several reasons, including the lack of administrative permission and other factors.
- Tensions with Local Singpho Tribesmen: Evictions and house burnings caused significant tensions and friction between Chakmas and the local Singpho community.

(c) Tangsa Encroachments and Conflicts:

The situation was made further complicated by encroachment and occupation of the plain areas in Namphuk Reserve Forest by members of the local tribes (Tangsas) abandoning their villages on the hill tops. The encroachment carried out by the Tangsas introduced an additional level of complexity to the Chakma settlement process in the Namphuk Reserve Forest. This situation led to competition between the Chakmas and Tangsas for the plain land and resulted in socio-economic conflicts as both groups aimed to establish their own villages and settlements.

(d) Lateral Movement and Internal Competition:

Migration from Chowkham, Deban, and Namdapha: Chakma families moved towards the Khagam (Diyun) area and the trans Noa-Dihing areas.

Increased Land Competition: Many Chakma families from areas like Chowkham and Deban migrated to the Khagam area, leading to fierce competition and internal conflicts for the best lands. This internal rivalry among the Chakma community, intensified by a rising number of migrants, became a prominent challenge for the local administration.

(e) Administrative Challenges:

This migration significantly increased the burden on both the land and the administration, which were already grappling with rehabilitation issues.

The local authorities' response to the issue was of bewilderment. The issue went beyond what could be managed by the Forest Department, which was responsible for the Chakma and Hajong migrant population settlement programme. Because the Deputy Commissioner was not completely informed about most of the initial aspects of the settlement operation, the Administrative Officer involved in the operation felt inadequate to alert the District Authority of the issue.

(3) Forest Settlements in Khagam and Dweep Area

The NEFA Administration took over 2,496 Chakma and Hajong families from the Assam Government to facilitate their final settlement in Tirap Division under schemes II, III, and IV. However, due to land scarcity, only 1,689 families were allotted land. Consequently, from the initial 2,496 families, 807 families did not receive any land settlement. Adding to this, around 300 families lost their lands because of erosion and silting by the Noa-Dihing river. This resulted in approximately 1,100 Chakma families remaining landless at the outset of the resettlement process.

As land scarcity persisted, many Chakmas in search of better land prospects migrated from Deban-Namdapha Settlement areas. They moved to regions like Diyun Reserve Forest, Namphuk Reserve Forest, and areas inhabited by the Singpho community. This migration trend continued over time.

A detailed report on Chakma settlements in Changlang district was prepared by Arun Goyal, IAS, Deputy Commissioner, Changlang District, after reviewing extensive records. This report, submitted to the Home Secretary of Arunachal Pradesh on September 8, 1990 (No. CA-108/89), reveals that around 700 out of 1200 landless families moved into the Dweep area of the Namphuk Reserve Forest and established villages.

The Dweep area is an island formed by trifurcation of the Noa-Dihing River below the Miao administrative headquarters and is locally known as "Dweep" area. Present day Dweep area comprises of Dharmapur-I, Dharmapur-II, Dharmapur-III under Miao Sub-Division, Milanpur, Ratanapur and Gulokpur in Kharsang Circle and Bijoypur-I, Bijoypur-II and Bijoypur-III under Bordumsa Sub-Division. This area of about 350 hectares of Namphuk Reserve Forest is an island between two rivers namely, Magantong/Buri Dihing and Kaikay.[87]

The Chakma migrants who settled in the Dweep area fell into two categories:

- Those who the Arunachal Pradesh Government could not provide land and were instead employed as forest workers in the Miao Forest Plantations.
- Those who voluntarily left their initial highland settlements in the Deban-Namdapha regions.

The Khagam-Diyun region saw a similar trend. Many Chakmas, initially settled in six blocks (Block No. 1 -6) of

---

[87] *A comprehensive note on Chakma settlers in Changlang district prepared by Arun Goyal, IAS, Deputy Commissioner,Changlang District, 1990*

the Khagam area, became landless due to environmental challenges, notably erosion and frequent flooding by the Noa-Dihing and its tributaries. This, combined with families not provided land by the government and those leaving unsuitable original settlements, led to the establishment of new villages like Jyotsnapur, Kamakhyapur and Rajnagar near the original six-block settlements like Moitripur (Block No. 1), Gautampur (Block No. 2), and Jyotipur (Block No. 4),, among others.

(4) Official Recognition and De-reservation of Chakma Settlements within Reserved Forests

Initially, the Chakma settlements in the Diyun and Namphuk Reserve Forests were seen as encroachments. However, over time, these areas were officially recognized as Chakma settlements to accommodate landless Chakmas migrating from Deban and Namdapha highland areas. This recognition aimed to rehabilitate those without land, giving them a fresh start.

The Chakma settlements in the Dweep area, namely Dharmapur, Milanpur, Ratnapur, and Gulokpur, within the Namphuk Reserve Forest, have been under the attention of the district authority from the beginning. The Conservator of Forests, Deomali, also addressed the matter through his communication No. SAC.19/72/2373-75 dated 27.06.1974, where he agreed to de-reserve these areas as Chakma settlement area. However, the land was not allotted systematically from one side to facilitate the marking and disposal of trees. Unfortunately, for reasons that remain unclear, no systematic land allocation was conducted, leading to an unregulated disposal of trees. Consequently, this lack of proper land allotment and regulated tree disposal created challenges in the process of de-reserving the area.

A pivotal meeting on 9th November 1976 held between DFO Jairampur and EAC Miao resulted in the recognition of Jyotsnapur village, comprising 72 families, as a Chakma village. Following this, the Arunachal Pradesh Government constituted a committee chaired by J.M. Syiem, the then Deputy Commissioner, Tirap district, between 07.05.1979 to 11.06.1979, to study and address the problems of resettlement areas in Miao Sub-Division.[88]

This Committee popularly known as J.M. Syiem Committee in its recommendations had made far reaching recommendations and had suggested de-reservation of areas of Namphuk and Diyun reserves on the ground that there is no alternative land available for resettlement of these 743 families. In fact, the committee had observed that in most villages land holding is quite small and there is no prospect of increasing it, hence the people will have to resort to intensive cultivation to get maximum yield. The Committee in its report has mentioned villages like Bijoypur, Joypur etc. which were established in the initial years of migration itself (i.e. late sixties or early seventies) as duly allotted areas.

The Committee also gave several reasons that led to encroachment in Namphuk and Diyun RF. As per the estimate of the Committee at that time, approximately 550 hectares of land had been encroached upon by the Chakmas in Diyun RF, 350 hectares of land in Namphuk RF and about 550 hectares of land had been occupied by them by direct negotiation with the three local villages of Mudoi, Innao and Kumsai. The Committee, after careful study had suggested/recommended the following:

*De-reservation of approximately 350 hectares of land in Namphuk RF which has been encroached by the villagers of Ratnapur, Milanpur, Gulokpur and Dharmapur.

*De-reservation of 550 hectares of land in Diyun RF encroached upon by the villagers of Jyotsnapur, Kamakhyapur and Rajnagar.

---

[88] *Report of the Committee about Resettlement in Miao Sub-Division, 1979 under the Chairmanship of J.M. Syiem, Deputy Commissioner, Tirap District*

The committee also observed that in most villages land holding was quite small and there was no prospect of increasing it. Hence the people will have to resort to intensive cultivation to get maximum yield.

A report by Arun Goyal, the Deputy Commissioner of Changlang district, dated September 8, 1990, indicates that the sudden implementation of the Forest Conservation Act, 1980 prevented the recommendations of the J.M Syiem Committee report from being executed. Some correspondence also suggests that the Arunachal Pradesh Government was largely in agreement with the Committee's recommendations.

The government eventually acknowledged and regularised these villages as Chakma settlements. Notably, since the onset of their resettlement, no Chakma village areas in Changlang district have been de-reserved or classified as non-forest land. As a result, most of these villages remain officially designated as RF or ARF areas to these days.

(5) Reasons for Abandonment in the Highland Settlements of Deban-Namdapha

Beyond administrative pragmatism and adhocism, a confluence of factors led to the Chakma abandoning their initial settlement areas in Deban and Namdapha and migrating to low lying areas in Khagam and Dweep area. These factors largely relate to geophysical challenges, human-wildlife interactions, and administrative shortcomings. They can be enumerated as:

Monsoon-induced Isolation: During monsoon, turbulent rivers made crossings treacherous. The airdrop zone for food grains was on the opposite riverbank, leading to several migrant deaths and initial food shortages. While domesticated elephants were employed to transport food grains, the fierce river currents during monsoon proved deadly. One notable incident involved a grain-carrying elephant drowning, amplifying the already present food scarcity, adding to the direness of the situation.

Furthermore, the Namdapha Firm Base settlement is situated in a Doab region, sandwiched between two turbulent rivers: the Deban and Noa-Dihing. This positioning hindered communication during rainy seasons, preventing food grain deliveries to migrant families.

Wildlife Challenges: This region was teeming with wildlife, and not uncommonly, human settlements lay within the path of elephant migratory routes. This created significant threats, with frequent human-elephant confrontations leading to loss of life, property damage, and environmental imbalances.

Agricultural Challenges: Wild elephant herds would regularly devastate crops during harvest season. Such events would emotionally and economically devastate the settlers, who depended on these crops for sustenance and livelihood. Such destruction not only poses a tangible setback but also instill a sense of despair, given their reliance on successful crop cultivation for sustenance and livelihood.[89]

Communication Hurdles: The remoteness of the settlements, over 30 kilometers away from any major market or administrative hub, compounded the migrants' challenges. This isolation hindered their efforts towards establishing a self-reliant community and prevented access to crucial services and trade opportunities.

Lack of road infrastructure and limited access to markets and administrative centres significantly impact migrants. They struggle with employment, obtaining essentials, accessing education and healthcare, and building social connections. This not only leads to economic difficulties and social isolation but also hampers their path to self-sufficiency, affecting their livelihoods and overall growth.

---

[89] *Report of the Committee about Resettlement in Miao Sub-Division, 1979 under the Chairmanship of J.M. Syiem, Deputy Commission, Tirap District*

Land unsuitable for wet rice cultivation: In the upper reaches of Deban settlement area, a vast chunk of land was unfit for wet rice cultivation and there was technical difficulty providing irrigation facilities. The undulating nature of soil had implications for water drainage, erosion patterns, and the suitability of the land for various uses such as agriculture or construction.

Monsoon Food Shortages: To support the food needs of migrants in the higher areas of Deban and Namdapha, food grains were airdropped during the dry season. However, the monsoon's relentless rains, coupled with a lack of motorable roads, disrupted this supply for about six months annually. This prolonged disruption significantly challenged the Chakmas, threatening their well-being and survival.[90]

Lack of Administrative Support for Jhum Cultivation: In the Deban-Namdapha region, many Chakma settlers were familiar with 'Jhum' cultivation from their homeland. However, the overseeing administration neither endorsed nor aided the Chakmas in continuing this traditional farming method.

The administration's failure to provide guidance on Jhum cultivation, particularly the stipulated norm of 20 acres per family (for two adults, one grown child, and two minors), was pivotal in the Chakma settlers' decision to abandon the highland areas of Deban and Namdapha.

Craving for plain land: The absence of persuasion by officials left the Chakmas yearning for the plains, where they envisaged a more stable agricultural practice through wet rice cultivation. Additionally, the allure of living closer to their kin further incentivized their move to migrate to the plains of Khagam area from highland settlement areas.

---

[90] *A Comprehensive Note on Chakma Settlers in Changlang District by Mr. Arun Goyal, IAS, Deputy Commissioner, Changlang enclosed in his letter No. CA-108/89 dated Changlang the 8th of September 1990 to the Home Secretary, Govt. of Arunachal Pradesh.*

Mismatch of Skills and Terrain for Hajongs: Approximately 200 Hajong families, originally from the plains of East Pakistan and familiar with wet rice cultivation, were misallocated to highland Jhum areas in Deban. Their unfamiliarity with Jhum cultivation prompted them to desert these regions.[91]

Abandonment of the Deban-Namdapha Region: By 1971-72, Chakmas had abandoned three villages (Ramrajpur, Budhha Bhakti, and Udaipuri) in the Namdapha Firm Base Settlement Scheme area, and by 1975, five more in the Deban Settlement Scheme area, including Sundarpur, Sumangal, Shivatola, Monmohini, and Jagatjyoti. The 1971 census showed a significant drop in the population, with only 705 families remaining from the original 1,355 in the Deban-Pakhan and Namdapha areas. By 1981, only 383 Chakma families were left in Deban. The abandoned villages of Ramrajpur, Budhha Bhakti, and Udoypuri are now part of the Namdapha Tiger Project within the Namdapha Wildlife Sanctuary.

(6) Landlessness: Beginning of Socio-Economic Conflicts

The unfolding socio-economic conflicts between the Chakmas and the Indigenous Singphos, Khamtis, and Tangsas of Arunachal Pradesh find their roots in intricate historical contexts, evolving demographics, land and resource dynamics, and interpersonal interactions.

The Chakmas were settled on lands unoccupied by local tribes and without individual or community ownership, and this was done with local people's consent. The North-East Frontier Agency (NEFA) administration sought approval from contemporary Singpho leaders before starting the settlement process.

---

[91] *Report of the Committee to study Refugee Settlements in Arunachal Pradesh constituted by the Govt. of Arunachal Pradesh under Memo No. POL.236/72, dated 08.12.1976*

However, bureaucratic challenges and other elements, such as the lack of support for jhum-based settlements, the desertion of specific highland regions in Deban and Namdapha, and significant erosion, left approximately 1,000 Chakma families without land and the means for agricultural livelihood.

Landlessness and the Emergence of Socio-Economic Tensions between Chakmas and Singphos: The Chakma community's inability to secure designated land for settlement became a key driver for socio-economic conflicts, particularly with the neighbouring Singpho tribe. Due to the lack of clear demarcation of settlement area, many Chakmas expanded their settlements beyond their designated areas into plain terrains within the reserved and unclassified state forests. This movement was not limited to those who were originally from designated settlement blocks; Chakmas from other areas also joined this quest for land. Over time, such expansions led to significant encroachments into key forest areas, including the Diyun and Namphuk Reserve Forests.

These encroachments not only raised environmental alarms but also sowed seeds of distrust among the Singpho and Tangsa tribes. As the Tangsa, migrating from higher terrains, also sought lands in the Namphuk reserved forest, a silent competition emerged between the Chakmas and the Tangsa for control over these plains.

Further complicating the situation were the unofficial agreements that some Chakmas made with local tribes. Enticed by monetary gains, some tribal locals collaborated with Chakmas to cultivate new lands. However, once the immediate benefits were reaped, some of these tribal collaborators would lay claim to the developed lands, leading to resistance from the Chakmas. This back-and-forth over land rights created significant friction between the Chakmas and the Singpho tribesmen. Occasional instances where tribal members sought administrative intervention or took matters into their own hands to evict them by burning down their houses, resulted in property damage against the Chakmas, only exacerbated the tensions.

Landlessness among the Chakmas, combined with the complexities of land agreements and competition for resources, laid the foundation for socio-economic conflicts with the Singpho tribe.[92]

[92] *A Note on Chakma Refugees in Arunachal Pradesh, MHA File No. 13024/5/73 AP-II (Archive of India)*

7

CATALYSTS FOR SOCIO-ECONOMIC CONFLICTS BETWEEN CHAKMAS AND LOCAL TRIBESMEN

In the early days of settlement, the relationships between the Chakmas and the local tribes were complex and multifaceted. Their shared history is full of varied interactions, some peaceful and many conflicted. These interactions are deeply rooted in regional history, cultural traditions, and changing socio-economic systems, presenting many challenges and complexities. While these conflicts might seem like simple cultural misunderstandings or disputes, they stem from many underlying factors.

This chapter explores the underlying causes of these issues. Disputes over land dynamics and reserve forests highlight the complexities of land ownership. Distrust from incidents of theft and animal killings shows how fragile coexistence can be when individual actions damage collective trust. Additionally, disputes over land ownership, complicated by historical claims, legal loopholes, and local customs, further complicate the situation. Criminal activities cast a dark shadow, affecting both the victims and the community's perception. Finally, there is a constant fear of domination, where one group worries that the other's rise might marginalise them.

As we journey through each of these sub-topics, this chapter aspires to provide a panoramic view, offering readers a holistic comprehension of the myriad forces fueling socio-economic tensions between the Chakmas and the local tribesmen.

(1) Catalysts

(a) Land Dynamics and Reserve Forests:

Without designated land, many Chakma families moved beyond their original areas into available plains within reserved and unclassified state forests. Some families from the highland settlement areas of Deban and the Namdapha scheme also joined this search for land. This led to frequent relocations and significant encroachments into forests, especially the Diyun and Namphuk Reserve Forests. These encroachments caused environmental concerns and increased tensions with the neighbouring Singpho and Tangsa tribes.

At the same time, a silent struggle for these lands began between the Chakmas and the Tangsa, who were also migrating from highland areas and expanding into the Namphuk reserved forest. Both communities' interest in the plains sparked competition between them.

It's important to note that Chakma land encroachments were not just because of a lack of designated settlement areas. Sometimes, they made deals with tribal locals who, tempted by financial incentives, helped the Chakmas develop new agricultural plots. However, this cooperation was temporary. Once the benefits were secured, some tribal members would later claim the cultivated lands, leading to resistance from the Chakmas. This struggle over land ownership significantly increased the tension between the tribes and the Chakmas. Tribal locals sometimes sought administrative help or took direct action, like destroying property, against the Chakma settlers, further intensifying the conflict.[93]

(b) Distrust Rooted in Theft and Animal Killings:

From the start of the Chakma settlements, some individuals were identified as sources of social disturbances, with rising incidents of theft and animal

---

[93] *A Note on Chakma Refugees in Arunachal Pradesh, MHA File No. 13024/5/73 AP-II (Archives of India)*

killings in their areas. Some Chakma migrants engaged in illegally killing domesticated animals, like buffalo and elephants, belonging to local Singpho and Khamti tribes. There were also reports of Chakmas participating in illegal wildlife hunting and using harmful methods, such as poisoning fishponds and rivers, which damaged marine life.

A significant event in the growing tensions between the Chakma and Singpho communities was the reported killing of an elephant owned by the respected Pisila Singpho. This incident symbolised the increasing conflicts because of the elephant's value and Pisila Singpho's high status in the Singpho community. Beyond the material loss, this act was seen as a direct insult to Singpho cultural values and their leaders.

Although these events were caused by a small number of Chakmas, they created mistrust and hostility between the Chakmas and Singphos. The actions of a few damaged the reputation of the entire community, leading to a breakdown in harmony. This was a significant turning point, with the Singphos feeling wronged, a sentiment that would affect future interactions between the two groups. While only a few individuals were responsible, the consequences affected everyone. The atmosphere became tense, replacing the previous peace and mutual trust.

These recurring incidents of theft and animal killings strained the socio-cultural bonds between the Chakmas and Singphos. These strains manifested in increased hostility and animosity, negatively impacting the overall community dynamics, and fostering suspicion.

The document "A Brief Note on the Anti-Social Activities of Chakma and Hajong Refugees who migrated from erstwhile East-Pakistan and settled in Arunachal Pradesh" includes Annexure-A, which lists 83 incidents that occurred between 1964 and 1980. These incidents involve killing animals, theft, fights, attempted robbery, assaults, gambling, encroaching on reserve forests, illegal logging, and not repaying loans.[94]

(c) Disputes related to land ownership:

In addition to encroachments in forest land, landless Chakma families entered into agreements with the Singpho and Khamti tribes, either purchasing land through cash transactions or using tribal land for sharecropping. This was primarily because the Chakmas either did not receive land allotments for settlement or chose to negotiate with the local tribals.

Attracted by the prospect of quick money, some Singpho and Khamti tribal landlords worked with landless Chakma families to clear new land for farming in their USF areas. They made agreements with the Chakmas, but then often tried to claim the land developed by the Chakmas for themselves. This caused resistance from the Chakmas, who felt their efforts were being undermined, leading to conflicts and disputes. The Chakmas protested, took legal action, or used other means to resist the landlords' claims, creating tension and animosity between the two communities.

Due to the opposition from a faction within the Singpho community towards certain landlords granting land to the Chakmas in their territory, situations have arisen where tribal members have requested assistance from the local administration to remove the Chakma families. Additionally, there have been instances where the tribal community has independently taken action to force the Chakma families out of these settlement areas, resorting to methods such as setting fire to their houses and physically pushing them away.

By means of such negotiation and agreement with Singpho landlords in the late 1960s, the landless Chakmas established a few villages like Chandrapur, Navajyotipur,

---

[94] *Report of the Committee to study Refugee settlements in Arunachal Pradesh, 1976*

Shakyapur and Balupather in Singpho Innao and Mudoi area. However, after 10 years of settlement in these villages, on 16th March 1979, 321 Chakma families were evicted from the area by burning their residential homes. The contention of Chakmas was that Singphos themselves invited them to settle in those villages and consequently, the local administration also appointed Chakma Gaonburahs under Assam Frontier Regulation (Administration of Justice, 1945) Act. and paid House Tax and land revenue.

(d) Criminal Activities and Their Impact:

The year 1977 marked a distinct rupture in the peaceful coexistence between the Chakmas and local Singpho and Tangsa tribes. A series of gruesome incidents severely strained their relationship.

On October 25, 1977, an altercation over land ownership spiralled out of control, resulting in a fatal attack on Chitra Mihu, the Circle Officer of Diyun, by a group led by Lalit Kumar Karbari from Udaipur.

Another heinous act took place on February 16, 1980, involving a Nepali man, who, by marriage, had become a member of the Tangsa community. This crime was allegedly committed by Jalanta Kumar Chakma in Bijoypur. Jalanta Kumar Chakma attacked the Nepali man and Kamtoi Mossang from Miao with a Dao (a type of knife) while they were searching for a cow belonging to Kamtoi Mossang. The Nepali individual lost his life and was disposed of in the river, whereas the Tanga person survived and was rescued by the village's Chakma Gaonburah (Headman).

As news of these crimes spread, feelings of anger, resentment, and mistrust grew within the Tangsa and Singpho communities. The senseless brutality displayed in these incidents caused a significant shift in their perception of the Chakma community. The crimes became a catalyst for generating animosity, as they were seen as a direct affront to the safety, and well-being of the Tangsa and Singpho people.

These violent episodes sowed seeds of anger and mistrust among the Tangsa and Singpho communities. Their sentiments towards the Chakma community, previously grounded in coexistence, transformed drastically. These incidents were not merely viewed as isolated crimes but were perceived as a reflection of a broader pattern of aggression and disrespect by the Chakmas. The harmony that had defined their earlier relationship was replaced by deep-seated animosity and suspicion.

(e) Population Growth and Its Implications:

A prevailing sentiment suggests that the Chakma community is undergoing a swift population surge, casting a shadow on the Singpho populace's demographic majority in the region. Such perceptions have occasionally led to hostilities between the two groups, with confrontations further deepening the divide.

The rising Chakma numbers have stirred unease within the Singpho and neighbouring communities. Anxieties stem from concerns that an expanding Chakma population might overshadow the Singpho's cultural, social, and political significance. Adding fuel to the fire, there are accounts of some Chakmas engaging in unlawful acts, deepening the Singpho community's sense of insecurity. Such events not only intensify the existing friction but also perpetuate negative stereotypes about the Chakma community.

A pivotal revelation came during the Arunachal Pradesh Council Meeting in December 1973. Claims were made that the deteriorating relationship between the two communities was fueled by Chakmas allegedly misusing their demographic advantage to coercively claim lands from local tribes. This perceived power imbalance and subsequent actions have only further embittered the Singpho community.

(f) Perceived threat of domination:

On May 18, 1973, a meeting of 60 Singpho and Tangsa Gram Panchayat leaders was held at Kharsang. They decided to form the "Tangsa-Singpho Committee," which would have the authority to issue eviction notices to Chakma settlers starting in August 1973.

The Chakmas have been actively advocating for the grant of citizenship, which would not only bestow upon them the right to vote but also enable them to participate fully in the political process. Additionally, they aspired to be recognized as Scheduled Tribes, which would provide them with certain legal protections and privileges. However, these aspirations have raised concerns among the Singpho and Tangsa tribals residing in the Miao area.

The Singpho and Tangsa tribals perceived the Chakmas' efforts to acquire citizenship as a cause for worry. They hold apprehensions regarding the potential consequences of granting citizenship to the Chakmas. The concerns stem from the Singpho and Tangsa tribes' perception that the Chakmas possess certain advantages over them in terms of education, intelligence, and economic status. This perception leads to the fear that once the Chakmas are granted citizenship, they might be able to exert dominance over local politics due to their perceived advantages.

The root of this mistrust is multifaceted. The Singpho and Tangsa tribes view the Chakmas, with their perceived educational, intellectual, and economic edge, as potential threats in the political arena. They worry that once equipped with citizenship, the Chakmas could capitalise on these perceived advantages, overshadowing the local tribes in matters of governance and political influence.[95]

The Singpho and Tangsa tribes' anxieties revolve around the potential of the Chakmas to reshape local politics and dynamics. The Chakmas' quest for citizenship and tribal

---

[95] *Development and Regulatory Measures-Settlement of Chakma Refugees in Arunachal Pradesh (MHA File No. 13024/5/73 APII), National Archives of India*

recognition, paired with their perceived societal advantages, has resulted in trepidation among local tribes, fearing a future shift in regional power dynamics.

(g) The First Eastern Buddhist Conference Controversy:

In May 1976, under the Leadership of Bhikkhu Karuna, a group of Buddhist monks in the Miao area organised the First Eastern Buddhist Conference. Despite clear instructions from the administration not to invite foreign nationals and Buddhist monks from outside the region, the organisers extended an invitation to the Thai Ambassador and other international dignitaries. This caused significant embarrassment for the government, as they had to intervene and advise the Thai Ambassador and other foreign invitees not to attend the conference.

During the first eastern Buddhist conference, another source of contention emerged when local Khamti and Singpho religious and sociopolitical leaders found themselves excluded from the event. Their absence led to feelings of marginalisation and suspicions that the conference was being leveraged for the Chakmas' exclusive sectarian agendas.[96]

Further aggravating the situation, the conference prioritised the celebration of the 68th birthday of Karmabir Pandit Jinaratan Mahathero, the spiritual mentor of Bhikkhu Karuna. Jinaratan Mahathero was conferred with a high-ranking monkhood honour during the event. This gesture was viewed critically by the Singpho-Khamti religious community, given their belief that other regional monks, with longer ordinations, held more spiritual merit and experience than Jinaratan Mahathero.

(h) Firearm Possession and Its Implications:

The actions of few Chakmas, such as animal killings and illegal hunting, along with the possession of firearms,

---

[96] *Development and Regulatory Measures-Settlement of Chakma Refugees in Arunachal Pradesh (MHA File No. 13024/5/73 APII), National Archives of India*

further reinforced negative perceptions and fueled a growing sense of apprehension and hostility.

Some Chakmas were discovered by the administration to be making and owning homemade muzzle-loaded firearms illegally. This led to grave consequences in how Chakmas interacted with local tribes. It increased fear, distrust, and hostility between them. Possessing firearms created a rift between Chakmas and local tribes, reducing trust and causing suspicion and animosity to grow in the community.

(2) The Ripple Effects of Socio-Economic Tensions

The continuous stream of disputes and confrontations between the Chakmas and Singphos has cultivated an environment of profound distrust and enmity. This intricate web of animosity has been woven thread by thread through each negative interaction that has transpired between the two groups.

Originating from a series of confrontations, the Chakmas find themselves in a vulnerable position. Facing eviction attempts from some Singpho landlords and witnessing antipathy from the wider Singpho community, they harbour feelings of vulnerability, anger, and scepticism. From their perspective, the looming shadow of the Singphos perpetually threatens their rights, land, and very livelihoods.

Conversely, the Singphos carry their own set of grievances. With concerns ranging from the perceived territorial overstepping by the Chakmas to the economic rivalry precipitated by their presence, many Singphos perceive the Chakmas as outsiders—interlopers who unsettle their traditional land claims and way of life.

This mutual animosity, deeply entrenched within the cultural memory of both communities, is perpetuated by a persistent cycle of scepticism, apprehension, and bitterness. These divisive sentiments overshadow the potential for unity, creating a chasm that hinders the prospects of genuine reconciliation or peaceful cohabitation between the two communities.

(3) The Amplification of Chakma-Hajong issues

The present state of the Chakma-Hajong issue is a magnified reflection of select unfortunate incidents and disputes that transpired on a micro-scale, implicating specific segments or individuals from the Chakma community. Yet, it is imperative to stress that the actions of a few should not overshadow the character of the entire Chakma community.

The anti-foreigner movement, which began its ascent in Assam around 1979, soon spilled its influence into the neighbouring Arunachal Pradesh. Organisations like the All–Arunachal Pradesh Students Union (AAPSU) and various political factions, inspired by the Assam Agitation Model, honed their focus onto the Chakma community, branding them as "outsiders" and "foreigners." This set the stage for a fervent call for their eviction.

The localised skirmishes and disputes between the Chakmas and tribal groups like the Singphos and Tangsas in the Diyun-Miao area were disproportionately highlighted, and often framed within a communal narrative. This skewed portrayal led to the unfair branding of the entire Chakma community based on the actions of a handful.

Groups with ulterior motives orchestrated a calculated campaign against the Chakmas, disseminating misleading narratives and casting them as foreign criminals. As part of this derogatory narrative, they perpetuated negative stereotypes about the Chakmas, likening them to pigs and suggesting they birthed uncontrollably. These narratives extended to assert that, if left unchecked, the Chakmas would soon overshadow all Indigenous tribes of Arunachal Pradesh, encroaching their lands and displacing their communities.

The primary objective of these campaigns was to distort public opinion, sowing seeds of mistrust and antagonism against the Chakma community. By depicting them as alien invaders and culprits, these factions aimed to evoke a palpable sense of threat among the indigenous populace. Their hyperbolic tales of the Chakmas' supposed ambitions to dominate only deepened the pre-existing animosity.

Such strategic misinformation not only perpetuated damaging stereotypes but also amplified the tensions between the Chakma community and other tribes within Arunachal Pradesh. By tarnishing the Chakmas' image and instigating fears of their rise to dominance, these groups hoped to rally support for their anti-Chakma stance, further sidelining and isolating the Chakma community.

One must draw a clear line between individual actions and a community's collective identity. Recognizing that individuals within any community can err, it remains fundamentally unjust to brandish an entire community based on isolated incidents, perpetuating undue stigma and prejudice.

8

LAND SETTLEMENT THROUGH DIRECT NEGOTIATIONS WITH SINGPHO TRIBESMEN

In areas like Namdapha and Deban Settlement Schemes, many Chakma migrant families found themselves unable to utilise the forest lands designated for their final settlement. This was due to various reasons including unsuitability of terrain, topographical challenges, and the looming threat of wild animals. Consequently, several of them shifted from their designated settlement scheme areas and ventured into the Singpho USF (Unclassified State Forest) areas, initially establishing themselves through tenurial or rental agreements and sharecropping practices.

Over time, after cultivating the land for several years, these previously landless Chakma families began to engage in direct negotiations with local Singpho landlords. These negotiations were aimed at achieving permanent land rights, and many of these agreements were formally documented. It's important to note that these arrangements typically involved monetary transactions between the Chakmas and the Singphos.

Through such mutual agreements, the Chakmas were successful in establishing several villages in areas like Diyun and Bordumsa Circle. Some notable settlements included Dumpather, Udaipur, Mudoidweep, Joypur, Balupather, Chandrapur, Chakyapur, and Navajyotipur in the Diyun region, and Bijoypur in the Bordumsa region. However, many of these villages later faced evictions due to administrative permissions and various other reasons.

(1) The Story of establishment of Dumpather Village:

In the late 1960s, around 28 Chakma families, mostly from the Teiya Goza clan, moved from their highland homes in Namdapha and Deban. They made a sharecropping deal with Engling Lah, also known as Kala Gaonburah, who was not only a landlord but also the respected chief of Dumba Singpho village.

After a year of cultivation in the land at what would later become Dumpather village, the forest department drew a boundary in April 1966, dividing the reserve forest from the Chakma settlement, which comprised six blocks. Following this, the government passed a directive halting the provision of food grain rations to migrants who moved outside the assigned settlement areas, compelling the 28 families to rely on daily wage jobs for sustenance.

In the subsequent year, 1967, a visiting Buddhist monk from Bordumsa delivered an enlightening sermon in Dumba village. He advocated the construction of a temple and illuminated the concept of "Bhumi Dana" within Buddhism. This act of land donation, he explained, holds significant spiritual merit and, when paired with moral righteousness, concentration, and comprehension, can lead to liberation from the cycle of rebirth.

Local Chakma elders remain convinced that Dumba Singpho Gaonburah was deeply influenced by this sermon, prompting his generous decision to grant land to the Chakma families who had settled beyond the previously defined boundaries, leading to the renaming and establishment of the area as Dumpather Chakma village.

Shortly after this pivotal sermon, Bisa Raja of Bordumsa reached out to Dumba Singpho Gaonburah, seeking labourers to aid in trapping elephant calves. The Gaonburah employed about 82 Chakmas from Dumpather for this expedition at Kharsang elephant corridor, remunerating them at 25 paise per day. They set up a traditional Khedda system there, and after a few months, successfully trapped a herd. While most were released, three young calves were retained. Two of these were kept by Bisa Raja, while one was gifted to the Chakmas in gratitude for their efforts.

Upon their return, in a gesture of deep appreciation and respect, the Chakma leaders, led by Durga Charan Chakma and few others, presented the gifted elephant calf to Dumba Singpho Gaonburah. Touched by their act, the Gaonburah reciprocated by granting the entirety of the present day Dumpather village to the Chakmas for their perpetual settlement.

The land gift was formalised through a deed, which was endorsed by notable figures like Engling Lah, the Gaonburah of Dumba, and Indingla Singpho, a Gaon Panchayat member, among others. This deed was validated by the competent authority and Durga Charan Chakma accepted the donation on behalf of the Chakma families. The gifted land was bordered by the Government Road to the North, Rezang Pani Nallah to the South, Block No. 6 Settlement Area to the East, and Bara Tula Gach (Big Cotton Tree) to the West.

A copy of the deed was sent to the Deputy Commissioner of Tirap and NEFA officials. In response, the Deputy Commissioner, along with the Agriculture Development Officer and other officials, visited the site. Their inspection led to the official recognition of Dumpather as a Chakma settlement village in 1976. Afterward, Durga Charan Chakma was appointed as the Gaonburah of this village, following the Assam Frontier (Administration of Justice) Regulation of 1945.

(2) The Story of establishment of Udaipur Village

Nestled in what was once an expansive Unclassified State Forest (USF), the Udaipur village tells a tale of cooperation, respect, and cultural significance. Originally owned by prominent Singpho tribal leaders such as Engling Lah-Goanburah from Dumba and others from Innao, this vast expanse saw the entrance of the Chakma families, specifically those from the Kambey Goza clan, around

1969-70. They ventured here after leaving their previous settlements in the upper terrains of Deban and began practising jhum (slash-and-burn) cultivation on a tenurial basis, paying a fixed rent either in cash or kind.

Adjacent to the burgeoning Dumpather village, the early Chakma settlers initially cultivated the land of Engling Lah, Goanburah of Dumba, located between the Rezang Pani Nalah and the Noa-Dihing river. As time progressed, the once dense jungle slowly transformed, revealing terrains suitable for wet rice cultivation, courtesy of the hard work and dedication of the Chakma settlers.

With dreams of permanent settlement and aspirations for further wet rice cultivation lands, the Chakma families approached the Singpho landlords with a proposition. Their gesture of negotiation was symbolised by the offering of "Tupula," a customary prayer plate carrying items such as money, rice, candles, and incense sticks. Leaders like Durga Charan Chakma, Suro Mohan Chakma, Amrityalal Chakma and Madan Joy Chakma spearheaded these negotiations. The Singphos, known for their generosity, acknowledged the plight of the landless Chakmas. Moved by the sincerity of the gesture, they agreed to part with their lands for a nominal amount of Rs. 22 per Chakma family, symbolising respect and gratitude.

The official handover took place on October 5, 1974, with the Singpho landlords formally donating lands that would soon become the Udaipur village. This agreement clearly delineated the boundaries of the land, stretching from Rezang Pani Nalah in the North to the Noa-Dihing River in the South, and from Block No. 6 Settlement area in the East to the iconic Kathal Gach (Jack Fruit Tree) in the West. Almost half of the acquired Udaipur territory was a gift from Engling Lah, Goanburah of Dumba Singpho, with the remainder coming from other Singpho landlords.

Post these negotiations, a gift deed was formalised in the presence of local administrative officials, marking the establishment and administrative recognition of Udaipur as a Chakma settlement village. Mr. Mahanta, a teacher from

Dumpani School, drafted this deed in the regional Assamese language, ensuring that the tale of Udaipur village became an indelible part of local history.

(3) The Birth of Bijoypur: A Harmony Forged in Adversity

In the backdrop of our previous chapter, many Chakma families lost their land due to environmental problems like flooding and silting, while others left the highland areas assigned to them under the Deban and Namdapha settlement schemes. In 1969, many of these landless Chakma families moved to what is now known as the Bijoypur area. Among the first to venture into this area was the family of Kiro Mohan Chakma (Mala Baab), along with his four brothers and Shanti Chakma, Dino Lal Chakma, and Monu Ram Chakma among othcr pcoplc.

Initially perceived as a reserve forest, the land was subsequently revealed to be under the ownership of Ombugam Maio of Bordumsa.

Undeterred, the Chakmas approached Maio with a proposition: they would cultivate the land in exchange for a share of the produce or cash. This arrangement marked the beginning of a symbiotic relationship that would profoundly shape the destiny of the community of Bijoypur.

This sharecropping arrangement continued for several years, during which many other landless Chakma families joined the newly reclaimed area. Through these interactions, a unique bond blossomed between Kiro Mohan Chakma and Ombugam Maio, transcending the boundaries of ethnicity and evolving into a deep familial connection. Ombugam became more than just a landowner; he became Kiro Mohan's revered godfather. This extraordinary relationship would prove to be the cornerstone of peace in the years to come.

However, a shadow fell over this burgeoning harmony. A clash between Singpho and Chakma men in around 1974-75 in the nearby Bet Camp (Cane Stock-up Camp) ignited tensions, culminating in attempts to evict the Chakma families from Bijoypur. Yet, the profound respect for the bond between Ombugam and Kiro Mohan prevailed, and the eviction was averted. Considering the familial relationship between Ombugam Maio and Kiro Mohan Chakma, the Singphos reconsidered their decision to evict them from the Bijoypur area.

After enduring hardships and working the Bijoypur lands for years, the Chakma families developed a cordial relationship with Ombugam deepened the roots of coexistence. Eventually, Ombugam made a momentous decision: he bestowed the land upon the Chakma families for permanent settlement. This generous act, solidified by a traditional "Tupula" offering made by Shri Kiro Mohan Chakma with the help of Shishir Kanti Dewan, who would later become the first Gaonburah of Bijoypur.

To provide governmental context to this settlement, official records indicate that the Deputy Commissioner of Tirap District, in his communiqué (No. REV 15/79/153) dated 22nd March 1979, addressed to the Extra Assistant Commissioner, Miao, confirmed the land agreement for Bijoypur. The letter detailed a consensus with Shri Ombugam Maio, ZPM of Bordumsa, Dumsagam, GB Bordumsa, Sikhet Lakhumla, and Inchai La of Bordumsa, stating they had agreed to give the land to the Chakma families. Additionally, the Chakmas could use the area encroached upon towards the west, but under no circumstances were they to encroach upon the forest area of Wakhetna and Borkhet villages.

This tale of Bijoypur is not just about land and settlement but also about the bonds of trust, compassion, and the indomitable human spirit. It is a story where the harsh realities of displacement and conflict are counterbalanced by the extraordinary power of human connection. The bond between Kiro Mohan Chakma and Ombugam Maio is a beacon of hope, illuminating the path towards reconciliation and coexistence.

(4) Mudoidweep Village - From Tenancy to Ownership:

Around 1974-75, a number of Chakma families who were rendered landless for various reasons including flooding, silting, non-allotment of land by government, abandonment of highland areas of Deban etc. were engaged in mustard cultivation in the Mudoidweep area on tenurial arrangement on fixed rent in cash or kind under landlords namely Milunong Singpho, Gam Ong Singpho (Goanbuarh, Wakhetna), Mili Nong Singpho, Khumpa Nong Singpho and Na Nong Singpho, of Wakhetna, Bordumsa. However, Khunki Nong Singpho, Gaonburah of Mudoi also claimed ownership of this area, so he asked the Chakmas to stop clearing the area the following season when they were doing so for Jhum cultivation. Subsequently, the Chakmas who were cultivating the land at Mudoidweep informed about the conflict to their landlord Milunong Singpho.

Milunong Singpho wanted to settle the land dispute in the Mudoidweep area peacefully. He went to Mudoi Gaonburah with some of his tenants, such as Khetra Mohan Chakma, Prabhat Chandra Chakma and Pratibha Ranjan Chakma, and offered him Tupula as a gesture of goodwill. Mudoi Gaonburah accepted the offer and agreed to give Milinong Singpho the ownership rights of a part of Mudoidweep area. The Chakmas continued to farm the land by paying rent to Milinong Singpho.

This agreement also paved the way for resolving the land ownership issue of other parts of Mudoidweep area among other claimants. They included Gam Ong Singpho (Goanbuarh, Wakhetna), Mili Nong Singpho, Khumpa Nong Singpho and Na Nong Singpho, who also collected rent from the Chakmas at an average rate of 2 Maunds (80 Kg) of paddy per family every season.

The Chakmas who initially entered tenurial arrangement based on fixed rent in cash or kind in Mudoidweep areas for

Jhum cultivation with the Singpho landlords included Khetra Mohan Chakma, Prabhat Chandra Chakma, Pratibha Ranjan Chakma, Nilo Kumar Chakma, Kamalya Chakma and Hangsadhar Chakma etc. before the 1974-75.

After years of cultivating the areas of Mudoidweep, in 1991 tenurial arrangement, Milunong Singpho entered into a mortgage agreement with the Chakma families of Mudoidweep represented by Dayal Ranjan Chakma, Sumati Ranjan Chakma and Ashok Kumar Chakma with respect to 85 Hectares of land under his ownership in consideration of payment of Rs. 50,000/- to him as repayable loan @18% interest per annum and with a condition that the Chakma families will be able to cultivate the said land without paying the rental, but the entitlement shall remain with Milunong Singpho.

Finally, on 16th September 2001, Milunong Singpho, Gam Ong Singpho (Goanbuarh, Wakhetna), Mili Nong Singpho, Khumpa Nong Singpho and Na Nong Singpho grant transfer of the title and ownership of said Mudoidweep village areas measuring 385 Hectare to the Chakmas with all rights appurtenant thereto forever. Following which, hundreds of families who were evicted in March 1989 from Milanpur, Ratnapur and Gulokpur after the local people burnt down their houses also settled in Mudoidweep. During the final negotiation, each Chakma family also had to pay Rs. 500 to the landlords.

The agreement or negotiation was later intimated to the local administration following which Mudoidweep was recognized as Chakma settlement village.

(5) Story of Settlement in Chandrapur, Chakyapur, Navajyotipur and Balupather

Background: The Government of India, along with the NEFA Administration, actively supported the resettlement of Chakma families. They planned for the rehabilitation of 1,200 Chakma families in Namdapha and Deban areas. However, these lands, while abundant, proved inhospitable. The sandy, rocky terrain defied cultivation. Added challenges were poor communication, crop destruction by wildlife, food shortages in the monsoon season, and lack of basic amenities. Consequently, many Chakma families were compelled to seek more hospitable terrains after investing years in trying to establish themselves.

Migration and Relocation: Starting from 1968, hundreds of Chakma families, originally from the Namdapha and Deban areas, migrated to the Diyun region under the Khagam Settlement Scheme area. Family connections allowed many to find a foothold, but the land soon became overstretched, struggling to accommodate the influx of Chakmas from Deban and Namdapha settlement scheme areas.

In their search for land, the Chakmas approached the Singpho community. Despite being a minority, the Singphos controlled vast areas, primarily marked as Unclassed State Forests (USF). Recognizing the Chakmas' plight, the Singphos, in many instances, allocated parts of their territories for the resettlement of Chakma families. These land agreements involved cash transactions, and in some cases, the Chakmas committed to periods of bonded labour in return.

Due to frequent devastating floods on the Noa-Dihing River, more families from the Khagam area migrated. They found refuge with their fellow Chakmas who had previously moved to the Singpho areas in Mudoi, Innao, and Kumchai, settling there through tenurial or sharecropping arrangements.

Transforming the Landscape:

What was once a deep jungle becoming the beating heart of several settlements. The Chakmas, resilient and determined, cleared forests, levelled lands, and transformed them into arable fields. Here they built homes, cultivated crops, and laid down roots, investing their very essence into the soil.

With Sangho's endorsement, several new Chakma settlements emerged. Some notable donations came from Khunkinong Singpho, the Gaonburah of Mudoi village. He granted parts of his lands for the creation of Chandrapur and Shakyapur.

The Singphos and Chakmas nurtured a symbiotic relationship, celebrating cultural exchanges and religious ties. This camaraderie earned official recognition for the Chakma villages, with prominent Chakma figures appointed as the village heads or Gaonburahs.

Khunkinong Singpho, the Gaonburah of Mudoi village on April 26, 1971, by writing gave or donated to Aswani Kumar Chakma, a group leader of these landless families, a part of land from Mudoi village for the Chakma families under him for their settlement that would later become known as Chandrapur. He also gave or donated a portion of land to landless Chakma families under Munindra Chakma for their settlement in Mudoi that would later become Shakyapur.

The Chakmas established themselves in these villages, with the explicit approval of the local Singphos, following traditional customs and conventions. This consent was grounded in both compassion and significant considerations.

As time passed, the Singphos and Chakmas cultivated a mutualistic bond. They engaged in cultural exchanges, and their shared religious values fostered mutual respect and collaboration. Recognized as Chakma settlements by the local authorities, the following individuals were designated as Gaonburah (Village Headman):

- Aswini Kumar Chakma oversaw Chandrapur with 122 families.
- Madan Mohan Chakma for Navajyotipur with 60 families.
- Munindra Chakma guided Shakyapur with 85 families.

- Kanta Moni Chakma leading Balupather with 30 families.

Controversy and Eviction:

Although these settlements grew into thriving Chakma villages, they faced controversy and eviction issues later. In late 1977, a resolution was passed by the singpho leaders, demanding that the Chakma families return to their original settlements in Deban and Namdapha.

On 29th and 30th November 1977, a pivotal meeting took place in Innao chaired by C.A. Gohain. A resolution was adopted demanding that the Chakmas from Chandrapur, Navajyotipur, Shakyapur, and Balupather, who had settled outside of government-designated 'Blocks', should return to their former blocks in the Deban and Namdapha settlement areas.

Following this, on 16th January 1979, the Extra Assistant Commissioner of the Miao Sub-Division issued a directive, via Notice Memo No. Misett-4/78/363-67, (A) 76/11018-27, for the Chakmas to leave the villages in Innao and Mudoi areas and revert to the Deban area. This was reiterated by a subsequent notice from the Deputy Commissioner of Tirap district on February 20, 1979, which stated that the villages must relocate to the upper regions of Deban.

The fallout was immediate and devastating. On March 16, 1979, a total of 321 Chakma families from these villages were forcibly displaced, their homes and cattle sheds burned, and their belongings destroyed.

When these Chakmas initially migrated from their native Deban-Namdapha highlands, some of their leaders directly negotiated with local inhabitants, primarily the Singphos, around Mudoi, Innao, and Kumchai villages. These negotiations led to varied agreements: while many were based on monetary transactions, some also promised bonded labour for a specified duration. To ensure clarity, most of these agreements were documented. As a result,

Chakma villages such as Jaipur, Chandrapur, Chakyapur, Navajyotipur, and Balupather were founded.

However, the resettlement of four villages - Navajyotipur, Chandrapur, Chakyapur, and Balupather - faced a setback in March 1978. Despite some of these villages having official Gaon Burah appointments, their resettlement was not sanctioned by the administration, leading to their eviction.[97]

Following the evictions, on May 16, 1979, the Chakmas petitioned the then Prime Minister, Home Minister, Rehabilitation Minister, President of Janata Dal and other MPs of India to seek remedy to the situation. Subsequently, the Ministry of Home Affairs sought a detailed report from the Government of Arunachal Pradesh on May 31, 1979, vide D.O. No. 13024/5/73-AP.

In response, the Government of Arunachal Pradesh furnished a concise note explaining its whole position on the subject that some of the Chakmas occupied land belonging to Singphos outside the allotted area without Government's permission. Consequently, resentment amongst the locals regarding unauthorised encroachments started gaining momentum. The note also further stated that Chakmas were found to be indulging in anti-social and criminal activities and criminal cases have been registered against about 100 Chakmas. Further that the Extra Assistant Commissioner, Miao wanted the Chakmas to shift back to the highland areas of Deban and Namdapha and since they were found to be adamant, it was gathered that the families might come back again after eviction, their houses were demolished.[98]

---

[97] *Report of the Committee about Resettlement in Miao Sub-Division, 1979 under the Chairmanship of J.M. Syiem, Deputy Commission, Tirap District*

[98] *Development and Regulatory Measures-Settlement of Chakma Refugees in Arunachal Pradesh (MHA File No. 13024/5/73 APII), National Archives of India*

The Chakma community contended that certain lands had been ceded to them by local tribes. In response, the Arunachal Pradesh Government clarified that under the Bengal Eastern Frontier Regulation of 1873, which remains in effect in Arunachal Pradesh, any land transaction is deemed invalid unless the recipient is an indigenous inhabitant and has received formal government approval. While there were some records, indicated by tribal fingerprints, suggesting land transfers to the Chakmas, the broader tribal community vehemently opposed and deemed such transfers as unlawful.

(6) Petroleum Mining and Eviction of Joypur village

In the early 1970s, 56 Chakma families under the leadership of Khudiram Chakma negotiated with a local leader, Raja Ningrunong Singpho of Dumba village. On November 20, 1972, Raja Singpho donated a square mile of his uncultivated jungle land to the Chakma families. The Raja specifically mentioned that the land which he proposed to donate was jungle land and it was not possible for him to cultivate the land as wild beasts created troubles by damaging crops. The Raja felt that if he donated the said land to the Chakma people, they would be able to clear the land and cultivate thereon and that would help him to protect his crops from wild beasts in his other land.

Subsequently, Khudiram Chakma was appointed the Village Headman (Gaon Bura) of the newly formed Joypur village by the Deputy Commissioner of Tirap District on November 20, 1975. The donation of this land received official recognition from the Deputy Commissioner, Tirap, as communicated by the Extra Assistant Commissioner, Diyun KVR Chari, in a letter dated April 26, 1976.

However, by 1977, Oil India Limited determined there were significant oil reserves in the area. An initial project was halted due to subsurface complications, but signs of hydrocarbon reignited interest. The State Government of Arunachal Pradesh granted a Petroleum Mining Lease to

M/s Oil, Duliajan starting November 27, 1983, for a 20-year term. From 1987 to 1993, OIL drilled 13 additional wells in the Kumchai field.

The tantalising possibility of successful petroleum mining and the allure of significant compensation stirred the local community to urge the Chakmas to vacate the area. This pressure led to a legal battle that spanned from the Guwahati High Court to the Supreme Court between 1992 and 1993.

However, the courts concluded that neither the Deputy Commissioner nor the Extra Assistant Commissioner possessed the legal authority to grant such approvals. Following this verdict, the Chakma residents of Joypur village faced eviction in the months of October and November in 1993. Of the evicted, 28 Chakma families found a new home in Jyotsnapur village. Lacking governmental support for land post-eviction, several other families sought refuge on the properties of their kin in Jyotipur, Avoipur, and neighbouring villages.[99]

[99] *1994 Sup (1) Supreme Court Cases 615 STATE OF ARUNACHAL PRADESH Versus KHUDIRAM CHAKMA (Civil Appeal No. 2182 of 1993)*

9

1964-79: REHABILITATION AND INDIANIZATION

India has a deep-seated tradition of assisting persecuted and displaced individuals, stemming from the cultural belief in safeguarding victims of persecution and ensuring they lead a dignified life. This commitment led to the establishment of the Ministry of Relief and Rehabilitation in September 1947, with the primary role of aiding those seeking refuge in India from the erstwhile undivided Indian territories.

In 1964, embracing this ethos, the Indian government initiated the rehabilitation of the Chakma people, aiming to provide them a respectable life in what was then known as the North Eastern Frontier Agency (NEFA), now Arunachal Pradesh. The government dedicatedly supported each Chakma family, ensuring their well-being as they transitioned through various transit camps until their permanent resettlement.

The Chakmas' final stop before official resettlement was the Ledo transit camp in Assam, after which the NEFA administration took charge of their final rehabilitation. Between 1964 and 1969, the government introduced five distinct settlement schemes, resulting in the establishment of areas in Deban, Namdapha, Khagam, Chowkham, and Kokila, distributed across three districts of the state.

1. Citizenship as a Fundamental Element of the Rehabilitation Policy:

In 1964, the Government of India observed parallels between the challenges faced by minorities in erstwhile East Pakistan and the harrowing experiences during the

1947 partition, particularly in West Pakistan. Both events saw mass migrations, communal strife, and the large-scale displacement of countless individuals.

Acknowledging these similarities and understanding the depth of the situation in 1964, the government introduced a comprehensive rehabilitation policy. This policy was not just a response to immediate crises; it was a holistic approach designed to address the wide range of challenges these minorities faced. This included providing legal, social, economic, and psychological support.

The implementation of such a robust policy highlighted the government's dedication to these affected communities. More than just immediate relief, the policy emphasised long-term integration, security, and overall well-being, ensuring that these minorities had the necessary foundation to rebuild their lives with dignity and stability.

De-facto Citizenship in the 1964 Rehabilitation Policy:

In 1964, the government's rehabilitation policy included de-facto Indian citizenship to the migrants of erstwhile East Pakistan. This means that although the Chakma migrants were not formally granted citizenship through the usual legal process, they were recognized as citizens of India for the purpose of rehabilitation. By recognising them as de facto citizens, the government ensured that they were entitled to the same rights and privileges as any other Indian citizen.

As rehabilitation policy had citizenship as a default component, a wide range of entitlements and privileges, such as the right to vote, access to education, healthcare, employment opportunities, social welfare benefits, and legal protections was extended to the Chakma migrants and other millions of such migrants. By doing so the government ensured that they could fully enjoy these rights and privileges, which are essential for their integration, well-being, and overall rehabilitation.

Recognizing citizenship as a default component of the rehabilitation policy demonstrates a commitment to providing a holistic and inclusive approach to rehabilitation. It acknowledged that rehabilitation goes beyond providing immediate relief or assistance and aims to restore individuals' lives in a comprehensive manner. Granting citizenship ensures that the Chakma migrants have a stable legal status and can fully participate in the social, economic, and political life of the country.

With regards to conferment of Citizenship to the migrants who entered India in 1964, the Ministry of Home Affairs on June 16, 1965, vide its express letter No. 4/366/63-IC issued instructions to the State Governments of Assam, West Bengal, Tripura, Manipur and Nagaland regarding policy and procedure regarding conferment of Indian Citizenship on migrants from East Pakistan. The letter states "it has been decided that such of thc migrants (whether they have come with or without migration certificates or without travel documents) as have severed their ties and connection with Pakistan and have settled in service, trade or profession in India, may be registered as Indian citizens under Section 5 (1) (a) of Citizenship Act, 1955, provided they fulfil such conditions laid down in rule 9 of Citizenship Rules, 1956".[100]

In reference to the aforesaid letter, the Ministry of Rehabilitation also wrote to the concerned states on this subject on June 28, 1966, vide letter No. 1(2)/65-RH. II/IV and on November 30, 1966 vide letter No. 16(10)/66-RH. II. stating that very few persons have, in fact, been able to acquire citizenship rights in terms of those orders. The main difficulty appeared to have been lack of knowledge on the part of the migrants and repatriates of the rules and procedures to be followed in the matter. The delay in registering the migrants as Indian Citizens was also hindering the process of their placement in various jobs

---

[100] *Development and Regulatory Measures-Settlement of Chakma Refugees in Arunachal Pradesh (MHA File No. 13024/5/73 APII), National Archives of India*

which, in turn, retards the rehabilitation programme. It further states that to accelerate the pace of rehabilitation of these migrants, it is essential that those migrants who satisfy the condition laid down in the Indian Citizenship Act, 1955, and the Citizenship rules, 1956 made thereunder are registered as Indian Citizens without delay. This will also help their speedy integration in Indian society.

The Ministry of Rehabilitation also wrote that unless a programme of registration is drawn up by each district authority and definite timetable is prescribed for completion of this special work, very few migrants are likely to come forward of their own accord for completing formalities required to acquire citizenship. It is therefore requested that necessary action instructions be issued to all concerned authorities in the matter so that the registration work is completed by the end of the year 1966 in respect of all new migrants and repatriates who have completed the minimum period of residence. [101]

2. Arunachal Pradesh Government's Citizenship Recommendation for Chakmas

In April 1973, Arunachal Pradesh's administration put forth a recommendation to grant Indian citizenship to Chakma and Hajong migrants who had been rehabilitated in Arunachal Pradesh in 1964. This aligned with the Ministry of Home Affairs' (MHA) guidelines about awarding Indian citizenship to those from East Pakistan (present-day Bangladesh). The MHA, in evaluating the recommendation, contemplated both the legal aspects and their standing policy on East Pakistan migrants.

The MHA also consulted the Intelligence Bureau (IB), an agency responsible for providing intelligence and security information to the Indian government. However, the IB expressed the opinion that the timing was not appropriate

---

[101] *Development and Regulatory Measures-Settlement of Chakma Refugees in Arunachal Pradesh (MHA File No. 13024/5/73 APII), National Archives of India*

for conferring citizenship on the Chakma and Hajong migrants.

Despite Arunachal Pradesh's recommendation and the MHA's review, the decision to confer citizenship was deferred, influenced mainly by the IB's reservations.

However, progress was made in November 1974 when the Rajya Sabha (India's upper parliamentary house) received assurances to expedite grant of citizenship to migrants from East Pakistan. Subsequently, the Ministry of Supply and Rehabilitation issued guidelines to State Governments and Union Territories. The directive was clear: fast-track the citizenship process for East Pakistan migrants who moved to India between January 1, 1964, and March 25, 1971.

The Ministry's instructions reflected the government's commitment to addressing the citizenship status of these migrants and facilitating their integration into Indian society. By setting a timeframe for their eligibility, the government aimed to streamline the process and ensure a timely resolution for the affected individuals.

1975: Deferral of Citizenship Decision for Chakma-Hajong Migrants

In 1975, the Secretaries Committee (Internal Affairs) convened a meeting and decided to defer the final decision on the matter of conferring citizenship to Chakmas for a year. This meant that the granting of citizenship to the Chakmas would be put on hold, and the issue would be reviewed in 1976.[102]

The decision to formally confer citizenship to these migrants encountered multiple delays. Reasons ranged from perceived security threats, the state's inaugural general elections, concerns about the Chakmas' behaviour, and the sentiments of the local populace.

---

[102] *Development and Regulatory Measures-Settlement of Chakma Refugees in Arunachal Pradesh (MHA File No. 13024/5/73 APII), National Archives of India*

3. Rehabilitation with Rights and Entitlements as Citizens

From the onset of the Chakmas' rehabilitation in Arunachal Pradesh (formerly NEFA), the Government consistently worked to empower the migrants, helping them become self-reliant. The objective was two-fold: to facilitate the Chakmas' self-sufficiency and to eventually reduce the government's long-term responsibility for their maintenance. This was achieved by granting them rights and entitlements typically reserved for citizens.

(a) Food Security Initiatives for Chakma Migrants:

- **Ration Cards:** Every Chakma migrant family received a ration card from their first year of settlement. This official document entitled them to buy subsidised food grains and essential items from government-operated fair price shops. This ensured that the Chakmas had a consistent, affordable source of food.
- **Fair Price Shops:** In tandem with ration cards, the government established fair price shops specifically for Chakma families. These are outlets where vital commodities, including food grains, are available at reduced rates. By catering to the Chakmas directly, the government made it easier for them to meet their dietary needs.

  Both these measures underscored the government's commitment to addressing the food security of the Chakma migrants. By providing affordable and readily available food resources, the government played a pivotal role in ensuring the Chakmas' nutrition and overall well-being during their rehabilitation phase.

(b) Land Allotment and Agricultural Assistance for Chakma Migrants

- **Land Allotment:** In the initial phase of rehabilitation, the government did not provide individual land plots to Chakma families. Instead,

Chakma group leaders, representing 40 to 100 families, were designated an area, often forest areas, which they were tasked with clearing and making arable. This collective approach is aimed at fostering community cohesion.

However, in 1970-80, the government shifted its strategy, acknowledging the benefits of individual land ownership for the Chakmas. As a result, each family was granted about 5 acres of land, giving them autonomy in their agricultural ventures. This move not only provided a sense of stability but also resonated with the Chakmas' agricultural background, enabling them to contribute to the local economy.

- **Agricultural Assistance:** Through land allotment and multifaceted agricultural assistance, the government took concrete steps to ensure the Chakma migrants' stability, empowerment, and self-sufficiency.
- **Tools & Implements:** The Chakma migrants, with agriculture being their primary occupation, were equipped with essential farming tools like ploughs, hoes, and sickles to ensure a smooth transition into their agricultural roles.
- **Seeds & Seedlings:** To kickstart their agricultural activities, the government provided the Chakma families with seeds and seedlings, essential for crop cultivation.
- **Livestock:** Some families were also given bullocks and cows, integral to farming activities, transportation, and dairy production. This support was geared towards enhancing agricultural productivity.
- **Financial Aid:** As a step towards ensuring their self-reliance, each Chakma family received a one-time cash grant of INR 4,200. This financial boost aimed

to help them settle economically and cater to immediate needs.

(c) Trade Licences for Chakma Migrants:

Recognizing the value of economic self-sufficiency, the government provided numerous Chakmas with trade licences. This initiative was designed to promote entrepreneurship within the Chakma community and reduce their dependence on government aid.

By issuing these licences, the government facilitated the Chakmas' entry into various economic sectors, allowing them to legally operate businesses. The goal was not only to boost their participation in the local economy but also to foster societal integration.

The strategic provision of trade licences had twofold benefits. First, it invigorated the Chakma community with a business-driven spirit, enabling them to generate income and contribute actively to the local economy. Second, it imbued the Chakmas with a sense of autonomy, self-worth, and dignity, as they could freely engage in their preferred trade or profession. This approach aimed to transition the Chakmas from being passive recipients of aid to active contributors to society and their own welfare.

(d) Employment Opportunities for Chakmas in Government Establishments:

To foster integration and economic independence, the government offered job opportunities within state government establishments to Chakmas with educational qualifications. This initiative enabled many Chakmas to serve in various departments such as Medical, Public Health & Malaria, Education, Public Health Engineering, Agriculture, and the Arunachal Pradesh Police (APP). Their inclusion in these critical sectors contributed to the broader welfare and societal development.

Moreover, Chakma youths found opportunities in defence establishments, including the Assam Rifles, CRPF, ITBP, and SSB. This not only displayed their commitment to national service but also provided them with consistent employment and career growth.

Reinforcing this commitment, the Ministry of Home Affairs, in its letter dated November 21, 1964 (No. 4/5 64-Estt.), urged state governments to offer concessions to the recent migrants from East Pakistan. The intention was to facilitate their assimilation into various state services and roles, as well as public undertakings under state purview.[103]

List of Chakmas and Hajongs employed in State Government Services

Sl. No. Name	Department	Year
1.Panja Joy Chakma	Civil Engineering	-
2.Amiyo Kumar Dewan	Food & Civil Supplies	-
3. Doyal Kumar Chakma	Arunachal Police	1976
4. Ranjit Kumar Chakma	Arunachal Police	1976
5. Ananta Talukdar	Arunachal Police	1976
6. Abhasta Moni Chakma	Arunachal Police	1976
7. Holodhar Chakma	Arunachal Police	-
8. Arunya Chakma	Arunachal Police	1984
9. Sushil Kumar Dewan	PWD	-
10. Prabhat Kr. Chakma	Medical & PH&M	-
11. Lalit Kumar Chakma	Medical & PH&M	-
12. Sudhamoy Chakma	Medical & PH&M	-
13. Maloti Chakma	Medical & PH&M	-
14. Sumoti Ranjan Chakma	Medical & PH&M	-
15. Sumoti Ranjan Talukdar	Dept. of Education	-
16. Sneha Kumar Chakma	Dept. of Education	1986
17. Pratap Ch. Chakma	Land Management	-
18. Rabi Dhan Chakma	Dept. of Forest	-
19. Samiran Chakma	Dept. of Forest	-
20. Chitta Ranjan Hajong	Dept. of Forest	-
21. Sneha Ranjan Talukdar	Dept. of Forest	-
22. Birendra Chakma	Dept. of Forest	-
23. Porimal Chakma	Dept. of Forest	-

[103] *Development and Regulatory Measures-Settlement of Chakma Refugees in Arunachal Pradesh (MHA File No. 13024/5/73 APII), National Archives of India*

24. Pradeep Kr Chakma Dept. of Agriculture -
25. Jubaraj Hajong Dept. of Agriculture -
26. Ishwar Ch Chakma Dept. of Agriculture -
27. Nibaran Hajong Dept. of Agriculture -
28. Yudhisthir Hajong Dept. of Agriculture -
29. Jayanta Chakma Dept. of Post/LDC Co Office -

(e) Subsidised Agricultural and Business Loans for Chakmas:

The government provided Chakma migrants with subsidised loans to encourage business and agricultural ventures. These loans, with reduced interest rates or other favourable terms, were designed to ease the initial capital burden and provide essential resources for their entrepreneurial efforts.

Specifically, Chakma entrepreneurs received financial support to establish sustainable businesses that contributed to the local economy. On the agricultural front, Chakma farmers benefited from loans tailored for purchasing farming inputs, leading to improved productivity. These provisions not only empowered Chakma farmers to be self-sufficient but also helped boost the region's agricultural sector with surplus production.

By facilitating subsidised loans for both business and agriculture, the government aimed to promote self-sufficiency, economic growth, and community empowerment among Chakma migrants.

(f) Educational Support for Chakma Students:

Chakma students were granted access to various educational facilities and scholarships, ensuring they received quality education and integrated seamlessly as Indian citizens. They benefited from free book grants, alleviating the financial strain of educational materials and enabling focused studies. Hostel facilities were also provided, creating an environment conducive to their academic progress.

Recognising their potential, scholarships were awarded to meritorious Chakma students. These incentives were in place to motivate them to achieve academic excellence and pursue higher education. Importantly, the Chakma students were treated on equal footing with other tribal students in the Arunachal educational system, promoting fairness, inclusivity, and integration.

The overarching goal behind these educational provisions was to integrate Chakma students as valued members of Arunachal society. Through these initiatives, the aim was to empower them educationally, allowing them to contribute positively to the nation and fostering a unified and harmonious society.

(g) Arms Training & Gun Licences for Chakmas:

In the early 1970s, guided by a strategic policy, the thousands of Chakmas underwent Village Level Training Programmes and Refresher Training Courses in civil defence by the SSB (formerly Special Service Bureau)[104]. The goal was to prepare Chakma villagers to defend their country when national exigency arises and potentially assume a "stay behind role" for the country. The training encompassed civil defence techniques, including small arms usage and self-defence methods. This initiative aimed to foster preparedness and resilience within the Chakma community.

Trained Chakma volunteers were invaluable to the SSB, serving as its on-ground informants. Their training

---

[104] *https://www.ssb.gov.in/index1.aspx?lsid=39&cid=0&lev=2&lid=11&langid=1*

facilitated their contribution to the region's security, underlining their integral role in its defence. Alongside, many Chakmas were issued gun licences, underscoring their role in self-defence and their integration into the larger security framework.

(h) Gaonburaship in Chakma Villages:

Post-settlement of Chakmas in Arunachal Pradesh, governance at the local level was established by appointing Gaonburas, or Village Headmen. Holding pivotal authority at the village level, Gaonburas play an essential role in managing development and upholding law and order.

Appointed by the District's Deputy Commissioner as per The Assam Frontier (Administration of Justice) Regulations of 1945, Gaonburas function as a bridge between the government and the villagers. Their duties span overseeing local development, liaising with government officials, implementing welfare programs, and addressing villagers' concerns.

A primary responsibility of the Gaonburas is maintaining village law and order. Collaborating with local law enforcement, they ensure the safety of the residents, foster communal harmony, resolve disputes, and address any criminal or unlawful activities.

As influential village figures, Gaonburas' insights and decisions are highly regarded. Representing the government, they convey the villagers' needs to higher authorities, advocating for their concerns. Their leadership drives the socio-economic advancement of their villages.

4. No Initial Pronounced Opposition to the Chakma-Hajongs in Arunachal Pradesh:

In the initial stages, Chakma and Hajong settlements in Arunachal Pradesh faced minimal opposition. Their presence became a topic of concern only after the late 1970s' anti-foreigner agitation in Assam, which subsequently spread to Arunachal Pradesh in 1979. Look for reference in the file.

Claims suggesting that the tribal inhabitants of Arunachal Pradesh were not involved in decisions regarding the Chakma-Hajong settlements in NEFA (North-East Frontier Agency) are questionable. Prominent leaders like Chow Khamoon Gohain Namshum, the first MP from NEFA, Daying Ering, a union Deputy minister and MP, and other local influencers were actively involved during the Chakma settlement phase.

Historically, Chakma resettlements in NEFA were pursued only after discussions with local leaders. Political officers or Deputy Commissioners earnestly sought the tribal leaders' consent for Chakma Settlement near their areas. Settlements were established where local leaders voluntarily allocated land. For instance:

In the Noa-Dihing area of the Tirap Division, consultations were conducted with Buddhist Singpho and Tikhak leaders before accommodating Chakmas.

In the Khamti area of Chowkham, Lohit Division, settlements were confirmed post discussions with Khamti leaders, including the noted Chow Khamoon Gohain, NEFA's first MP.

Before settling in Hollongi-Dirgha, Subansiri Division, the administration sought local community leaders' approval and proposed the rehabilitation of 400-500 Chakma families.

Notably, certain proposed settlements in frontier regions were rejected by local leaders, leading the administration to forego those plans.

The Chakma resettlement phase in NEFA paralleled a time of political evolution. Efforts were made to incorporate NEFA's residents into decision-making, as evidenced by the 1967 North-East Frontier Agency Panchayat Raj Regulation Act. This Act set up an Agency Council as the supreme governing body, with Zilla Parishads, Anchal Samitis, and Gram Panchayats functioning at district, block, and village levels respectively. Traditional village councils, acknowledged under the 1945 North-East Frontier Administration of Justice Regulation, were upgraded to Gram Panchayats. [105]

The Agency Council, formed to advise the Governor of Assam on NEFA affairs, functioned similarly to other state legislative assemblies. With 20 members, its first meeting was on 3rd December 1969, inaugurated by Sri B.K. Nehru, the Assam Governor. Subsequently, the Agency Council took over the role of making policies for NEFA, representing the people who lived there.[106]

Upon Arunachal Pradesh's recognition as a union territory in January 1972, the Agency Council transitioned into the Pradesh Council on 1st August 1972. Later, it evolved into a provisional legislative assembly on 15th August 1975.

During the transition from the Agency Council to the Pradesh Council and later to the Legislative Assembly until 1979, there was little opposition from the local people of the state regarding Chakma settlements. The main concern raised was about not settling additional refugees, ex-

[105] https://web.archive.org/web/20090410004725/http://arunachalpradesh.nic.in/rural/html/glance.htm
[106] https://namsai.nic.in/history/

servicemen, or people from outside in Arunachal Pradesh. There was no discussion about deporting or relocating the existing Chakma residents to other states.

In the inaugural session of the Pradesh Council, from 2nd to 6th October 1972 in Shillong, the policy regarding the settlement of outsiders in Arunachal Pradesh was debated. Varied viewpoints emerged, leading to a decision to defer the discussion to the next session and, in the interim, gather the perspectives of Zilla Parishads and Anchal Samitis members.[107]

At the council's second session from 23rd to 25th January 1973 in Along, a resolution emerged, recommending the administration to assess the situation of outsiders settled before 1972. Any activities of these settlers should be regulated, especially concerning potential forest encroachments. Moreover, any future outsider or refugee settlements should only proceed after consultation with local Panchayat Raj Bodies, ensuring genuine cases are addressed.

Throughout these discussions, the Chakma settlements faced no significant opposition.

5. AAPSU's Stance on Chakma-Hajongs in Arunachal Pradesh Prior to 1979

Before 1979, the All–Arunachal Pradesh Students' Union (AAPSU) did not vocalise significant opposition to the Chakma settlements. Despite its prominence as a student organisation, AAPSU refrained from raising concerns about the Chakma community's presence in Arunachal Pradesh. This suggests that, for the student

[107] *Recommendations of the Inaugural Session of Pradesh Council of Arunachal Pradesh held at Shillong from 2nd to 6th Oct' 72*

union, the Chakma settlement was neither contentious nor a primary concern during this period.

Founded in 1959 as the All NEFA Student's Union (ANSU) with its headquarters in Pasighat, AAPSU underwent a name change in 1972. This shift followed NEFA's renaming as Arunachal Pradesh and its status update to a Union Territory. Consequently, the name transitioned from ANSU to AAPSU, with the student politics hub centred at Pasighat's Jawaharlal Nehru College.

Up until 1979, AAPSU primarily focused on issues such as the Assam-Arunachal boundary dispute and student-centric concerns. Their demands encompassed the establishment of more advanced educational institutions, a switch in the medium of instruction from Assamese to English, an increase in student stipends, reserved seating in scientific and technical institutions, and administrative enhancements. They also sought the upgrade of the NEFA administration to Union Territory status, the creation of more administrative centres, and a relocation of its headquarters from Shillong to a location within NEFA.

In a file note, M.L. Kampani, Joint Secretary (NE) at MHA, astutely captured the sentiment of the local populace regarding the settlement of the Chakmas. ***"The local tribals, in the hope that at a later stage they would be able to throw them out of the area have overreacted towards the Chakmas, but there has been no pronounced opposition to their being there. In the Arunachal Pradesh Council the emphasis has been on preventing further induction of refugees or for that matter any non-Arunachalis into the Union Territory."***[108]

[108] *Development and Regulatory Measures-Settlement of Chakma Refugees in Arunachal Pradesh (MHA File No. 13024/5/73 APII), National Archives of India*

According to Joint Secretary (NE), MHA notation, the local tribal communities held a belief that, in the future, they would have the ability to remove the Chakma people from the area. As a result, their interactions with the Chakmas were marked by an excessive and exaggerated response. However, it is important to note that this response did not manifest as overt and explicit opposition to the presence of the Chakmas.

Within the context of the Arunachal Pradesh Council, the focus primarily centred around preventing any further influx of refugees, including the Chakmas, as well as any individuals who were not considered Arunachalis. This indicates that the emphasis was on controlling the demographic composition of the Union Territory, rather than specifically targeting the Chakma community.

6. A Unique Exemption from the Foreigner's Act 1946

Arunachal Pradesh granted the Chakma community a unique exemption from the Foreigner's Act 1946, distinguishing them from other refugees, such as the Tibetans. Although no formal statutory order directly exempts the Chakmas from the Foreigner's Act 1946 or the Foreigner's Order of 1948, historical records and government directives provide clarity on this exception.

On 3rd January 1964, through Letter No. 21/48/62-F. IV(B), the central government issued guidelines to all state governments, specifically regarding Pakistani Nationals from minority communities. This directive mandated that such individuals should not be prosecuted under the Passport (Entry into India) Act 1920 or the Foreigners Act 1946 without prior consent from the Government of India, aiming to shield persecuted minorities.

Consequently, Chakmas in Arunachal Pradesh received an exemption from the Foreigner's Act 1946 provisions, distinguishing them from other refugees like the Tibetans. This exception underlines India's distinct approach to refugee policies, emphasising both the historical context and humanitarian considerations for the Chakma community. It stands as a testament to the government's dedication to ensuring the safety and rights of persecuted minorities from their homeland.[109]

[109] *MHA File No. 13024/5/73-AP-II, Development and regulatory measures, Security matters - Settlement of Chakma Refugees in Arunachal Pradesh*

10

1979-96: DE-INDIANIZATION & DE-REHABILITATION

Prior to 1979, the Chakma and Hajong communities in Arunachal Pradesh coexisted relatively peacefully with the local populace and faced little opposition from the All–Arunachal Pradesh Students' Union (AAPSU), as discussed in the previous chapter. The primary focus of the administration during this period was demographic control within the Union Territory, aiming to prevent further influx of outsiders, including ex-servicemen, Chakmas, and Hajongs. Notably, there was no significant antagonism directed towards the Chakma and Hajong communities at this time.

However, the landscape shifted dramatically in 1979. The emergence of the anti-foreigner movement in neighboring Assam had a profound impact on Arunachal Pradesh, igniting a surge in opposition to Chakma and Hajong migrants. This pivotal year also witnessed the establishment of Dera Natung Government College in Itanagar, marking a turning point for AAPSU. The relocation of the student union's headquarters from Pasighat, predominantly Adi, to Itanagar, primarily Nyishi, transformed AAPSU's stance on the Chakma-Hajong issue. This geographical shift coincided with a hardening of the union's position, ushering in a new era of activism centered around opposition to these communities.

A Ministry of Home Affairs note (UO No. 13024/5/73-AP, dated 9th August 1982) reveals that Chief Minister Gegong Apang attributed the sudden spotlight on the "foreigners issue" in Arunachal Pradesh to AAPSU's alliance with the All Assam Students Union and opposition members of the Arunachal Pradesh Assembly. He also hinted at a potential, albeit undisclosed, influence from missionaries in Assam, Shillong, and Nagaland swaying students to address this issue.[110]

On October 6, 1982, Amar Roy Pradhan, the MP from Cooch Behar raised a question in Lok Sabha whether the government had received a proposal to remove Tibetans and Chakmas from Arunachal Pradesh, along with the withdrawal of their trade licences, and sought clarity on any decisions made in this regard.

Mr. Nihar Ranjan Laskar, the Minister of State in the Ministry of Home Affairs, responded by acknowledging recent demands put forth by the AAPSU (All Arunachal Pradesh Students' Union), which included requests for the removal of foreign nationals and the withdrawal of trade licence from non-Arunachalees. Laskar clarified that the Chakmas had been settled in Arunachal Pradesh under various rehabilitation schemes. He explicitly stated that the question of their removal did not arise, indicating that their settlement was not under consideration for alteration.[111]

1. Shift in Discourse: The Beginning of De-Indianization and De-Rehabilitation of Chakmas

1979 was a watershed year when AAPSU, for the first time, broached the Chakma-Hajong topic in Arunachal Pradesh. Their reformulated charter of demands included:

- Identification and expulsion of foreign nationals from the territory.
- Revocation of land allotment permits, and trade licences granted to non-Arunachalis.

---

[110] *Development and Regulatory Measures-Settlement of Chakma Refugees in Arunachal Pradesh (MHA File No. 13024/5/73 AP Vol. III), National Archives of India*

[111] *MHA File No. 9/12/82-AP Lok Sabha Starred Question No. 541 for 6.10.82 by Shri Amar Roy Pradhan regarding proposal to remove Tibetans and Chakmas from Arunachal Pradesh. (National Archives of India)*

- Implementation of effective measures to prevent further infiltration of foreign nationals.

(a) A Turn of Events: AAPSU's Stance on Chakma-Hajongs in 1979 and Beyond

The year 1979 was a defining moment as AAPSU began adopting a hardline stand against the Chakma-Hajongs, often branding them as "foreign nationals." This shift signified the onset of de-indianization and de-rehabilitation process for the Chakma and Hajong communities, undoing the rehabilitation groundwork laid by the Government of India in 1964.

De-indianization refers to the deliberate strategy to alienate the Chakma and Hajong communities from their Indian roots and rights, even though they had established their identities as citizens before 15th August 1947. This stance starkly contradicted the Government of India's earlier initiatives, which intended to provide these displaced communities with a secure abode and the promise of a brighter future within Indian territories.

AAPSU's persistent campaign against the Chakmas and Hajongs significantly altered the state's perception and treatment of these communities. By categorising them as foreign nationals and calling for their identification, removal, and the revocation of their land and trade licences, AAPSU effectively obstructed the rehabilitation of these communities and their assimilation into Arunachal society.

To amplify their demands, AAPSU orchestrated its inaugural two-day Bandh in early 1980 – a protest characterised by a halt in economic activities being done by Chakmas and Hajongs. Arunachal Pradesh, for the first time, witnessed a robust movement against the Chakma and Hajongs. The momentum from this protest eventually swayed the state government to accede to AAPSU's demands. This sequence of events underscores the fluctuating narratives and policies determining the fate of these communities in Arunachal Pradesh.

(b) AAPSU's Evolving Tactics and its Influence in Arunachal Pradesh

In response to increasing pressure from the All–Arunachal Pradesh Students' Union (AAPSU), the state government issued a discriminatory order on September 29, 1980 (No. Pol-21/81). This order prohibited Chakmas and Hajongs from securing employment in state government positions, exacerbating tensions and negatively impacting the two communities.

A significant outcome of AAPSU's advocacy was the inception of the "Bandh Culture" in Arunachal Pradesh. The effectiveness of their Bandh in achieving desired results laid the foundation for subsequent protests in the state, establishing Bandhs as a potent tool in the regional socio-political landscape.

Starting in 1985, AAPSU shifted from simply petitioning the government to taking more direct action. Instead of just making appeals, they began using confrontational tactics to voice their concerns. Led by figures like Mr. Jarbom Gamlin and Larbin Nashi, AAPSU organised many district-level Bandhs to push their demands. This change was partly inspired by the success of the anti-foreigner movement in Assam, which grew into a significant movement. As a result, AAPSU intensified their efforts to call for the deportation of the Chakma and Hajong communities.

The signing of the Assam Accord in 1985, which included AASU (All Assam Students Union) as a stakeholder, further bolstered AAPSU's position. Under the leadership of Nabam Rebia and Tabin Taki, the union embraced a more rigid stance on the Chakma-Hajong issue. This era saw an escalation in AAPSU-led activities, with frequent Bandhs, protests, marches, and hunger strikes becoming commonplace.

By the 1990s, AAPSU's relentless campaigns on state boundary disputes and Chakma-Hajong deportation had successfully galvanised public sentiment. Their increasing influence posed a challenge to the Congress party, which began to view AAPSU as a political contender. Rumours suggest that to counteract AAPSU's burgeoning influence, Mr. Gegong Apang recruited several prominent former AAPSU leaders into the Congress, providing them with political avenues.

(c) Strengthening the narrative of continued influx of Chakmas in Arunachal Pradesh:

In 1986, a significant humanitarian crisis unfolded when over 56,000 Chakma refugees fled to South Tripura district, India, from Bangladesh. India provided temporary shelter and aid to these refugees. Diplomatic efforts were initiated to create conditions for their safe repatriation to Bangladesh. This process began in 1994 and concluded in 1996.[112]

The All–Arunachal Pradesh Students' Union (AAPSU) capitalized on this situation to bolster its claims about the ongoing influx of Chakmas into Arunachal Pradesh. By highlighting the large number of Chakma refugees, AAPSU argued that unchecked migration posed a threat to the demographic balance of the state, implying a potential risk of the indigenous population being outnumbered.

(d) Politicisation of the Chakma-Hajong Issue in Arunachal Pradesh

In a bid to address AAPSU's concerns, the state government restricted the issuance of ration cards to the Chakma-Hajong community, as evidenced by directive No. FP-5D/90-91 dated October 31, 1991.

This move signalled the onset of the Chakma-Hajong issue's politicisation in Arunachal Pradesh. Politicians, many of whom were former AAPSU leaders, placed the Chakma-Hajong matter at the forefront of their campaigns,

---

[112] *Ministry of Home Affairs, Govt. of India, Departments of Internal Security, States and Home (Annual Report 1995-96)*

promising decisive actions like deportation if they secured power.

The 1995 Assembly elections saw the Chakma-Hajong issue leveraged as a primary campaign topic. Politicians wielded rhetoric and false narratives around the issue to gain votes, embedding it deeply into the state's political fabric and inadvertently fostering xenophobia. Although political manifestos didn't directly address the Chakma-Hajong issue, it became intertwined with the Arunachal-Assam boundary topic as a significant election issue, serving as populist topics to rally public support.

Dr. Kuku Panyang, in his 2017 paper titled ALL ARUNACHAL PRADESH STUDENTS' UNION: A STUDY OF ITS HISTORY AND LEADERSHIP (IJRSSH) 2017, Vol. No. 7, Issue No. I, elaborates on this trend. [113]

Dr. Kuku Panyang, in his paper titled ALL ARUNACHAL PRADESH STUDENTS' UNION: A STUDY OF ITS HISTORY AND LEADERSHIP (IJRSSH) 2017, Vol. No. 7, Issue No. I. He writes, *"Since student"s associations, particularly All Arunachal Pradesh Students" Union, posed a serious challenge to the government and the Congress party, the then chief minister changed his tactics - from confrontation to appeasement. The selective policy of appeasement was offered to some of the top leaders of AAPSU by inducting them in the party and the government. The chief minister, Gegong Apang, adopted such a policy to achieve twin objectives- to get rid of his political opponents by replacing them with young leaders; and to weaken the AAPSU movement by offering political opportunities to its leaders".*

"Many of the former AAPSU leaders were initiated into the political arena through this policy. Former AAPSU presidents Jarbom Gamlin and Takam Sanjoy went on to become the state"s chief minister and Member of Parliament respectively. Nabam Rebia, another former AAPSU resident, presently a

---

[113] *ALL ARUNACHAL PRADESH STUDENTS' UNION: A STUDY OF ITS HISTORY AND LEADERSHIP (IJRSSH) 2017, Vol. No. 7, Issue No. I*

legislator, was the speaker of Arunachal Pradesh Legislative Assembly. Tater Kipa, a former president, was a minister in Apang"s Council of Ministers, while Larbin Nasi, former general secretary, went on to become an MLA. However, it must be clear that some of them did not have the blessing of Gegong Apang".

(e) AAPSU's Resurgent Campaign and the Chakma-Hajong Crisis of 1994

Bolstered by political backing during the elections, AAPSU reignited its campaign in early 1994, advocating for the deportation of Chakmas and Hajongs. While the Assam-Arunachal Boundary issue was highlighted in the Congress party's manifesto, AAPSU shifted their focus entirely to the Chakma-Hajong issue, prompting multiple inter-state dialogues to seek a resolution.

In a significant mobilisation, May 1994 saw a 400-strong AAPSU delegation initiate the "Delhi Chalo Movement." They organised rallies, aiming to catch the Central Government's eye. Strengthening their cause, AAPSU partnered with the North Eastern Students Organization (NESO), garnering support from prominent regional student associations.

In a dramatic escalation, AAPSU released a "Quit Arunachal Notice" to the Chakmas and Hajongs on August 1, 1994. They were given a deadline of up to September 30, 1994, to voluntarily leave the state. This was accompanied by a series of rallies in Chakma-inhabited areas, including Kokila on August 21, 1994, and Miao on September 7, 1994. AAPSU's message was unequivocal: they would use force if necessary.

Meanwhile, Assam's Chief Minister, Hiteshwar Saikia, added to the crisis by authorising a "shoot at sight" directive to deter any potential Chakma-Hajong migration into Assam. This left the Chakma-Hajong community trapped amidst clashing powers, heightening their vulnerability.

In a desperate plea for intervention, the situation was brought before the National Human Rights Commission

(NHRC). Given the challenging circumstances, the NHRC petitioned the Supreme Court, advocating for specific protective measures for the Chakma-Hajongs.

Amid this intense climate, another blow came. On October 11, 1994, authority positions held by Gaonburahs from Chakma villages under the Assam Frontier (Administration of Justice) Regulations, 1945, were annulled by the Deputy Commissioner of Changlang District, further destabilising the community's standing vide order No. GA-3/GB/DYN/88/16045-67.

(f) AAPSU's Campaigns and the Escalation of the Chakma-Hajong Issue in 1995

In 1995, the intensity of AAPSU's movement against the Chakma-Hajong community was evident in their "Quit Certificate Movement." Intending to underline their demands, AAPSU proposed that students surrender their academic certificates. This initiative, however, did not gain traction as students recognized the long-term repercussions on their careers.[114]

On September 20, at Naharlagun, a pivotal referendum rally took place. A unified front of AAPSU, the public, and politicians convened, pressuring both state and central governments to mandate the Chakma-Hajong community's removal from Arunachal Pradesh by January 1, 1996.

The referendum rally also called for the government to ban CCRCAP, a Chakma rights organisation, and PRO, a human rights organisation. It urged the authorities to refrain from entertaining any representations or granting audience to the Chakma-Hajongs. The rally issued a warning that if their demands were not met, there would be mass resignations from the primary membership of political parties.

A state-wide directive was also put forth by AAPSU, urging the Indigenous population to withhold all support or

---

[114] *Student Movements in Arunachal Pradesh: S. Dutta (ISBN-81-86393-17-X)*

services to the Chakma-Hajongs. Any indigenous individual found defying this directive would risk societal excommunication.

An all-party meeting took place on December 20, 1995, in Itanagar. The meeting included the Chief Minister of the state, other ministers, Members of Legislative Assembly, student leaders, and civil society representatives. Its purpose was to express strong condemnation regarding the National Human Rights Commission (NHRC) filing a writ against the State of Arunachal Pradesh in the Supreme Court for alleged human rights violations against the Chakma-Hajongs.

During the meeting, it was decided that the Chief Minister should attend a meeting convened by the union Home minister to discuss the Chakma-Hajong issue. The main demand in this regard was the prompt removal of Chakma-Hajongs from Arunachal Pradesh, and it was emphasised that granting them citizenship should not be considered by the Home Ministry. [115]

The movement led by the All–Arunachal Pradesh Students' Union (AAPSU) advocating for the deportation of the Chakma-Hajong community from Arunachal Pradesh has had multiple repercussions. Firstly, it stalled the Chakma-Hajongs' efforts towards social integration and acceptance within Arunachal's society, a process we can term "De-Rehabilitation."

Furthermore, influenced by AAPSU's strong advocacy, the State Government revoked many of the rights and privileges the Chakma-Hajongs had acquired since their settlement in 1964. This roll-back not only signifies a regression in their societal standing but also underscores how AAPSU's actions have hindered the Chakma-Hajongs' integration into Arunachal society.

---

[115] *White Paper on Chakma and Hajong Refugee Issue, Govt. of Arunachal Pradesh, 1996*

Compounding these challenges, the Chakma-Hajongs have grappled with a diminished sense of dignity and self-worth. The consistent societal pressure, coupled with the loss of rights, has adversely affected their psychological well-being and their sense of security within the state.

2. Influence of AAPSU's Campaign against Chakma-Hajongs on State Policy

As Arunachal Pradesh was nurturing its young democracy and establishing its governance infrastructure, AAPSU's campaign resonated deeply with the public. Notably, their stance on the Boundary issue garnered widespread support, which naturally extended to the Chakma-Hajong matter. As a result, the state government and politicians endorsed AAPSU's agenda, aiming to retain public trust and remain in alignment with popular sentiment.

AAPSU's relentless actions against the Chakma-Hajongs, including strikes, protests, and rallies since 1985, created a ripple effect across the state. What initially seemed insignificant, grew into a larger and potentially dangerous situation, fueled by the dissemination of false narratives and incorrect perceptions.

(a) Two primary misconceptions emerged during this time:

- The Chakma-Hajongs were erroneously equated with Tibetan refugees, and further, they were unfairly associated with illegal Bangladeshi migrants in Assam.
- There was a strategically amplified concern suggesting the Chakma-Hajongs endangered the state's demography, culture, and indigenous populace. AAPSU claimed an ongoing illegal influx of Chakmas, projecting a future where native residents might become a minority. AAPSU asserted that the Chakma-Hajongs' settlement was

both temporary and unauthorised, arguing it bypassed indigenous consultation and breached the Bengal Eastern Frontier Regulations Act of 1873 and the Chin Hills Regulation Act of 1896.

Over time, the state government implemented a policy that systematically restricted the rights of the Chakma-Hajong people, resulting in discriminatory treatment by the local administration. The discriminatory actions unfolded in various stages.

(b) Curtailment of Rights and Entitlements:

- **Employment Restrictions (1980):** The state prohibited the Chakma-Hajongs from taking up state government jobs, limiting their public employment prospects and access to governmental benefits.
- **Legislative Assembly's Resolution to remove Chakmas (1980):** Succumbing to AAPSU's pressures Arunachal Pradesh Legislative Assembly adopted a resolution on 23rd September 1980 for removal of Chakmas from Arunachal Pradesh. [116]
- **Ration Card Denial (1991):** The Chakma-Hajongs were denied ration cards, essential tools for obtaining subsidised essentials, further alienating them.
- **Termination of Gaonburaship (1994):** Orders appointing Gaonburahs, village representatives, from Chakma communities were revoked, diminishing the community's voice in administrative matters.
- **Document Accessibility:** While general issuance of birth certificates and other pivotal records by local offices was stopped, some individuals with

---

[116] *MHA File No. 9/12/82-AP Lok Sabha Starred Question No. 541 for 6.10.82 by Shri Amar Roy Pradhan regarding proposal to remove Tibetans and Chakmas from Arunachal Pradesh. (National Archives of India)*

connections could bypass these constraints, creating disparities within the community.

- **Economic Impediments:** Trade licences granted to Chakma-Hajongs were recollected and terminated under the guise of renewal, obstructing their economic pursuits. Concurrently, their access to local departmental benefits dwindled, intensifying their socio-economic challenges.

  These successive restrictive measures entrenched the discrimination against the Chakma-Hajong community, severely restricting their access to basic services, job opportunities, and essential documentation required for everyday living.

3. Local Repercussions of AAPSU's Campaign on the Chakma-Hajongs

Under the influence of AAPSU's campaign, local authorities, especially the police, allegedly misused their power, particularly targeting Chakma activists and susceptible members through intimidation and threats. Regular misconducts included unlawful detentions, sidestepping standard police protocols, and filing baseless charges against the Chakma-Hajongs.

Community perception drastically shifted, with Chakma-Hajongs being branded as "foreigners" and "outsiders." Such stigmatisation turned them into social pariahs, subjected to frequent harassment and prejudice in public spaces. This discrimination infiltrated every facet of their lives, intensifying their sense of alienation and vulnerability in society. The community lived in perpetual anxiety, fearing for their safety and overall well-being.

Economically, the Chakma-Hajongs grappled with a blockade, barring them from trading their goods in both Assam and nearby markets. This severely hampered their economic prospects and diminished their trade opportunities.

Socially, they faced heightened discrimination in public places. Local youths would routinely screen buses, singling out Chakma passengers, instilling a climate of fear and intimidation. A prevailing unwritten code emerged, compelling Chakma passengers to relinquish their seats for local tribal members on buses. Such practices further isolated the Chakma-Hajongs, undermining their sense of equality and inclusion.

4. The AAPSU's Impact on the Chakma-Hajong Community

The Chakma-Hajong community encountered a vast range of discrimination, from economic restrictions to daily public humiliations, intensifying their societal marginalisation. The AAPSU's campaign against this community led to severe consequences, both tangible and psychological.

In March 1980, tragedy struck Bijoypur, a Chakma settlement village under the Bordumsa circle, when local tribals razed it, rendering 400 Chakma families homeless. The wave of violence did not stop there. On February 15, 1983, six Chakma villages under the Balijan Circle in Subansiri District were destroyed, with 160 family houses burnt to the ground, plunging the community further into turmoil.

This antagonism seeped into the educational realm. Tribal-dominated schools frequently witnessed tribal students ganging up against Chakma students, breeding an environment of intimidation. On July 13, 1982, a prominent politician, accompanied by AAPSU members from Miao, barged into Chakma student accommodations and their hostel. They not only threatened the students but also coerced them into supporting AAPSU's "All Arunachal Bandh" protest from July 17th to July 20th, 1982.

Miao Town saw a surge in derogatory posters with messages like "Go Back Shameless Bangladesh Refugees" and "Arunachal Schools for Arunachal Tribal Students". On July 17, 1982, tensions escalated as roughly 800 protestors converged in Miao Town, targeting the Chakma community. They encircled a school housing Chakma student. Thankfully, the situation was defused with the intervention of the Extra Assistant Commissioner (EAC) of Miao and the CRPF. However, the atmosphere of hostility persisted, affecting even the Sompoi Middle English School, where Chakma students were enrolled, as it got caught in the ripples of the Miao Town incident.

5. The Chakma Students' Ordeal

Chakma students, for a long time, experienced a climate of persistent animosity in their educational pursuits, an environment marked by fear, discrimination, and emotional turmoil. Such hostility affected not only their academics but also their mental health. These students grappled with an overshadowing fear—physical, emotional, and psychological, every time they entered their schools.

Various forms of discrimination confronted them, from verbal assaults and social ostracization to physical violence. The focus on their ethnicity hampered their academic experience and potential.

In March 1989, three Chakma villages—Milanpur, Ratnapur, and Golakpur, under the Miao Circle—were torched by locals. 185 affected families were displaced. Many took temporary shelter by the Dihing River, while others found refuge in Bijoypur village under Bordumsa Circle. Due to local tensions, these communities had to relocate multiple times, with some families eventually settling in the Diyun Circle.

During the first fortnight of June 1989, Nishing (Nyishi) individuals from the Capital area visited Chakma villages in Kokila, Balijan circle (Lower Subansiri District), issuing threats for the Chakma community to immediately vacate the area. They surveyed Chakma-allocated lands, asserting sole ownership by local Nishing and expressing intentions to occupy these lands. This led local authorities to heighten police patrolling in the Kokila area.

In an earlier event on April 4, 1989, senior students from Changlang District convened a meeting in Miao to deliberate on Chakma settlement areas within the district. As a result of this meeting, a decision was made to submit a memorandum to the Chief Minister of Arunachal Pradesh in alignment with AAPSU's demands.

Further developments emerged on June 25, 1989, when senior students at Miao HS School in Changlang District decided to restrict new admissions of Chakma students in the school. Simultaneously, they drafted a memorandum to authorities, urging the establishment of a separate school in the Miao area exclusively for Chakma students.

Between July 9 and 10, 1989, Shri Tabin Taki and Dolum Sora, President and Vice President respectively of AAPSU, visited Miao in Changlang District and later proceeded to Lohit, Dibang Valley District in Arunachal Pradesh. During their Miao visit, they engaged with senior students from Miao HS School, encouraging heightened AAPSU activities in the area. They also urged the formation of a district-level AAPSU executive body for Changlang District and advocated for fundraising from local businesspeople.

Subsequently, on July 17, Shri Tabin Taki and Dotum Sora, President and Vice President of AAPSU, issued a press release from Naharlagun criticising the Arunachal Pradesh government for admitting refugee students such as Chakma and Tibetans into various government schools in the state. Simultaneously, tribal students from Miao HS School in Changlang District circulated a directive, instructing Chakma students to refrain from attending classes starting July 29.

Amid escalating tensions, on the night of August 1, 1989, local tribal students armed with weapons allegedly forced their way into the Chakma students' hostel at Miao HS School, reportedly assaulting at least 17 Chakma students. The Miao police registered a case under several sections of the Indian Penal Code against the accused individuals, with an ongoing investigation into the incident.

On August 10, 1989, approximately 100 Chakma students from Miao in Changlang District gathered for a meeting with local public leaders from Diyun Circle. They collectively decided to approach both the Government of Arunachal Pradesh and the Government of India to request separate educational facilities specifically for Chakma students.

During the latter half of August 1989, the local tribal student's union at Miao HS School presented a demand to the Chakma students. They requested the withdrawal of the case filed against tribal students concerning the assault on some Chakma students on the night of August 1. This demand stipulated a deadline of August 16. However, the Chakma students chose not to withdraw the case, leading to agitation among the tribal students of Miao who contemplated their next steps against the Chakma students. Additionally, external Chakma students advised those from Miao against withdrawing the case filed against the tribal students.[117]

Arun Goyal, the Deputy Commissioner of Changlang District in 1990, noted in his comprehensive report on the Chakma settlers that incidents of Chakma student hostels being targeted, and students harassed by local youths were common, especially in Miao and Bordumsa. He writes ***"almost every year, incidents of Chakma hostels being set on fire in Secondary and Higher Secondary Schools and unwarranted harassment inflicted upon Chakma students by local youths are reported. Despite the district administration's efforts to provide sufficient protection to the Chakmas, there is significant discontent, particularly in the Miao and Bordumsa regions. It is recommended that the government take immediate action to construct dedicated hostels for Chakma students in the Miao and Bordumsa areas. Additionally, the government may also consider***

[117] *Fortnightly Confidential Report from Government of Arunachal Pradesh. MHA File No. 7/14/89-AP (National Archives of India)*

establishing separate Secondary and Higher Secondary Schools in Chakma-populated regions."[118]

A grim illustration of this ongoing conflict transpired in 1994 at the Miao Higher Secondary School. A violent altercation broke out between Chakma and local tribal students, leaving several Chakma students brutally injured. A particularly tragic aftermath of this event saw a Chakma student drown in the Noa-Dihing river while trying to flee from the violence. After the incident, Chakma students were barred from Miao Higher Secondary School and its hostel services were withdrawn, compelling many to abandon their education.

Even within schools in Chakma regions, racial prejudice was evident. Derogatory slogans like "Go Back Chakmas" adorned public spaces, and efforts to erase them met with severe backlash. An illustrative case is that of Sunil Kumar Chakma, a student at Govt. Secondary School in Innao, who was mob-lynched by local students and the public for attempting to counter such acts.

This continuous cycle of violence and discrimination highlighted the dire need for inclusivity, understanding, and mutual respect within the educational milieu.

6. The Chakma-Hajong Crisis in the Diyun Area

In the Diyun region, even though Chakmas made up over 75% of the population, with the local tribal community being less than 10%, a stark display of dominance emerged from local leaders. They passed a resolution in the Circle Officer's chamber excluding Chakma-Hajong from agricultural, contractual, and business activities, as detailed in Circular No. DYN/JUD-1/97 from October 31, 1997.

This era saw Chakma-Hajong discrimination escalate to levels reminiscent of Apartheid. Their rights as Indian citizens eroded in a process of "de-Indianisation", with

---

[118] *A Comprehensive Note on Chakma Settlers in Changlang District authored by Arun Goyal, Deputy Commissioner, Changlang District, 1990*

basic privileges steadily revoked. The systemic prejudice rendered the state almost uninhabitable for them due to the hostility and lack of peace.

The Chakma-Hajong issue was intensified to critical levels by political leaders and the All–Arunachal Pradesh Students' Union (AAPSU). There are reports suggesting that Gegong Apang, the Chief Minister at the time, made a commitment to deport the Chakma-Hajongs, even implying that he would resort to wearing a Mekhela, a traditional female garment, as a symbolic gesture if he did not fulfil this promise.

The 1990s were marred with severe human rights violations. Several Chakma women were subjected to heinous gang rapes and assaults and most of these cases were un-reported, which instilled fear within the community.

In addition to the sexual violence, there were also cases of Chakma men and women disappearing and being brutally murdered, yet these incidents went unreported and largely unnoticed by the authorities. The lack of reporting and attention to these cold-blooded murders further highlighted the vulnerability and marginalisation experienced by the Chakma community during that time.

A sinister undercurrent involved coercing Chakma-Hajong families into trading their documentation for cash and abruptly departing from the state. This alleged strategy, possibly backed covertly by local administration and police, intended to displace as many families as possible. Tragically, a few Chakma individuals were complicit in this scheme, betraying their kin.

Within the Chakma community, this scam has left an indelible mark, reminding them of a time when some, motivated by fear or personal gain, betrayed their own. This painful memory has given rise to whispers and hushed voices, referring to these collaborators as the "Apangs' Agents." Even today, the weight of this betrayal weighs heavily on the collective heart of the Chakma people.

This narrative highlights a grim reality for the Chakma-Hajong community, pressured into abandoning their identity and rights. The alleged involvement of state machinery and the treachery from within the Chakmas intensified the community's sense of injustice and betrayal.

7. The Silent Suffering of the Chakmas

The peak of the anti-Chakma movement was marked by a dark chapter of widespread violence and brutality inflicted upon the community. Countless acts of cruelty, often concealed from public view, caused immeasurable suffering and left enduring trauma that continues to affect the Chakma people.

Chakma individuals frequently faced public physical attacks, enduring not just the assault but also the humiliation that accompanied such public acts. This was not just violence; it was an orchestrated attempt to degrade their dignity and humanity.

Heartbreakingly, some of these unprovoked acts of violence culminated in death, tearing families apart and leaving communities steeped in grief.

Many Chakma women, unfortunately, bore significant suffering during this time. Beyond the physical and verbal assaults, many were victims of heinous sexual crimes, their personal boundaries breached with alarming audacity. Among the most harrowing of these were instances of gang rapes, which left survivors with deep physical and emotional wounds.

This dark phase of hidden crimes against the Chakmas is a sombre reflection of the depths of human prejudice and animosity. It underscores a crucial chapter in Chakma history that demands recognition, justice, and a collective commitment to ensuring such atrocities remain in the past.

9. The Chakma Camouflage: Survival Through Adaptation

Confronted with pervasive discrimination and the looming threat of violence, the Chakma community found themselves pressured to mask their cultural identity in public. This was a protective response to the frequent targeting by local youth and tribesmen, who sought out Chakma individuals in buses, markets, offices, and other communal areas.

Chakma men blended in by wearing local attire, like the traditional Lungi, or chose neutral clothing such as trousers and shirts to minimise attention to their origins. Chakma women similarly adapted, often choosing the Mekela, a wrap-around cloth, to obscure their distinct Chakma attire.

This adaptive camouflage was more than just a fashion choice; it was a vital strategy for self-preservation in a climate rife with hostility. Reflecting on this era, many Chakmas poignantly refer to it as the "Mekela Days".

11

1996-2024: A TIME OF TURBULENCE, RELIEF AND QUEST FOR RIGHTS

The early to mid-1990s was a tumultuous period for the Chakmas and Hajongs in Arunachal Pradesh. Their experiences were like the persecution and suffering faced by religious minorities in Islamic East Pakistan during the 1960s, which forced millions, including Hindus, Christians, and Buddhist Chakmas, to seek refuge in India.

The situation reached a crescendo on August 1, 1994, when the All–Arunachal Pradesh Students' Union (AAPSU) served a "Quit Arunachal Notice" to the Chakmas and Hajongs, demanding they leave by September 30, 1994.

This posed a dire choice: abandon their homes or endure potential consequences. This ultimatum put immense pressure on the Chakmas and Hajongs, leaving them with a difficult and heart-wrenching decision to either uproot themselves from their homes or face the consequences. They found themselves caught in a precarious situation, feeling alienated in the very place they had called home for generations.

Adding to this pressure, the Assam Government issued a "shoot at sight" order against any Chakma and Hajong attempting to enter from Arunachal Pradesh. This move effectively closed off a potential escape route for the Chakma and Hajong communities.

As a result, the Chakma-Hajongs were trapped between two opposing forces. On one side, they faced the threat of violence and expulsion from their homes in Arunachal Pradesh, and on the other side, they confronted the risk of being met with lethal force if they tried to seek refuge in Assam. The communities were stuck in a precarious and dangerous situation, with little support or protection from the authorities.

These events led to a grave humanitarian crisis, raising concerns about the violation of human rights, displacement, and violence against marginalised communities. The situation attracted attention and criticism from various human rights organisations and advocacy groups.

On September 9, 1994, the People's Union for Civil Liberties in Delhi raised this issue with the NHRC, prompting the Commission to send inquiries to the Chief Secretary of Arunachal Pradesh and the Home Secretary of the Government of India. On September 30, 1994, the Chief Secretary of Arunachal Pradesh responded via fax, assuring that the situation was completely under control, and adequate police protection had been provided to the Chakmas.

Then, on October 15, 1994, the Committee for Citizenship Rights of the Chakmas of Arunachal Pradesh (CCRCAP) lodged a complaint with the NHRC, highlighting the persecution faced by the Chakmas. The petition included a press report from "The Telegraph" dated August 26, 1994, which mentioned that the All–Arunachal Pradesh Students Union (AAPSU) had issued "quit notices" to all alleged foreigners, including the Chakmas, ordering them to leave the State by September 30, 1995. Subsequently, again on October 28, 1995, the CCRCAP urgently sent petitions to the NHRC, alleging immediate threats to the lives of the Chakmas.

Considering these complaints, the NHRC advised the State Government to stay its hands and allow the status quo to be maintained. The directions were conveyed separately to the Governor, the Chief Minister, and the Chief Secretary of Arunachal Pradesh, as well as to the union Home minister and the Ministry of Home Affairs.[119]

[119] https://nhrc.nic.in/press-release/archives-human-rights-cases

1. SUPREME COURT'S 1996 JUDGEMENT: PROTECTING THE CHAKMAS

In response to the rising tensions, the National Human Rights Commission (NHRC) filed a writ petition in the Supreme Court [National Human Rights Commission vs State Of Arunachal Pradesh & Anr (Equivalent citations: 1996 AIR 1234, 1996 SCC (1) 742)]. This action emphasised the fundamental rights of "aliens" in India, underscoring that they should neither be deprived of their right to live nor face unjust treatment as per Article 21 of the Constitution. This was particularly pertinent given the implicit support AAPSU's actions seemed to receive from Arunachal Pradesh's authorities.

The Supreme Court ruled affirmatively, mandating the Arunachal Pradesh government to ensure the safety and personal liberty of the Chakma residents. It ruled against any attempts by groups, especially AAPSU, to evict or threaten the Chakmas. The State was directed to resist such efforts, even deploying paramilitary or police forces if necessary. If more forces were needed, the Union of India was to be approached, and it was obligated to provide the required support. The ruling also emphasised that Chakmas' rights to their homes and to live without threat should not be infringed upon, except within legal limits.

Thanks to the NHRC's proactive step, the Supreme Court's ruling provided much-needed protection for the Chakmas' rights and safety.

(a) SUPREME COURT'S 1996 JUDGEMENT: A TURNING POINT FOR CHAKMA-HAJONGS

On January 9, 1996, the Supreme Court delivered a groundbreaking judgement that ensured the safety and security of the Chakma-Hajong community. This ruling countered the ongoing threats of eviction they faced from groups like AAPSU.

Key outcomes of the judgement:

- **End of Threats:** The ruling quashed AAPSU's campaigns, severing their collaborative efforts with the State Government and local leaders.
- **State Responsibility:** The state government was mandated to protect the life and liberty of every Chakma within its jurisdiction. This meant thwarting any forcible eviction attempts by groups. If necessary, the state could call upon paramilitary or police forces.
- **Central Government's Role:** In situations where the state needed additional forces for protection, the central government was obligated to assist.
- **Protection of Lives and Liberty:** The Chakma-Hajong community was granted the right to remain in their homes unless legal provisions dictated otherwise. This reaffirmed their rights to a domestic life and comfort, effectively ending AAPSU's persistent demands for their deportation.
- **Path to formal Citizenship:** The court directed the State Government to forward any Chakma citizenship applications to the Central Government for review.[120]

In conclusion, acknowledging the circumstances that led to the Chakma-Hajongs settling in India, and recognizing the Central Government's decision to grant them citizenship, the Supreme Court issued comprehensive directions, as highlighted in paragraph No.21 of the NHRC case, to ensure the community's safety and rights.

[120] *National Human Rights Commission vs State Of Arunachal Pradesh & Anr on 9 January 1996 Equivalent citations: 1996 AIR 1234, 1996 SCC (1) 742*

"21. In view of the above, we allow this petition and direct the first and second respondents, by way of a writ of mandamus, as under:

(1) The first respondent, the State of Arunachal Pradesh, shall ensure that the life and personal liberty of each and every Chakma residing within the State shall be protected and any attempt to forcibly evict or drive the mouth of the State by organised groups, such as the AAPSU, shall be repelled, if necessary by requisitioning the service of paramilitary or police force, and if additional forces are considered necessary to carry out this direction, the first respondent will request the second respondent, the Union of India, to provide such additional force, and the second respondent shall provide such additional force as is necessary to protect the lives and liberty of the Chakmas;

(2) except in accordance with law, the Chakmas shall not be evicted from their homes and shall not be denied domestic life and comfort therein;

(3) the quit notices and ultimatums issued by the AAPSU and any other group which tantamount to ·threats to the life and liberty of each and every Chakma should be dealt with by the first respondent in accordance with law;

(4) the application made for registration as citizen of India by the Chakma or Chakmas under Section 5 of the Act, shall be entered in the register maintained for the purpose and shall be forwarded by the Collector or the DC who receives them under the relevant rule, with or without enquiry, as the case may be, to the Central Government for its consideration in accordance with law; even returned applications shall be called back or fresh ones shall be obtained from the persons concerned and shall be processed and to forwarded to the Central Government for consideration;

(5) while the application of any individual Chakma is pending consideration, the first respondent shall not evict or remove the person concerned from; is occupation on the

ground that he is not a citizen of India until the competent authority has taken a decision in that behalf; and

(6) the first respondent will pay the Petitioner cost of this petition which we quantify at Rs 10,000 within six weeks from today by depositing the same in the office of the NHRC, New Delhi."

(b) THE CHAKMA-HAJONG ISSUE: A CONTINUING CHALLENGE

Following the Supreme Court's verdict, the State Government released its "White Paper" in 1996 concerning the Chakma-Hajong matter. This official policy document shed light on the government's standpoints regarding the issue. Despite the years, unfortunately, the central disagreements persist, keeping the issue in limbo."

The State Government's policy documents suggest that the Chakma-Hajongs were settled in the state by a hasty decision of the then Governor of Assam on April 10, 1964, and did not take into consideration the legal protection of the indigenous tribal people and their traditions, culture and customs. It also alleges that Chakma-Hajongs were settled in the state in contravention of various legal provisions that provide protections to the indigenous local people of the state. The state government also views the settlement of Chakma-Hajong people as temporary in nature, whereas the Central Government is of the view that the settlement was permanent.[121]

Although the Supreme Court's order in 1996 instilled a semblance of peace in Chakma areas, shielding them from threats and daily adversities, misconceptions about the Chakma-Hajongs persist at the local level. Manifestations of discrimination, akin to apartheid, remain, both in societal attitudes and state policies.

The longstanding grievances and past adversities remain vivid in collective memories, leading to the Chakma-

---

[121] *White Paper on Chakma and Hajong Refugee Issue, Govt. of Arunachal Pradesh, 1996*

Hajongs' struggle for complete acceptance in Arunachal Pradesh. This issue remains one of the state's most volatile subjects.

Chakma community continues to endure:

- **Employment Discrimination:** Chakmas are systematically denied access to government jobs, limiting their chances for economic advancement, and hindering their participation and presence in state government roles and thus their socio-economic progression.
- **Restricted Benefits:** The state's discriminatory stance extends to various privileges and benefits available through trade licences and state and central schemes. The Chakmas are often denied fair and equal access to these programs, which further hampers their socio-economic development and opportunities for growth.
- **Documentation Challenges:** Basic rights that most citizens take for granted, such as obtaining Birth Certificates and residential certificates, are not easily accessible to the Chakmas. This bureaucratic obstacle severely affects their legal identity and hinders their ability to access essential services and benefits that require such documentation.
- **Limited Food Security:** Access to food security is another fundamental right that continues to be denied to the Chakma community. Lack of access to government welfare schemes and subsidised food programs further exacerbates their vulnerable position and perpetuates their socio-economic disparity.

While time has moved on, the state's policies still marginalise the Chakmas, curtailing their advancement and depriving them of rights that other citizens enjoy seamlessly.

2. VOTING RIGHTS GRANTED TO "BY-BIRTH" CHAKMA-HAJONG CITIZENS

Born in Arunachal Pradesh, the new generations of Chakma and Hajongs secured Indian citizenship "by birth" in line with the Citizenship Act, 1955. Motivated by this legal recognition, during 1998-2000, thousands sought their democratic right to vote by applying for inclusion in the electoral rolls using Form No. 6.

Despite their legitimate claims, the state authorities continually rejected their applications. To challenge these rejections, the Committee for Citizenship Rights of the Chakmas and Hajongs of Arunachal Pradesh (CCRCHAP) filed Writ Petition (No. 886 of 2000) in the Delhi High Court.

Their primary contention was clear: Chakmas and Hajongs born in India from 1964 to 1st July 1987 qualify for Indian citizenship under Section 3 (1) (a) of the Citizenship Act, 1955. Hence, they argued for their rightful inclusion in Arunachal Pradesh's electoral rolls, emphasising their democratic right to vote.

The Writ Petition not only aimed to validate the citizenship rights of these Chakmas and Hajongs but also addressed the systematic denial of their electoral representation. Their intention was to assert their rightful place as Indian citizens and ensure their political participation and representation in the state's democratic affairs. [122]

In a counter-affidavit, the Union of India referenced Section 3 of the Citizenship Act, 1955, asserting that every person born in India is entitled to citizenship.

- *On or after 26th day of January 1950 but before the commencement of Citizenship (Amendment) Act, 1986 (in short the Amendment Act)*

[122] https://ccrchap.wordpress.com/

- *On or after such commencement and either of whose parents is citizen of India at the time of his birth, shall be a citizen by birth.*

CHAKMA-HAJONG CITIZENS BY BIRTH: A MILESTONE IN POLITICAL REPRESENTATION

The Central Government clarified that individuals who migrated to Arunachal Pradesh post-1964 but prior to the 1986 amendment of the Citizenship Act are considered Indian citizens.

Following this declaration in the form of an affidavit by the Central Government, the Delhi High Court's decision on September 28, 2000, affirmed the "by birth" citizenship status of Chakmas, paving the path for eligible Chakma and Hajong individuals to join the electoral rolls.

After the High Court's verdict, the Election Commission of India introduced "special and additional guidelines" for the revision of the Electoral Rolls in four Arunachal Pradesh constituencies with substantial Chakma and Hajong populations. This led to the establishment of new polling stations in their villages, resulting in the addition of 1,497 Chakma and Hajong voters to the state's electoral roll. Consequently, in the 2004 elections, they cast their votes in both parliamentary and assembly elections for the first time.

Before the General and Assembly elections in April 2024, the inclusion of Chakmas and Hajongs had increased, with 9,401 people now on the electoral list in 3 different assembly constituencies (49 Bordumsa Diyun, 50 Miao & 14 Doimukh). This marks a significant rise in their political participation and representation. This election is the fifth consecutive time that the Chakmas have exercised their right to vote.

3. AAPSU CHALLENGES CHAKMAS' INCLUSION IN ELECTORAL ROLL

In 2010, AAPSU filed a PIL in the Gauhati High Court to challenge the Election Commission's additional guidelines issued in 2005 and 2007 for the special revision of Electoral Rolls in four assembly constituencies of Arunachal Pradesh. These constituencies comprised areas with a substantial population of Chakma and Hajong communities, who had migrated from erstwhile East Pakistan (now Bangladesh) during the 1960s and sought refuge in the then Union Territory of NEFA, now Arunachal Pradesh.

AAPSU contended that the guidelines were discriminatory and violated Constitutional and statutory provisions. They highlighted the legal protections for Arunachal Pradesh's Indigenous people, referencing The Bengal Eastern Frontier Regulations (1873), the Scheduled District Act (1874), the Assam Frontier Tracts Regulation (1880), and the Chin Hills Regulation (1896).

Central to AAPSU's argument was the significance of the Inner Line Pass for Chakmas in Arunachal Pradesh. Without this pass, they maintained that Chakmas should not be recognized as typical residents of the said constituencies and hence, shouldn't be eligible for inclusion in the state's electoral rolls.

The contested guidelines by the Election Commission clarified that any person born in India between January 26, 1950, and July 1, 1987, is a citizen of India by birth under Section 3 (1)(a) of the Citizenship Act, 1955. Birth certificates issued by competent authorities, indicating the place of birth in India, were to be accepted as material proof of Indian citizenship, regardless of any technical deficiencies in such certificates. The guidelines further specified that claims for inclusion in the electoral roll filed without supporting documents should not be automatically rejected but should undergo verification through local enquiry.

The High Court based its decision on the judgement of the Hon'ble Supreme Court in the case of National Human Rights Commission vs. State of Arunachal Pradesh & Anr.

[(1996) 1 SCC 742]. In that landmark case, the Apex Court had issued specific directions to protect the interests of the Chakma migrants for whom the Government of India consciously decided not to repatriate but to settle them in various parts of the country, including Arunachal Pradesh, and grant them Indian citizenship.

The High Court upheld the Election Commission's additional guidelines, authorised by Article 324 of the Constitution, as non-discriminatory. These guidelines were designed to protect the rights of the Chakma migrants and their descendants, ensuring their legitimate right to vote as genuine citizens. The court clarified that once the Chakmas were permitted by the Government of India to reside in Arunachal Pradesh, it implicitly acted as granting them an "Inner Line Permit/Pass."[123]

Further, the Court also stated that in view of the policy decision taken by the Government of India to settle the Chakmas in different States and also in Arunachal Pradesh in consultation with the authorities of the Arunachal Pradesh, and also to confer Indian citizenship, the contention of the petitioners (AAPSU) that the aforesaid guidelines have the effect of violating the provisions of law in terms of lack of Inner Line Permit or violation of provisions of section 13 of the Registration of Births and Deaths Act, 1969 does not hold water. We are of the view that once a decision had been taken to settle these Chakma refugees in Arunachal Pradesh in consultation with the authorities of Arunachal Pradesh, they would become residents of Arunachal Pradesh and would not require the Inner Line Permit/Pass. Otherwise also, once they have been allowed to settle in Arunachal Pradesh, it would be deemed that such permits had been granted to them and in our considered opinion, any other view would negate and defeat the policy decision taken by the Government of

---

[123] *Landmark Judgements on Election Law (A compilation of Important Judgements pronounced by the Supreme Court of India, High Courts and Election Commission of India) Volume - V by Election Commission of India*

India in consultation with the Arunachal Pradesh authorities to settle these Chakmas in Arunachal Pradesh.

4. JHPC: A Glimmer of Hope for the Final Resolution of the Chakma-Hajong Issue

A beacon of hope emerged for the decades-long Chakma-Hajong settlement issue in Arunachal Pradesh with the formation of the Joint High-Power Committee (JHPC) on August 10, 2010. Chaired by the Joint Secretary (NE) of the Ministry of Home Affairs, the JHPC's mandate was far-reaching: to delve into the complexities of Chakma-Hajong settlement, explore the possibility of granting Indian citizenship to eligible individuals, and recommend concrete actions for the Central Government.

With representatives from crucial stakeholders – the Ministry of Home Affairs, the Arunachal Pradesh government, the Chakma-Hajong community, and the All–Arunachal Pradesh Chakma Students Union (AAPSU) – the JHPC promised a platform for comprehensive dialogue and potential resolution.

The first meeting, held on January 9, 2012, in Itanagar, witnessed a breakthrough amidst the long-held tensions. AAPSU under the leadership of Takam Tatung, a key voice in the issue, expressed conditional acceptance of Chakma-Hajongs who settled between 1964-69, subject to thorough field verification. Recognizing the importance of ensuring accuracy and mutual trust, the JHPC Chairman, Mr. Shambhu Singh, readily agreed to the joint verification proposal.

This initial agreement signifies a crucial step towards finding a lasting solution. The JHPC's commitment to inclusivity, transparency, and evidence-based verification offers a glimmer of hope for a future where the Chakma-Hajong community and the people of Arunachal Pradesh can coexist peacefully and contribute to the state's progress.

The second JHPC meeting on October 26, 2012, marked a critical juncture in the Chakma-Hajong issue. After what could be described as a "spirited discussion," a crucial decision was made – the formation of a State Level Core Committee. This committee, tasked with conducting the joint verification survey, comprised crucial stakeholders:

(i) Secretary (Political), Government of Arunachal Pradesh
(ii) Representatives of AAPSU
(iii) Chakma-Hajong community members (CCRCHAP)
(iv) District Administration: Providing logistical and ground-level support.

Their mission was clear: to definitively identify the Chakma refugees who settled in Arunachal Pradesh between 1964 and 1969.

On November 3, 2012, the newly formed Core Committee convened its first meeting. They diligently established a set of objective criteria to identify eligible refugees:

- **Cut-off year:** Only those who settled between 1964 and 1969 would be considered.
- **Chitta register:** This document, detailing Chakma families during the stipulated period, would serve as primary verification evidence.
- **Refugee Index Register**: Another crucial record to corroborate claims of residency.
- **Government-issued documents:** Identity cards, relief eligibility certificates, and other relevant paperwork issued during 1964-1969 would add further weight to claims.

AAPSU: A Shift in Leadership:

However, a significant development arose after the Core Committee's first meeting. There was a complete change in the AAPSU executive body, bringing in new faces and potentially, new perspectives on the Chakma-Hajong issue. Kampta Lapung assumed the role of President, ushering in a new era of student representation in the ongoing dialogue.

The formation of the State Level Core Committee and the establishment of objective verification criteria laid the groundwork for a crucial phase in the JHPC's journey. With AAPSU undergoing a leadership shift, their renewed stance was a huge setback impacting the quest for a resolution.

The State Level Core Committee, established with hope, faced its first major hurdle on March 12, 2013. A recent communal flare-up between Singphos and Chakmas at Mpen cast a dark shadow over the meeting, creating a tense atmosphere and preventing any considerable progress.

On June 20, 2013, the State Level Core Committee convened with two crucial developments:

- **Expanding Representation:** Recognizing the concerns of the Tai-Singpho community, the Committee agreed to seek approval from the JHPC Chairman to include them in their deliberations. This decision aimed to broaden the dialogue and ensure all relevant voices were heard.
- **AAPSU's New Priorities**: The student body, now under new leadership, expressed a different approach. Instead of immediate verification, they emphasised the need for a comprehensive study. This study would assess the living conditions of Chakma-Hajongs, analyse the law-and-order situation, and gauge the state of inter-community relations. Based on this information, AAPSU believed more productive discussions could take place.

Acknowledging AAPSU's concerns, the Committee agreed to a joint survey starting in July 2013. This survey would provide data on the settlement areas, potentially paving the way for the comprehensive study proposed by AAPSU.

Following the survey, a preliminary report was submitted by the JHPC Core Committee, laying the groundwork for further investigation and analysis.

Joint High Power Committee Progress Grinds to a Halt

While the Joint High-Power Committee (JHPC) once offered a beacon of hope for the long-standing Chakma-Hajong issue in Arunachal Pradesh, progress toward a lasting solution has unfortunately stagnated. This lack of movement leaves both communities in limbo and raises critical questions about the commitment to finding a resolution.

Initially, the JHPC, with its inclusion of the Central Government, represented a significant step forward. The conditional acceptance of Chakma-Hajongs who settled between 1964-69 by AAPSU, a key stakeholder, during the first meeting in January 2012, seemed to pave the way for progress. However, the subsequent handover of the initiative to the State Level Core Committee marked a turning point.

Several factors appear to be contributing to the current impasse:

a. Lack of Central Government initiative: Despite the JHPC's initial promise, the Central Government's current absence from the process leaves a crucial gap in leadership and resource allocation.

b. Evolving stance of AAPSU: The change in leadership within AAPSU has seemingly led to a shift in their position. Their emphasis on a comprehensive study before verification suggests a possible retreat from the conditional acceptance expressed earlier.

This lack of progress is deeply concerning for the Chakma-Hajong community, who face the continued uncertainty of their status and rights in Arunachal Pradesh.

The onus now lies with all stakeholders, including the Central Government, state authorities, and community leaders, to reignite the spirit of cooperation and actively seek a solution that respects the rights and concerns of all parties involved.

5. SUPREME COURT'S ORDER ON CHAKMA-HAJONG CITIZENSHIP IN 2015

4,637 Chakmas and Hajongs, who were original migrants from East Pakistan, submitted citizenship applications between February 18, 1997, and January 22, 2003 (not including those born in India for clarity). However, both the Central and State Governments failed to process these applications. Consequently, the Committee for Citizenship Rights of Chakmas and Hajongs (CCRCHAP) approached the Supreme Court in 2007. They referenced a 1996 order from Writ Petition (C) No. 720 of 1995 titled "National Human Rights Commission vs. State of Arunachal Pradesh" and filed a contempt petition, which evolved into Writ Petition No. 510 of 2007.

The Union of India clarified during the hearings through a counter affidavit that directly received applications by the Ministry of Home Affairs from Chakmas and Hajongs were forwarded to the Government of Arunachal Pradesh. Most of these applications were not returned, except for a few that received negative recommendations. The rejected applications were then sent back to the Government of Arunachal Pradesh. In response to the situation, the Ministry of Home Affairs advised the state government to comply with the court's judgement and take appropriate actions regarding the citizenship applications of the Chakmas and Hajongs.

The state of Arunachal Pradesh responded with a counter affidavit, stating that certain laws applicable within the state were not considered during the settlement of the Chakmas and Hajongs. These laws include the Government of India Act, 1870, the Bengal Eastern Frontier Regulation,

1873, the Scheduled District Act, 1874, the Assam Frontier Tract Regulation, 1880, the Assam Frontier Forest Regulation, 1891, the Chin Hills Regulations, 1896, and the Assam Frontier (Administration of Justice) Regulation, 1945 (1 of 1945).

Finally, the Supreme Court acknowledged, based on the stance of the Government of India, that the Chakmas have the right to be granted citizenship, provided the proper procedure is followed. The court also recognized through its judicial decisions that the Chakmas settled in the State of Arunachal Pradesh are not required to obtain any Inner Line permit.

On September 17, 2015, the Supreme Court issued a directive to the Government of India and the State of Arunachal Pradesh, instructing them to expedite the process of granting citizenship rights to eligible Chakmas and Hajongs. Additionally, they were tasked with ensuring the implementation of directions provided in earlier judicial decisions to safeguard the life and liberty of the Chakmas and Hajongs and prevent any form of discrimination against them.

The court emphasised the urgency of the matter and urged both parties to complete the process promptly, preferably within three months from the date of the order.

Even though an order was issued on September 17, 2015, mandating the completion of the conferment of citizenship rights for eligible Chakmas and Hajongs within three months, there has been no progress made in processing the Citizenship application forms.

The court has heard the matter on several occasions to inquire about the state's actions regarding the Citizenship application forms. In response, the state frequently requested extensions of time, and it was only on September 06, 2016, when a status report was finally filed.

On December 12, 2017, the Court issued directives to the Member Secretary of the Arunachal Pradesh State Legal Services Authority (APSLSA) to examine the dispute between the parties regarding the implementation of the Court's order. The Member Secretary, APSLSA, was also instructed to take into consideration the perspectives of both the government and the petitioners. The Court granted the Member Secretary, APSLSA, the authority to give appropriate directions in the matter and complete the proceedings within forty-five days.

Despite these instructions, the Member Secretary, APSLSA, faced challenges in fulfilling the Court's directions and requested multiple extensions of time. Ultimately, on November 02, 2018, the Registry was directed to provide the report of the Member Secretary, Arunachal Pradesh Legal Services Authority, to the respective counsels of both parties. However, since then, no substantial action has been taken by the State and Central Government regarding the finalisation of granting citizenship rights to eligible Chakma and Hajong migrants.

The Supreme Court judgement of September 2015 garnered significant attention and coverage in both local and mainstream media. It was a highly anticipated ruling that had the potential to bring about significant changes in the lives of the Chakmas and Hajongs, as it pertained to the conferment of citizenship rights to eligible individuals from these communities.

The Supreme Court's September 2015 ruling on this issue drew considerable media attention, both locally and nationally. The judgement, which held the promise of transformative change for the Chakmas and Hajongs, was eagerly awaited. Yet, despite the widespread media coverage and the communities' hope, the on-ground results were disappointing.

A primary reason for this limited impact was the vague timeline in the Court's order. While the judgement recommended finalising citizenship rights within three months, it lacked a firm deadline. This vagueness paved the way for delays. The authorities, without a strict mandate, didn't prioritise the implementation, leaving the affected communities in a continued state of limbo.

This ambiguity in the timeline created uncertainty and allowed for delays in the implementation process. Consequently, there was no immediate and tangible change in the situation of the affected communities. The absence of a specific deadline gave leeway to the authorities responsible for the process, which resulted in a lack of urgency and priority in its execution.

As a result, despite the optimistic expectations generated by the Court's ruling, the process of conferring citizenship rights on eligible Chakmas and Hajong migrants remained slow and inadequate. The affected individuals faced continued uncertainty and lack of clarity regarding their status, which further compounded their challenges and hardships.

In cases like this, where the Court's judgement has the potential to bring transformative changes, it becomes crucial to have clear and concrete directives, including a definite timeline for implementation. Such specificity not only ensures prompt action but also provides the affected parties with a sense of security and assurance. When timelines are left open-ended, the process can languish and result in little practical impact, leaving the affected communities still waiting for the promised change to materialise.

6. STATUS OF CITIZENSHIP APPLICATIONS:

On February 28, 2018, the Office of the Member Secretary of the Arunachal Pradesh Legal Services Authority furnished the subsequent information about the status of citizenship applications, alongside the corresponding order.

The Commissioner, Home representing the Government of Arunachal Pradesh, communicated that a total of 4637 applications for citizenship acquisition from the Chakmas and Hajongs were received by the state government through the Ministry of Home Affairs, Government of India.

Among these 4637 citizenship applications, 271 applications were with the Ministry of Home Affairs (MHA), while 3827 applications have been scheduled for evaluation and hearing by three Deputy Commissioners overseeing Papumpare, Changlang, and Namsai Districts. Additionally, 539 applications from Changlang District were missing.

In the subset of 3827 applicants whose cases are under evaluation, only 1798 applicants participated in the hearings facilitated by the respective Deputy Commissioners for the purpose of granting citizenship. After the procedural process executed by the State Government, these cases were transmitted to the Ministry of Home Affairs.

The remaining 2029 applications out of the 3827 evaluated were identified as instances of duplicates, triplicates, or mutilated applications, as well as cases where applicants were absent, deceased, or had relocated. The break-up of 2029 applications are shown below:

Absent:	915
Expired:	919
Shifted:	06
Duplicate Applications:	178
Triplicate Applications:	10
Mutilated applications:	01
Total	**2029**

Out of 539 missing applications, 452 applications were traced out and submitted to the MHA by the Govt. of Arunachal Pradesh. However, the details of the remaining 87 missing applications out of 539 could not be traced out.

The detail status of the Citizenship applications as furnished are as follows:[124]

(i) Total citizenship applications:	4637
(ii) Application already forwarded to MHA:	- 271
	4366
(iii) Missing applications:	- 539
(iv) Applications taken up for hearing:	3827
(v) Absent/Expired/duplicate/mutilated applications etc. (including 915 absent applicants and 1 mutilated):	2029
(vi) Applications forwarded to MHA after hearing:	:1798

The Chakma citizenship issue has been mired in consistent legal delays, with tangible progress remaining notably absent. Despite sporadic appearances on the Supreme Court's agenda, the resolution for the 10% of Chakma migrants from East Pakistan in 1964 remains unaddressed.

This extended legal inertia has placed the Chakma community in a perpetual state of uncertainty. Their quest for a clear citizenship status is thwarted by system inefficiencies, prolonging their vulnerability and instability.

[124] *Order of Member Secretary, Arunachal Pradesh State Legal Services Authority, Itanagar in SC Case-Writ Petition (Civil) No. 510/2007*

12
THE POLITICAL APPEASEMENT AND DENIAL OF RIGHTS TO CHAKMAS

The State Government's refusal to acknowledge the Chakma-Hajongs as rightful Indian citizens stems from a need to appease tribal sentiments in Arunachal Pradesh. These sentiments have historical roots linked to the migration of the Chakma-Hajong community to the state. Over time, local communities began to view the Chakma-Hajongs as outsiders and potential threats. To maintain harmony and minimise friction between the Chakmas and Indigenous communities, the State Government has adopted a policy that limits the rights of the Chakma-Hajongs. This approach seeks to resonate with local tribal communities who regard the Chakma-Hajongs as foreign entities, potentially jeopardising their traditional way of life.

Legally, the Chakma population in Arunachal Pradesh falls into two primary categories:

- **Chakma Citizens by Birth:** Descendants of the original Chakma migrants born in Arunachal Pradesh after 1964. They account for approximately 90% of the Chakma and Hajong population in the state and are recognized as Indian citizens by birth under section 3 (1) (a) of the Citizenship Act of 1955.

- **Chakma Migrants from Former East Pakistan:** The original Chakma migrants who came to India in 1964 from what was then East Pakistan fall under the second category. Although most of this group has since passed on, they now account for less than 10% of the present population. Even with their limited numbers, they are safeguarded by the esteemed Supreme Court of India's 1996 and 2015 ordering, assuring them citizenship rights.

Despite the legal status of the majority of Chakmas as citizens by birth, the State Government remains adamant in not recognizing their citizenship. This approach lumps together both categories of the Chakma community, disregarding their distinct legal standings.

1. The Chakma Citizenship Impasse: State Policy and its Implications

Despite over 90% of the Chakma population being born in Arunachal Pradesh and having legal status as citizens by birth, the State Government continues to deny them recognition. This denial is perplexing given that most Chakmas in Arunachal Pradesh are indisputably citizens due to their birthright. However, the State Government has combined both Chakma categories - those born in the state and the migrants from the former East Pakistan in 1964 - into a single category. This merging of distinct groups not only overlooks their unique circumstances but also creates a policy framework that does not address the specific needs of each.

The implications of such a policy are manifold:

- It restricts Chakmas' access to public services, limits job opportunities, excludes them from welfare schemes, and diminishes their political participation avenues.
- The policy adversely affects the well-being of the Chakma community, limiting their integration into society and exacerbating inequality and marginalisation. Such conditions deter them from contributing significantly to the state's growth.

The underlying reasons for the State's stance on the Chakma-Hajongs are multifaceted, involving historical, social, and political dynamics. Key among these.

(a) Tribal Identity and Autonomy: Arunachal Pradesh boasts a rich tapestry of Indigenous tribes, each with its distinct culture and history. Safeguarding tribal identity and autonomy remains paramount. Recognizing the Chakma-Hajongs as citizens might be seen as a threat to this identity. To avert potential conflicts from these tribes, the State Government has chosen appeasement over recognition, thereby complicating the Chakma-Hajongs' path to citizenship.

(b) Land and Resource Concerns: For many tribal communities, land and its resources form the crux of identity and sustenance. The state government might fear that acknowledging the Chakma-Hajongs as citizens could spark land disputes or heighten competition for resources. By leaning into tribal sentiments, the intent is likely to avert potential conflicts tied to the Chakma-Hajongs' integration.

(c) Political Dynamics: Government decisions are invariably influenced by political motives. To ensure political stability and retain support, the state might prioritise indigenous tribal concerns, potentially at the expense of the Chakma-Hajongs' citizenship rights.

(d) Historical Context: The migration of the Chakma-Hajong community from the former East Pakistan to Arunachal Pradesh brings with it historical complexities. This backstory, coupled with challenges in their settlement and integration, has heightened existing tensions. The appeasement policy could be the state's response to these layered challenges, seeking to maintain the status quo.

(e) Maintaining Harmony: Recognizing the Chakma-Hajong community could incite social or political discord, especially if Indigenous tribes feel their position is threatened. By adopting an appeasement stance, the state government likely hopes to dodge such unrest and ensure continued peace.

While the state government's approach seeks to safeguard tribal identity and rights, it inadvertently fosters disparity and marginalisation for the Chakma-Hajong community. Such a policy, although possibly well-intentioned for immediate peace, has long-term implications, notably compromising the rights of the Chakma-Hajongs as Indian citizens.

2. PRIORITISING TRIBAL APPEASEMENT OVER CHAKMA CITIZENS' RIGHTS

The Government of India's rehabilitation policy inherently included citizenship for displaced individuals as a "by-default" component. In its commitment to the long-term resettlement of these groups, the Ministry of Rehabilitation & Relief (R&R) renamed itself by dropping "relief", a term suggesting transience.

Given the impracticality of issuing formal citizenship certificates to the millions of displaced persons across India through the standard procedures was beyond the government's logistical capabilities, these displaced individuals were allowed to reside as citizens without the need to obtain formal citizenship certificates.

In alignment with this approach, the Ministry of Home Affairs issued explicit instructions to the State Governments of Assam (including NEFA), West Bengal, Tripura, Manipur, and Nagaland on June 16, 1965. The instructions pertained to the policy and procedure for granting Indian citizenship to migrants from East Pakistan. These guidelines stated that migrants who had severed their ties with Pakistan and had settled in various occupations in India could be registered as Indian citizens under Section 5 (1) (a) of the Citizenship Act, 1955, provided they met the conditions outlined in rule 9 of the Citizenship Rules, 1956. This allowed migrants to become citizens even if they arrived without migration certificates or travel documents.[125]

(a) Streamlining Citizenship for Migrants: An Urgent Directive from the Ministry of Rehabilitation

Considering the letter sent to the State Governments regarding citizenship for migrants, the Ministry of Rehabilitation took further steps to ensure clarity. They communicated through letters (No. 1(2)/65-RH. II/IV on June 28, 1966, and No. 16(10)/66-RH. II on November 30, 1966) to the Chief Secretaries of various states, emphasising the limited success in registering migrants for citizenship. The primary barrier appeared to be the migrants' unfamiliarity with the necessary rules and procedures.

This lack of awareness not only delayed their citizenship registration but also their job opportunities, adversely affecting the overarching rehabilitation initiative.

To accelerate the rehabilitation of these migrants and facilitate their integration into Indian society, the Ministry emphasised the urgent need to promptly register those individuals who met the conditions prescribed in the Indian Citizenship Act, 1955, and its associated rules. Doing so would enable their seamless assimilation into Indian society and accelerate the overall rehabilitation process.[126]

Furthermore, the Ministry of Rehabilitation expressed its concern that without a comprehensive registration program devised by each district authority, and a clear timetable set for completing this process, only a limited number of migrants would voluntarily step forward to fulfil the necessary formalities for obtaining citizenship.

---

[125] *MHA Letter No. 4/366/63-IC dated June 16, 1965, to the State Government of Assam, West Bengal, Tripura, Manipur and Nagaland.*

[126] *Ministry of Rehabilitation letter No. 16(10)/66-RH. II dated November 30, 1966, to the Chief Secretaries of Assam, West Bengal/Nagaland, Tripura, Manipur*

Therefore, the Ministry requested that appropriate action instructions be issued to all relevant authorities to ensure that the registration process is concluded by the end of the year 1966 for all new migrants and repatriates who have fulfilled the minimum period of residence.

(b) Arunachal Pradesh's Evolving Stance on Citizenship Recommendation on Chakmas

Acting upon the guidelines for granting citizenship to migrants from East Pakistan provided by the Ministry of Home Affairs (MHA) and the Ministry of Rehabilitation, the Arunachal Pradesh Administration forwarded a recommendation in 1972. They urged the MHA to expediently consider granting citizenship to the Chakma-Hajongs of Arunachal Pradesh. (Reference: File No. 26013/100/73-I.C) [127]

In response, the MHA sought insights from the Intelligence Bureau (IB) to ensure a comprehensive understanding of the situation before deciding on the Chakma community's citizenship.

The IB reports, submitted to the MHA on April 3 and August 18, 1973, painted a complex picture. They revealed tension between the Chakma settlers and local tribal communities, primarily due to land aspirations. Disturbingly, approximately 1000 Chakma families had settled unlawfully in the Dweep area, disregarding the instructions of the local civil administration. Furthermore, the report noted that the Chakma settlers showed a strong interest in the affairs of Bangladesh, particularly concerning their fellow Chakmas residing there.

The report underscored the Chakmas' active pursuit of Indian citizenship and their aspiration to be recognized as Scheduled Tribes. This raised eyebrows among the local Singpho and Tangsa tribes in the Miao region. These tribes feared that the Chakmas, being more educated, clever, and

---

[127] *Note for the Secretaries' Committee on Internal Affairs" vide No. 13024/5/73-AP dated November 4, 1975 (National Archives of India)*

economically well-off, would exert dominance in local politics once they acquired Indian citizenship. [128]

Reacting to the Intelligence Bureau's findings about these tribal apprehensions, the Arunachal Pradesh administration reconsidered its earlier recommendation of swiftly granting Indian citizenship to the Chakmas. Instead, they advised the Ministry of Home Affairs to defer this decision, suggesting a period of close observation of the Chakma community's actions.

In response to the Intelligence Bureau report, which highlighted the "perceived fear" among the tribal Singpho and Tangsa communities in the Miao area, the Arunachal Pradesh administration reconsidered its earlier stance where they had previously advocated for granting Chakmas Indian citizenship as soon as possible. The Arunachal Pradesh administration conveyed to the Ministry of Home Affairs stating that considering various circumstances, the decision on granting citizenship rights to the Chakmas should be postponed for a few years. Throughout this period, the administration would closely monitor the activities of the Chakma community.[129]

The Arunachal Pradesh administration's change in stance, deferring the decision on granting citizenship to the Chakma community, was primarily driven by the desire to appease the sentiments of the local Singpho and Tangsa tribes. These tribes expressed strong apprehensions and concerns about the potential implications of providing Indian citizenship to the Chakma settlers in the region.

To assuage these tribal concerns and in hopes of preserving regional harmony and sidestepping potential discord, the administration opted to prioritise the local tribes' sentiments over the Chakma community's rights and

---

[128] *Intelligence Bureau Report No. D.I.B. UO No. 17/Tribe(Q)/72/(13) dated 03/04/1973 (National Archives of India)*

[129] *Arunachal Pradesh Administration Letter D.O. No. POL.236/72 dated June 22, 1973 (National Archives of India)*

aspirations. While this choice was made to maintain peace, it consequently protracted the Chakmas.

It is crucial to recognize the repercussions of the appeasement strategy. By delaying the decision and giving precedence to the local tribes' sentiments, the Chakma settlers' rights and interests were sidelined. This posed questions about the potential marginalisation of the Chakmas and the curtailment of their rights.

Upon the Arunachal Pradesh administration's recommendation to delay citizenship for the Chakma migrants, the Ministry of Home Affairs sought another review from the Intelligence Bureau on October 4, 1973, through U.O. No. U-13024/5/73-AP. They inquired if the current moment was suitable for contemplating citizenship for the Chakmas in Arunachal Pradesh.[130]

Subsequently, the Intelligence Bureau in its report from March 5, 1974, under U.O. No. 18/Tribe(Q)/73(8), recommended that the time was not opportune for the grant of citizenship to the Chakma refugees because there was growing opposition to the continued settlement of the Chakma migrants in Arunachal Pradesh.

After reviewing the situation, the Joint Secretary (UT) recommended postponing the decision on Chakma's citizenship until after Arunachal Pradesh's inaugural Assembly elections. The underlying rationale was the potential influence of the approximately 18,000 Chakmas on the local Panchayati system if they were granted Indian citizenship.

Granting citizenship would naturally lead the Chakmas to seek adequate representation in the Pradesh Council and Zila Parishad. This would empower them to voice their demands for improved settlement and development facilities. Given their relatively higher level of education and political awareness, they might not shy away from

---

[130] *Ministry of Home Affairs letter to Intelligence Bureau vide U.O No. U-13024/5/73-AP on October 4, 1973*

resorting to agitational activities to pursue their aspirations. Therefore, it was important to carefully assess the potential impact of their inclusion in the political system before deciding on granting them citizenship.

The report further proposed that during this period, all necessary measures should be implemented to ensure the proper settlement and development of Chakmas. This approach aims to address a significant portion of their current grievances, thereby potentially easing tensions between the Chakmas and the indigenous tribal population of Arunachal Pradesh. This proactive approach could also promote the Chakmas' assimilation with the indigenous tribes.

Furthermore, the report recommended settling Chakmas in smaller groups rather than concentrating them in one location. This strategic dispersal would help mitigate the possibility of any potential agitational activities and contribute to a smoother integration process. By dispersing the settlement, a more harmonious coexistence between the Chakmas and the local communities could be fostered.[131]

On November 22, 1974, the Minister for Supply and Rehabilitation assured the Rajya Sabha that the process of granting citizenship to the new migrants from East Pakistan, who arrived in India between January 1, 1964, and March 25, 1971, would be expedited. This assurance was based on the established procedure outlined by the Ministry of Home Affairs and the Ministry of Rehabilitation.

After the Minister of Rehabilitation's commitment in the Rajya Sabha, the Ministry of Rehabilitation reached out to all relevant State Governments through letters dated February 11, 1975 (Letter No. 1(2)/74-RH. I) and March 18, 1975 (Letter No. 25(14)/75-RH. II). In these letters, the State Governments were instructed to promptly take the

[131] *Intelligence Bureau Report dated the 5th of March 1974 vide U.O. No. 18/Tribe(Q)/73(8) (National Archives of India)*

necessary steps to grant citizenship to the settled Chakmas and other migrant families. The State Governments were asked to issue appropriate instructions to Project Officers and Rehabilitation Officers to collect applications from the migrant's seeking citizenship. These applications were then to be forwarded to the respective Collectors for further action.

With the affirmation from the Minister and directives from the Ministry of Rehabilitation, the onus of actioning the citizenship process for the migrants squarely fell on the State Governments.[132]

Following the Rajya Sabha's assurance on November 22, 1974, and subsequent issuance of instruction by the Ministry of Rehabilitation, the question of grant of Citizenship to Chakmas rehabilitated in Arunachal Pradesh was examined in an inter-departmental meeting held between Joint Secretary (NE) MHA, Joint Secretary, R&AW, Joint Secretary, MEA, Joint Director, IB, Deputy Secretary (AM), MHA on July 29, 1975.

The Joint Secretary (NE), MHA provided an overview of the Chakmas' settlement in Arunachal Pradesh, noting that despite living in the country for around 11 years, they hadn't been granted Indian citizenship. Given the political shifts and the anticipated elections, some Chakmas were advocating for Indian citizenship and voter enrollment to exercise their democratic rights. The Joint Secretary stressed that if integration was the goal, this was the opportune moment, or else it would foster resentment among the Chakmas.

The IB was of the view that while there is a case for granting the Chakmas Indian citizenship and the right to franchise to keep them contended and help in their assimilation process with the local tribals. The IB Wanted

---

[132] *Ministry of Rehabilitation letter No. 16(10)/66-RH. II dated November 30, 1966, to the Chief Secretaries of Assam, West Bengal/Nagaland, Tripura, Manipur (National Archives of India)*

the matter to be settled in a way to keep Chakmas contended and contained.

Conversely, the Ministry of External Affairs expressed reservations that in view of the renewed influx from Bangladesh and the continued propaganda that India keeps an "open house" for such refugees, grant of Indian citizenship to the Chakmas at this juncture would be inadvisable as it would increase further migration.

R&AW were of the view that Chakma roots were still in Bangladesh and as their links are likely to improve with growth of communications in the areas, it would not be wise to have this large chunk of people in the border area, whose loyalty may be questionable. It was also felt that if practicable the Chakmas should be moved away from Arunachal Pradesh to Southern India where the possibilities of their assimilation would be better.

The question of shifting the Chakmas to other parts of the country and rehabilitating them afresh was also discussed and there was a general feeling that it would require considerable financial and organisational effort. Further complications may arise if the Chakmas resisted the move.

The general feeling, therefore, was that the question of allowing the Chakmas to continue to stay in Arunachal Pradesh should be considered de-novo. As their assimilation would be interlinked by the ethnic ties with the remaining Chakmas in Bangladesh, it may be advantageous if possibilities of settling them outside Arunachal, far away from the borders, are explored.

Amid divergence of opinions expressed during the inter-departmental meeting, the Joint Secretary, MHA presented a note on November 4, 1975, to the Secretaries' Committee on Internal Affairs. The note, marked No.13024/5/73-AP, raised two primary concerns:

- Should the Chakmas be relocated from Arunachal Pradesh?

- Should the decision on granting them Indian citizenship be postponed?[133]

During their meeting on December 16, 1975, the Secretaries Committee on Internal Affairs deliberated on the issue of Settlement of Chakmas in Arunachal Pradesh and conferment of Indian citizenship upon them. Considering the lack of suitable land in the South, the Committee concluded that relocating the Chakmas from Arunachal Pradesh was not necessary. However, they agreed to postpone the citizenship decision for an additional two years, subject to a one-year review. Meanwhile, it should be conveyed to the Chakmas that "the conferment of citizenship would depend upon their good and peaceful neighbourly behaviour."[134]

On January 12, 1976, the Ministry of Home Affairs communicated with the Government of Arunachal Pradesh through letter No. U-13024/5/73-AP, informing them of the decision made by the Committee of Secretaries on Internal Affairs. The decision stated that "there is no need to relocate the Chakmas from their current habitation." As for the matter of granting citizenship to the Chakmas, the Committee decided to defer this decision for a couple of years, with a plan to review it again after one year.

During this period, the Chakmas should be informed in an appropriate manner that the granting of Indian citizenship would be contingent upon their good behaviour and maintaining peaceful neighbourly relations. [135]The Arunachal Pradesh Administration was also requested to take necessary action in accordance with these decisions.

---

[133] *Note vide No.13024/5/73-AP dated November 4, 1975, from MHA to Committee of Secretaries of Internal Affairs (National Archives of India)*

[134] *Minutes of the Meeting of Secretaries Committee on Internal Affairs held on 16 December 1975. Doc No. CD-1255/75 (National Archives of India)*

[135] *MHA letter No. U-13024/5/73-AP to the Government of Arunachal Pradesh on January 12, 1976, (National Archives of India)*

Pursuing the issue of the Chakmas' settlement in Arunachal Pradesh and the potential conferment of Indian citizenship upon them, the Ministry of Home Affairs, through its letter No. U-13024/5/73-AP on November 9, 1976, reached out to the Arunachal Pradesh Government, seeking their views. This was done to aid the Home Ministry in its review process.[136]

In response, on November 17, 1976, the Arunachal Pradesh Government decided in a cabinet meeting to form a committee. This committee's purpose was to meticulously assess all aspects of Settlement of Chakmas in Arunachal Pradesh to make specific recommendations.

On December 9, 1976, in a reply to the Home Ministry's letter, the Chief Secretary of Arunachal Pradesh, via D.O. No. POL. 236/72, conveyed **that *"the question of the behaviour and attitudes of the Chakma settlers has been reviewed. We find it premature to grant them Indian Citizenship as decided earlier to defer it for a couple of years. Further, complaints against the Chakmas from the local people and their elected representatives continued to be received about their tendency to migrate and encroach widely outside the settlement areas allocated to them".***

To address these issues comprehensively, the administration had established a committee tasked with conducting an in-depth study of all problems related to the Chakmas.[137]

Meanwhile, the Chakma delegations engaged in meetings and correspondence with various ministers, leaders and people's representatives in both the Union Territory (UT) and Central Government, seeking grant of Citizenship and Rights to Franchise. Copies of these appeals

---

[136] *MHA letter to Government of Arunachal Pradesh vide No. U-13024/5/73-AP dated November 9, 1976 (National Archives of India) National Archives of India*

[137] *Letter D.O. No. POL. 236/72 December 9, 1976, of the Chief Secretary, Arunachal Pradesh to Dy. Secretary, MHA (National Archives of India)*

were endorsed to the Arunachal Pradesh Government by the Ministry of Home Affairs (MHA), prompting the state government to provide an updated stance on the critical issue of "Conferment of Citizenship on the Chakmas."[138]

In accordance with the decision made at the Committee of Secretaries on Internal Affairs meeting on January 12, 1976, the Ministry of Home Affairs (MHA) consistently sought a report from the committee that the Arunachal Pradesh Government had established to assess Chakma settlement issues. Beginning on March 19, 1977, the MHA made this request, followed by subsequent reminders on April 19, 1977, and May 25, 1977.

Available records indicate that the MHA persistently reached out to the Chief Secretary of Arunachal Pradesh, using teleprinter messages, urging the prompt release of the findings from the committee investigating Chakma settlement issues. These communications also sought the government's stance on granting citizenship to the Chakmas. These reminders were dispatched on various dates: 09.09.1977, 23.09.1977, 27.10.1977, 28.11.1977, 22.12.1977, 16.01.1978, and 06.02.1978.

Responding to these messages, the Chief Secretary of the Arunachal Pradesh Government sent a ciphered message on February 18, 1978 (ref No. POL-IV/89/72). It mentioned that the matter of granting Indian citizenship to the Chakmas was still under consideration and would require additional time for resolution. The MHA would be notified promptly once a decision was finalised.

Later, on April 18, 1978, the MHA, in its letter No. 13024/5/73-AP, forwarded two letters (dated 10.03.1977 and 23.08.1977) from the Eastern Buddhist Welfare Society to the Lt. Governor of Arunachal Pradesh. The MHA asked the Union Territory (UT) Government to provide feedback on the issues highlighted in these letters

---

[138] *MHA letter No. U.13024/5/73-AP to the Secretary of the Lt. Governor, Government of Arunachal Pradesh on July 15, 1977 (National Archives of India)*

related to the Chakmas' citizenship. Furthermore, the MHA sought the state government's comments on the committee's report, which had been established by the Arunachal Pradesh Government to scrutinise the potential citizenship grant to the Chakmas.

After their previous letter, the Ministry of Home Affairs (MHA) once again reached out to the Chief Secretary of the Arunachal Pradesh Government on June 7, 1978, emphasising the need for the committee's findings on the Chakmas' citizenship status.

After a considerable wait, the Committee report was eventually submitted on June 14, 1978, to the Ministry of Home Affairs (MHA) by the Government of Arunachal Pradesh, as indicated in their communication with reference Letter No. POL-236/72.

However, the report failed to address the most crucial question at hand—the issue of granting citizenship to the Chakmas. This matter was of utmost importance and had been eagerly anticipated by the MHA, who had been waiting for a comprehensive review of the Chakma citizenship situation.

Despite the MHA repeated requests for inputs from the Arunachal Pradesh Government and to actively seek resolution and clarity on the citizenship matter for a considerable period, the Committee's report did not touch upon this central aspect, leaving the MHA with lingering uncertainties about the issue.

Contrary to the expectations and specific inquiries of the Ministry of Home Affairs (MHA) regarding the conferment of citizenship to the Chakmas, the submitted Committee report primarily centred on various other aspects of concern. Instead of addressing the crucial question of citizenship, the report primarily delved into the socio-economic conflicts between the Chakmas and local tribal communities. It also examined the unverified links the Chakmas had with their original homelands, issues related to criminal activities, and challenges surrounding land settlement.[139]

The Government of Arunachal Pradesh, while forwarding a copy of the report stated that the question of grant of citizenship to the Chakmas has political and social implications. They also noted that this topic had been a recurrent subject of debate in their Assembly sessions. Consequently, they mentioned that the regional Cabinet plans to discuss the citizenship grant more extensively, and they promised to share subsequent decisions on this pivotal issue.

In their communication dated June 14, 1978, the Arunachal Pradesh Government alluded to their cabinet's forthcoming deliberations on the Chakmas' citizenship status. Considering this, the Ministry of Home Affairs (MHA) dispatched multiple letters on September 8, October 21, November 21, December 27 of 1978, and January 17, 1979, addressed to the Chief Secretary of the Arunachal Pradesh Government. These letters sought updates on the state government's stance and any developments related to the Chakmas' citizenship issue.[140]

In response to the MHA's persistent queries on the issue of Grant of Indian Citizenship to Chakmas, the Arunachal Pradesh Government replied with two letters dated January 4, 1979, and February 14, 1979:

- In the January 4, 1979, correspondence, referenced as No. POL-236/72, the Arunachal Pradesh Government communicated that they were actively examining the matter and would relay their final decision to the MHA once it was established.
- Subsequently, in their letter of February 14, 1979, also under No. POL-236/72, the state government

[139] *Chief Secretary, Arunachal Pradesh Letter No. POL-236/72 on June 14, 1978, to Ministry of Home Affairs (National Archives of India)*

[140] *MHA letter to Govt. of Arunachal Pradesh vide No. 13024/5/73-AP on various dates. National Archives of India*

> conveyed that their administration was still analysing the issue, promising to share their conclusion when the timing was appropriate.

Pursuing the issue, the Ministry of Home Affairs sent a series of letters to the Arunachal Pradesh Government on March 13, April 25, August 2, and August 29 of 1979, all under the reference D.O. No. 13024/5/73-AP. These correspondences sought updates on the cabinet's deliberation about granting citizenship to the Chakmas.[141]

In reply to this string of communications, the Arunachal Pradesh Government, through a letter dated August 20, 1979, and referenced as No. POL.236/72, communicated that the subject of the Chakmas' citizenship was still being actively reviewed. As of that communication, they had not yet reached a decision.

Further, on November 19, 1979, the Ministry of Home Affairs reached out again, under the reference D.O. No. 13024/5/73-AP, seeking an update from the Arunachal Pradesh Government on any advancements made on the citizenship question for the Chakmas.

Replying on November 30, 1979, with reference No. POL.236/72, the state government conveyed that they continued to deliberate on the matter, factoring in the diverse intricacies of the situation. They further informed the Ministry that a census was underway for the Chakmas to issue them identity cards, a measure likely intended to assist in comprehensively evaluating the situation and making an informed decision on the issue of conferment of citizenship to the Chakmas.

Conclusion: The correspondence over the years reveal a shift in the position of the Arunachal Pradesh Government regarding granting citizenship to the Chakmas. Initially, in 1972, the government seemed supportive of the idea, especially when opposition to the

---

[141] *MHA Letters to Chief Secretary, Govt. of AP vide Do. No. 13024/5/73-AP on various dates. National Archives of India*

Chakmas was minimal. However, the scenario changed when an Intelligence Bureau (IB) report highlighted concerns from the local Singpho and Tangsa tribes. This report raised the alarm that the Chakmas, owing to their higher education levels, astuteness, and economic prosperity, could potentially overshadow local politics if granted citizenship.

This "perceived fear," as highlighted by the report, caused the Arunachal Pradesh Government to pivot from their initial stance. In response to the apprehensions of the Singpho and Tangsa tribes, the government adopted a policy of appeasement. This meant sidelining the Chakmas, curbing their potential political influence and socioeconomic advancements by withholding citizenship rights.

By the time the topic of the Chakmas' citizenship was deliberated by the Committee of Secretaries on Internal Affairs on January 12, 1976, the prevailing concerns of the local tribes, especially the Singpho and Tangsa, became a focal point. These tribes were wary that the Chakmas, once given citizenship rights, would rise to prominence due to their perceived edge in education, intelligence, and financial status. Given these apprehensions, the committee chose to postpone the decision on Chakmas' citizenship.

Although the Committee of Secretaries had plans to reassess the issue in a year, this did not materialise. The Arunachal Pradesh Government, in their bid to appease the local tribes, sidestepped the Chakmas' citizenship issue. Thus, the matter lingered unresolved, mainly driven by the state's efforts to prioritise the sentiments of the local tribal communities.

The extensive correspondence between the Ministry of Home Affairs (MHA) and the Arunachal Pradesh administration from 1976 to 1979, amounting to over 50 exchanges, underscores the Central Government's determination to address the Chakma rights issue. This dedication stemmed from the central policy focused on the rehabilitation of migrants from East Pakistan.

Throughout these years, the MHA consistently inquired about the progress regarding the Chakma citizenship, signalling its genuine intention to resolve the matter. This reflects the Central Government's intent to ensure proper rehabilitation and grant citizenship to the Chakmas.

On the other hand, the Arunachal Pradesh administration seemed to frequently sidestep and delay the issue, becoming increasingly evident through their recurrent hesitations and non-committal responses to the MHA's probes.

The situation remained in a standstill and grew into a significant political concern within the state. This impasse can be largely attributed to the Arunachal Pradesh government's inclination to placate tribal sentiments. Their strategy, it seems, was to avoid unsettling the local tribal populace, even if it meant leaving the Chakma's fate hanging in the balance.

13

CHAKMA-HAJONG ISSUE: EVOLVING NARRATIVES THROUGH TIME

Before the upheaval of the Anti-Foreigner Movement, the Chakma-Hajong issue in Arunachal Pradesh had been relatively stable. The anti-foreigner agitation spearheaded by the All-Assam Students' Union (AASU) in Assam had ripple effects throughout the North Eastern States. As the movement intensified, its reach extended into Arunachal Pradesh by 1979, marking the beginning of a sequence of events that would drastically alter the state's social equilibrium and unity.

As the unrest spread to Arunachal Pradesh, the All–Arunachal Pradesh Students' Union (AAPSU) rose to prominence. They championed a large-scale movement aimed at identifying and deporting foreigners from the state. In this process, the Buddhist Chakma community and the smaller Hajong Hindu tribal group were mistakenly branded as "foreigners," which placed them in the crosshairs of discrimination and animosity.

The tensions escalated as the negative sentiment of hostility and prejudice against these communities spread. The Chakma and Hajong people, who had been residing in Arunachal Pradesh for decades, faced unwarranted suspicion, prejudice and were unjustly labelled as intruders. This misplaced classification led to their alienation, resulting in considerable hardship and turmoil for these groups.

1. Changing Narratives: From Granting Citizenship Rights to Demanding Deportation

In the earlier chapters and through deep dives into archival records, a resounding truth emerges about the initial narrative and intent surrounding the Chakmas of Arunachal Pradesh. The initial narrative was clear-cut: extend formal citizenship, intertwine them within the fabric of the state's population, and assist their assimilation, aligning perfectly with the rehabilitation policy designed for displaced minorities arriving in India from the once undivided India. The overarching vision was empowerment, self-reliance, and inclusion.

However, the landscape dramatically shifted with the ripple effects of the vehement anti-foreigner protests in Assam, casting an ominous shadow over the Chakmas in Arunachal Pradesh. Suddenly, a stark transformation occurred in the narrative. No longer were the Chakmas viewed through the lens of inclusion and rightful citizenship; instead, a disturbing rhetoric emerged, branding them as foreigners and illegal migrants. This shift has led to an alarming demand for their deportation from the state, a sharp departure from the initial aspirations of affording them full-fledged rights and recognition as citizens.

This change in the storyline from integration and citizenship to outright labelling and calls for deportation from the state marks a troubling deviation from the initial ethos of assimilation and support. It is a testament to the powerful sway that broader socio-political movements can exert on individual communities, drastically altering the narrative from one of inclusion to exclusion, leaving the Chakmas in a precarious position, caught amidst shifting tides of perception and policy.

Even amid the growing bias and prejudice sparked by the anti-Chakma sentiments, the Ministry of Home Affairs remained unwavering in its mission to provide the Chakma community with proper rehabilitation and citizenship. The Ministry consistently engaged with the Arunachal Pradesh Government, asking for updates regarding the "Grant of Citizenship to the Chakmas." This commitment to the Chakma's well-being stood firm, irrespective of the broader societal discord and hostility resulting from the prejudiced movement.

Because of the prolonged indecision concerning the "Grant of Citizenship to the Chakmas," the Ministry of Home Affairs dispatched additional inquiries on February 14, 1980, March 11, 1980, and March 26, 1980, under reference No. 13094/5/73-AP. These communications emphasised the need for pertinent details and suggestions from the Arunachal Pradesh Government to effectively resolve the issue.

Responding to these inquiries, Gegong Apang, the then Chief Minister of Arunachal Pradesh, conveyed in his letter dated April 22, 1980 (ref D.O. No. CM/AP/R/80) to the Indian Home Minister, "With the intensification of the agitation concerning foreigners in Assam, the Students' Union of Arunachal Pradesh has initiated a similar movement. A key demand of theirs is the expulsion of Chakma and Tibetan refugees from Arunachal Pradesh."

It further clarified that the Government of Arunachal Pradesh have explained to the public leaders, they youth and students that the Chakmas and Hajongs have not entered this territory surreptitiously but were settled under the regular rehabilitation schemes sponsored by the Government of India and have taken various steps to tighten the security measures and have also issued orders to ensure that the refugees do not encroach into the economic activities of the local people. It has also been decided by local administration not to issue any trading licences in future to the Chakmas and Tibetan refugees outside their settlement areas. It is further ensured that employment opportunities are not afforded to Chakmas or Tibetan Refugees at the cost of Tribal people.

While the question of grant of Indian Citizenship to Chakmas was still under consideration of Arunachal Pradesh, the Chief Minister of Arunachal Pradesh in his letter to the Home Minister has taken the stand that as foreigners, Chakma and Tibetan refugees cannot exercise power of adult franchise in Arunachal Pradesh. In order to prevent unauthorised entry of Tibetan and Chakmas, the Government of Arunachal Pradesh have decided to introduce the system of identity cards to refugees and such cards are in the process of issue. He had also suggested dispersal of these refugees in other parts of the Country so that the Tribal people of Arunachal Pradesh are not exploited.[142]

The Chief Minister Gegong Apang's letter to India's Home Minister represents a pivotal moment in the State Government's stance on the Chakma community and their entitlements. Whereas previous discussions centred around granting the Chakmas citizenship rights, this letter emphasised a new direction: a call for their relocation out of the state. This change marked a significant shift in the discourse around the Chakma community's place in Arunachal Pradesh.

This shift in stance reflects a major departure from the earlier objective of granting citizenship rights and instead adopts a more exclusionary and discriminatory approach. The change in narrative suggests a shift in the government's perception of the Chakma community, moving away from an inclusive and equitable policy towards a more hostile and unwelcoming one.

The letter indicates that the shift in narrative and focus was influenced by the prevailing anti-Chakma movement led by the All–Arunachal Pradesh Students' Union (AAPSU). The sentiments and demands of this movement likely played a role in shaping the government's official stand, which now aligned with the anti-Chakma sentiments propagated by the student union.

The shift in governmental approach appears to have roots in the tactic of placating tribal sentiments for political gains. By courting the favour of specific tribal factions or seeking their political backing, the government seemingly adopted a tougher stance on the Chakma community, overlooking their rights and welfare in the process.

As a result, the central discourse around granting citizenship rights to the Chakmas took a detour. The narrative transitioned from ensuring their rights and

---

[142] *Letter of the Chief Minister of Arunachal Pradesh to the Home Minister of India vide D.O. No. CM/AP/R/80 on April 22, 1980 (MHA File No. 13024/5/73 AP Vol. III), National Archives of India*

assimilation into the state to advocating for their removal, casting the Chakma community in an unfavourable light, as outsiders undeserving of equitable rights and opportunities.

Further highlighting this wavering stance, the Government of Arunachal Pradesh, in letters dated April 29, 1980, and May 5, 1980, bearing reference No. POL.236/72 about Chakma citizenship, communicated to the Ministry of Home Affairs that the state's decision remained pending.

2. Distorting Historical Facts: An attempt to Misrepresent the Past

Following the Chief Minister of Arunachal Pradesh's letter, India's Home Minister responded on July 19, 1980, under reference No. 13024/5/73-AP. II, shedding light on the historical context of the Chakma settlements in Arunachal Pradesh. The Home Minister elucidated that the decision to settle Chakma migrants in Arunachal Pradesh stemmed from the imperative to alleviate refugee burdens in certain North-Eastern states. Thus, it was agreed that Arunachal Pradesh should share the responsibility of rehabilitating these refugees.

The Government of India, in collaboration with the Arunachal Pradesh Administration, had taken this decision after engaging in consultations with the local population to determine suitable settlement sites. It was a thoughtful process that involved considering the views and concerns of the people residing in the state.

The Home Minister also highlighted a practical challenge, stating that displacing the Chakma population at this stage and resettling them in other parts of the country would be difficult. Therefore, the letter emphasised the need to convince the people of Arunachal Pradesh regarding the settlement of the Chakmas, acknowledging the importance of gaining the support and understanding of the local population for a successful resolution to the issue. [143]

On August 18, 1980, the Chief Minister of Arunachal Pradesh penned a response to the Home Minister of India's elucidation regarding the Chakma settlement. The Chief Minister rebutted that when the Chakmas were initially settled in Arunachal Pradesh, it was conveyed to them that this arrangement was temporary. The intention was to repatriate them to their homeland once normalcy was restored there.

Furthermore, the Chief Minister shed light on reports implicating the Chakmas in a series of anti-social activities, some of which bordered on criminality. Such activities purportedly fostered a sense of unease among the indigenous tribes. Consequently, echoing previous sentiments, the Chief Minister recommended the relocation of the Chakmas to alternative regions in the country, aiming to avert potential adverse outcomes in the forthcoming years.

The Chief Minister's correspondences with the Home Minister seemingly underscore a narrative divergence, insinuating a possible manipulation or misinterpretation of historical background concerning the Chakmas' settlement in Arunachal Pradesh.

Firstly, the Chief Minister's approach of conflating Tibetan Refugees with the Chakmas is a glaring misrepresentation. By suggesting that both groups were provisionally settled with an intent for repatriation once their native regions stabilised, the Chief Minister contradicts established records. These clearly state that the Chakmas' resettlement in the state was a strategic and permanent rehabilitation move, rooted in the Government of India's policy towards migrants fleeing the 1964 communal unrest in East Pakistan.

---

[143] *Home Minister's letter D.O. No. 13024/5/73-AP. II on July 19, 1980 to the Chief Minister of Arunachal Pradesh (MHA File No. 13024/5/73 AP Vol. III), National Archives of India*

Secondly, the Chief Minister's correspondences with the Home Minister seem to be less about presenting accurate historical records and more about craftily reshaping the narrative of the Chakma settlement in Arunachal Pradesh. This appears to be a deliberate endeavour to skew the true origins and nature of their relocation.

Lastly, the Chief Minister's consistent mischaracterization, pairing Tibetan Refugees and Chakmas as two sides of the same coin, is misleading. By positing that both were temporary settlers awaiting a return to their homelands, he not only misconstrues facts but blatantly contradicts established historical documentation.

The historical records clearly demonstrate that the Chakmas' settlement in Arunachal Pradesh was not an ad-hoc arrangement but rather a meticulously designed rehabilitation plan. This initiative, rooted in the Government of India's policy, aimed to assist migrants who had sought refuge in India following the 1964 communal discord in East Pakistan (present-day Bangladesh). The intent was clear: offering the Chakmas a permanent sanctuary and a new lease of life in India.

However, the Chief Minister's attempt to lump Tibetan Refugees and Chakmas into one category and misstate the settlement's rationale obfuscates the genuine narrative surrounding the Chakma resettlement. Such dubious assertions not only challenge the legitimacy of the Chakma community's presence in Arunachal Pradesh but also cast a shadow of doubt over the Chief Minister's intentions. The underlying question looms: Why present a skewed version of events to the Home Minister?

What accentuates this contradictory stance of the state government is the conflicting actions and demands. While the Chief Minister vociferously argued for the Chakmas' relocation from Arunachal Pradesh, in stark contrast, the Director of Rehabilitation from the same state government requested a budgetary sanction of Rs. 1.8 Crore. This substantial sum was intended for comprehensive integration and upliftment of the Chakma community, spanning sectors like Housing Assistance, Education,

Medical and Health Care, and more. This glaring inconsistency not only highlights the incongruous stand of the state government but also underscores a potential lack of coherence and alignment in its policies and actions.

On August 19, 1980, the Director of Rehabilitation of the Arunachal Pradesh Government, through letter No. DRS/SSSA/36/80, addressed the Ministry of Supply and Rehabilitation concerning the Chakma settlements and the challenges they faced. Detailing the background of their settlement and various associated schemes, the state underscored the pressing need for comprehensive measures to facilitate the Chakma community's proper integration. Essential areas highlighted included Housing Assistance, Education, Medical and Health Care, Water Supply, Agriculture and its allied services, Animal Husbandry, Cottage and Small-Scale Industries, Marketing Cooperatives, enhancement of internal road networks, Transport, and other Establishment and Miscellaneous needs. In line with these requirements, the state also proposed a financial allocation of Rs. 1.8 Crores from the Central Government's budget.[144]

Amid concerted efforts to reshape the historical narrative of the Chakma settlements, along with escalating demands for their relocation, the Ministry of Home Affairs, through its letter No. 13024/5/73 AP dated August 30, 1980, reached out to the Arunachal Pradesh Government. The Ministry sought comprehensive data regarding the contentious issue of granting citizenship to the Chakma community.

A few days later, on September 2, 1980, Shri P.V. Narasimha Rao, the Minister of External Affairs, forwarded a significant letter to Giani Zail Singh, the Minister of Home Affairs. This letter, originally addressed to the Prime Minister, echoed concerns voiced by various Members of Parliament regarding the treatment meted out to the

---

[144] *Director of Rehabilitation, AP letter No. DRS/SSSA/36/80 on August 19, 1980, to Ministry of Supply and Rehabilitation (MHA File No. 13024/5/73 AP Vol. III), National Archives of India*

Chakma tribals in India. Authored on July 26, 1980, by respected figures like Kushok G Bakula from the Minorities Commission, MHA, and MPs P. Namgyal (LS), Chandra Pal Shailani (LS), and Sathiavavi Muttu (RS), it highlighted the pivotal issues surrounding Chakma citizenship and sought urgent redress.

In a striking display of inconsistency, while the Chief Minister of Arunachal Pradesh was actively pushing for the relocation of the Chakmas, the Director of Rehabilitation & Settlement of the state, in a subsequent move on October 23, 1980, under letter No. DRS/SSSA/36/80, reached out to the Ministry of Supply & Rehabilitation. The Director sought approval for a previously tabled proposal, requesting a significant amount of Rs. 1.8 Crores to cater to the developmental needs of the Chakma community.

A day later, on October 24, 1980, the Ministry of Home Affairs, in response to the state's request, penned a letter back to the Arunachal Pradesh Government. Through D. O No. 12/1/80-Desk.IV, the Ministry sought clarity on the state's seemingly contradictory stance. They questioned how the state government could simultaneously recommend enhanced amenities and support for the Chakma settlers while also advocating for their removal from the state.[145]

In a defensive response to the Ministry of Home Affairs, the Government of Arunachal Pradesh, via a letter No. DRS/SSSA/36/80 dated December 17, 1980, detailed the challenges the state confronted due to the presence of a significant Chakma population. Highlighting the socio-political, economic, and law and order issues stemming from the Chakmas' presence, the state underscored that depriving Chakmas of essential amenities within their designated settlement zones would lead them to constantly migrate within the state. Such movement, they reasoned, would intensify the insecurities and apprehensions of the local indigenous populace. This, the government argued,

[145] *MHA letter D. O No. 12/1/80-Desk.IV dated October 24, 1980, to Govt. of Arunachal Pradesh*

was the rationale behind the Chief Minister's appeal to the Home Ministry for Chakmas' relocation to other parts of the country.

Parallelly, concerning the complexities around the Chakmas' settlement in Arunachal Pradesh and the associated financial provisions, the Ministry of Home Affairs on November 24, 1980, via D.O. No. 13024/5/73-AP, reached out to the Ministry of Rehabilitation, Government of India. They requested a comprehensive brief on the matter. In return, the Ministry of Rehabilitation responded with D.O. No. 12/1/80-Desk-IV on December 9, 1980, enclosing an informative note on the settlement of Chakma refugees in Arunachal Pradesh.[146]

3. Normalisation of New Construct

In a remarkable and unparalleled step towards the removal of the Chakmas from Arunachal Pradesh, the state government, on December 29, 1980, communicated with the Ministry of Home Affairs through letter No. POL-24/80. This correspondence specifically proposed the dispersal of Chakmas from the state. As evidence of the state's intent, the letter included a private member's resolution from the Arunachal Pradesh Legislative Assembly dated September 23, 1980. This resolution explicitly endorsed the removal of Chakmas, with a clear directive "urging the Government to initiate measures to expel Chakmas from Arunachal Pradesh."[147]

In a letter dated February 12, 1981, the Ministry of Rehabilitation communicated with the Arunachal Pradesh government about their earlier request for sanction of additional funds for the Chakmas. Using reference No. 12/1/80-Desk.IV, the Ministry lucidly noted, ***"The scheme for settlement of Chakma families in Arunachal Pradesh were originally formulated by the then N.E.F.A.***

---

[146] *MHA letter D.O. No.13024/5/73-AP on November 24, 1980, to the Ministry of Rehabilitation*

[147] *Private Member's Resolution of Arunachal Pradesh Legislative Assembly on September 23, 1980*

Administration/State Government and were recommended by them for consideration of the Rehabilitation Ministry. These were accordingly sanctioned by the Ministry of Rehabilitation. After implementation of these schemes, the work relating to this settlement of the Chakma families was normalised by the then N.E.F.A. Administration in April 1968 vide letter No. RR/5/68, dated 8th April 1968, issued to various Deputy Commissioners concerned. Consequently, these families are now a part and parcel of the local population and if any additional facilities are to be provided for them, these may be provided by the State Government from its own resources. [148]

Subsequently, on February 25, 1981, the Director of Rehabilitation of Arunachal Pradesh reached out to the Ministry of Supply and Rehabilitation. In the letter, referenced as No. DRS/SSSA/36/80, he beseeched the government to swiftly approve the essential funds aimed at enhancing facilities within the Chakma settlements. This plea was substantiated by recounting his recent tour of the Chakma regions, where the community's representatives, including students, openly shared the severe challenges they grappled with. A copy of this letter was also duly forwarded to the Ministry of Home Affairs.[149]

On February 12, 1981, the Ministry of Home Affairs, through communication D.O. No. 13024/5/73-AP (Vol.III), approached the Intelligence Bureau for an in-depth assessment regarding the potential citizenship grant to the Chakmas, intending to present a comprehensive viewpoint to the Home Minister.

Responding on March 7, 1981, via Letter No. 34/0/80(20)-823, the Intelligence Bureau conveyed its

---

[148] *Ministry of Rehabilitation Letter No. 12/1/80-Desk.IV dated February 12, 1981, to the Govt. of Arunachal Pradesh (MHA File No. 13024/5/73 AP Vol. III), National Archives of India*

[149] *Director of Rehabilitation, AP letter to Ministry of Supply and Rehabilitation & MHA vide No. DRS/SSSA/36/80 dated February 25, 1981 (MHA File No. 13024/5/73 AP Vol. III), National Archives of India*

opinion on the matter of granting of Citizenship to the Chakmas of Arunachal Pradesh to the Ministry of Home Affairs. *"Since the Chakma refugees have been staying in Arunachal Pradesh for over 15 years, their request for grant of Citizenship is a very genuine one. However, their concentration at three places only in the state has caused population imbalance giving rise to genuine fear and resentment among local tribals against these refugees. In view of the very anti-Chakma feelings obtaining at present among the tribals in Arunachal Pradesh, we would recommend that this legitimate demand of the Chakmas should be considered only after they have been rehabilitated in small groups in Arunachal Pradesh and some other states so that the present pattern of local population is not disturbed beyond reasonable limits. If that is done, much of the opposition among the tribals against the Chakmas would be diluted."*[150]

On April 2, 1981, through communication D.O No.DRS/SSSA/36/80, the Government of Arunachal Pradesh reached out to the Ministry of Home Affairs. Highlighting the need for financial support related to the settlement of Chakma families, they enclosed a correspondence from the Director of Rehabilitation, Arunachal Pradesh. The letter stressed that the proposed funding should come directly from the Central Budget, rather than imposing it on the state's resources, to support the Chakma community's development.

Responding to this on July 17, 1981, via D.O. No. 13024/5/73-A.P. Vol.III, the Ministry of Home Affairs addressed the Ministry of Supply and Rehabilitation earlier request dated 12.02.1981. The reply noted the continuous clamour from Arunachal Pradesh's native population for relocating the Chakmas. Given the prevailing tensions stemming from the foreigner agitation in Assam, it was deemed unwise to proceed with such a move. Further, the Ministry acknowledged that allocating funds from the

---

[150] IB's opinion on the matter of grant of citizenship vide Letter No. 34/0/80(20)-823 dated March 7, 1981, to MHA (MHA File No. 13024/5/73 AP Vol. III), National Archives of India

state's budget might be met with local disapproval. Thus, they suggested that the additional resources required for the Chakma community should be allocated from the Ministry of Rehabilitation.

Meanwhile, during the National Convention of Buddhists convened on April 11th and 12th, 1981, there was a unanimous show of support for the rightful demands of the Chakma Tribal Buddhists in Arunachal Pradesh regarding the granting of citizenship. This consensus was subsequently communicated to Gianai Zail Singh, the Home Minister of India, by Narain Chand Parashar, MP (LS) on April 23, 1981.

On October 15, 1981, the Home Ministry dispatched a letter to the Lt. Governor of Arunachal Pradesh, under reference No. 13024/5/83-AP, providing a detailed backdrop of the Chakma settlement in Arunachal Pradesh dating back to 1965. The Lieutenant Governor of Arunachal Pradesh acknowledged this correspondence on October 24, 1981, through DO No LG-PS-P/81.

In all, 5 schemes were sanctioned for settlement of 2902 families at a cost of Rs. 1.30 Crores. Before settlement these families were screened by the SIB, Shillong.

In 1972, Arunachal Pradesh Government themselves had recommended grant of citizenship to the Chakma families. Subsequently, the Administration recommended that the question of grant of Citizenship be stayed for a few years more because Chakma settlers were reported to have maintained their links with Bangladesh.

Reports reaching us from time to time indicate that the youth in Arunachal Pradesh have been demanding effective control on the influx of Chakmas in Arunachal Pradesh and eviction of the existing population to other parts of the country. According to our information, there has been no further influx into the territory.

It may also be recalled that the question of settlement of Chakmas had come up for consideration in 1973 before the Home Ministry's Advisory Committee for

Arunachal Pradesh. It was observed that these migrants from East Pakistan could neither be repatriated to Bangladesh nor to any other part of India, rather effort should be made to assimilate them in the area and also ensure these people don't encroach upon lands possessed by the local people.[151]

The question of grant of Citizenship to these refugees is yet to be settled. Since they have been staying in Arunachal Pradesh for over 15 years they cannot return to Bangladesh. Uprooting them for resettlement elsewhere will cause misery and will be an expensive project. It would also be undesirable to keep them unsettled for such a long time without grant of citizenship.

On January 16, 1982, the Ministry of Rehabilitation informed the Ministry of Home Affairs vide D.O. No. 12/1/80-Desk IV that the Ministry has decided to send a small team to visit Arunachal Pradesh and to make on-the-spot assessment of the conditions of Chakma refugees. The Government of Arunachal Pradesh had proposed a programme of visit as per their D.O. No. DRS/SSSA/36/80 dated January 4, 1982.[152]

Again, on February 8, 1982, Ministry of Rehabilitation vide D.O. No. 12/1/80-Desk IV also requested the Ministry of Home Affairs to send representatives to the proposed visit to Arunachal Pradesh from 11.02.1982 to 19.02.1982 to assess the need for further assistance to Chakmas as it is also vitally concerned about the matter.

Following the visit of the Central team comprising of members from Ministry of Rehabilitation and Ministry of Home Affairs, a meeting took place on February 16, 1982, in the residential office of the Chief Minister, Arunachal Pradesh where the Chief Minister requested the Central

---

[151] *MHA Letter No. 13024/5/83-AP to the Lt. Governor of Arunachal Pradesh on 15.10.1981 (MHA File No. 13024/5/73 AP Vol. III), National Archives of India*

[152] *Ministry of Rehabilitation Letter D.O. No. 12/1/80-Desk IV dated January 16, 1982 (MHA File No. 13024/5/73 AP Vol. III), National Archives of India*

team to give a resume of the impressions of the team on their visit to the rehabilitation areas. He also wanted to know the policy of Govt. of India regarding the Chakmas.

The Central Team visited Chakma settlement in Diyun and Chowkham however could not visit Deban area but some of the Chakmas from Deban came and met the team in Miao Circuit House and represented their grievances. N.R. Hota, Joint Secretary, Ministry of Rehabilitation indicated that Chakmas in Deban appeared to be not doing well due to lack of irrigational facilities and that some Chakmas had in fact migrated from this settlement to other areas.

In the Diyun area, the Chakma settlers were found to have done well. They constructed their houses and were cultivating the agricultural lands quite well. He also highlighted the requirement for more teachers and higher secondary schools. In the Chowkham area, the team indicated that the Chakmas did not appear to have taken much interest in resettlement. A large part of the area is still unreclaimed and the settlers indicated that they were mostly working as agricultural labourers on the land of the Khamtis in neighbouring villages. They were also doing sharecropping on Khampti land. This area needs specific attention regarding reclamation of land, layout of the settlement, development of land and introduction of proper agricultural practices. He also mentioned the grievances of the Chakmas that included denial of citizenship rights, non-availability of employment opportunities as well as trading rights, developmental schemes etc.

Shri Hota mentioned that the Chakmas had been brought into Arunachal Pradesh in 1964-65 by the Government of India and settled here at Govt's instance. These people did not come as infiltrators. In fact, infiltrators from Bangladesh after 1971 are not being treated as refugees and not given any assistance as per Govt. policy. He, therefore, stated that the genuine needs of these people who came prior to 1971 be met either by Arunachal Pradesh Govt. from their budget or by special sanction from the Ministry of Rehabilitation if that is necessary. Regarding the policy for the Chakmas, **Shri Hota stated that *after 17 years of having settled them in Arunachal Pradesh there would be no case for throwing them out.***

Shri B.P. Mishra, Deputy Secretary, Ministry of Home Affairs said that the infiltration in Assam and the settlement of Chakmas in Arunachal Pradesh stood on a different footing. The Chakmas were registered refugees who came in 1964 and were settled by the Govt. of India in consultation with the then Arunachal Pradesh Administration. He further referred to the fact that the agitating leaders in Assam also have accepted those who were registered refugees, particularly those who have been settled by the Government. Shri Mishra said that in the case of Chakmas of Arunachal Pradesh there was no infiltration and the Chakmas had been settled by the Govt. once and for all. Removal of Chakmas would not be possible as there would be repercussions in other parts of the country and more so in Assam. As regards Govt.'s policy on dispersal Shri Mishra said that refugees who came before 25th March 1971 cannot be deported in view of various policy instructions issued by the Govt. of India from time to time on the subject as well as the international commitments.

He also referred to the lack of developmental assistance to the Chakmas, the difficulties in relation to their education including stipends, employment etc and felt that because of the neglect, frustration was growing and that this could be one of the reasons for some criminal activities.[153]

Gegong Apang, the Chief Minister also explained the position of the state government that local people had not been consulted before the settlement of Chakmas in the state in 1964. A number of resolutions have been passed by the Agency Council and State Legislative Assembly against their settlement. He also opined that earmarking some

---

[153] *Minutes of the Meeting held in the Residential Office of the CM, Arunachal Pradesh on 16.02.1982 (MHA File No. 13024/5/73 AP Vol. III), National Archives of India*

funds in the development sphere for the Chakmas is likely to spark off further resentment by the local people and therefore, the State Government would not like to accept the Central fund for the development of Chakmas rather the fund should be diverted to the developmental programs relating to the indigenous people of Arunachal Pradesh. He also opposed grant of Citizenship to the Chakmas and suggested that the only solution lay in their shifting out from the state.

On April 14, 1982, N.R. Hota, the Joint Secretary of the Ministry of Rehabilitation, communicated with his counterpart in the Ministry of Home Affairs through D.O. No. 12(1)/80-Desk. IV. He enclosed a copy of the report prepared by the Rehabilitation Department's team, accompanied by the minutes from their meeting with the Chief Minister of Arunachal Pradesh. The documents also contained their endorsement to bestow citizenship upon the Chakmas.

On May 3, 1982, the Lieutenant Governor of Arunachal Pradesh, H.S. Dubey vide D.O. No. Pol.236/72 replied to the Ministry of Home Affairs in reference to an earlier dated letter regarding grant of Indian Citizenship to the Chakmas of Arunachal Pradesh in which he reiterated the position of the Chief Minister of the state. He also highlighted the complaint of encroachment by the local people, and the tendency of Chakmas to stray outside settlement, giving rise to tension between the Chakmas and the local people. Further, the Committee constituted by the Government of Arunachal Pradesh in 1976 to review the entire situation also confirmed that there was a feeling of resentment among the local people and had apprehension that the Chakmas would dominate them both economically and socially if they are conferred citizenship and political rights. Based on the Committee's report and in pursuance of the resolution adopted by the Arunachal Pradesh Legislative Assembly, this government decided to defer the question of citizenship to the Chakmas and to suggest to the

Ministry to make alternative arrangements for settlement of these Chakmas.[154]

In a confidential document from the Ministry of Home Affairs, dated August 9, 1982 (referenced as MHA UO No. 13024/5/73-AP), it's revealed that the Chief Minister of Arunachal Pradesh highlighted concerns regarding the alliance between students from Arunachal Pradesh and the All-Assam Students' Union, as well as with Opposition Members of the Arunachal Pradesh Assembly. This collaboration occasionally led to complications surrounding the foreigner issue in Arunachal Pradesh. The Chief Minister also subtly insinuated that missionaries operating in Assam, Shillong and Nagaland might be influencing students to bring the foreigner issue to the forefront.

On August 14, 1982, as referenced in D.O. No. CM(AP)/9/82, Arunachal Pradesh's Chief Minister addressed the Prime Minister, raising concerns about the growing unrest spurred by student agitations on the Chakma issue, threatening the state's peace and stability. He highlighted that opportunistic element from the Opposition, particularly from the United People's Party, had exploited his absence, manipulating student leadership to fuel the protest. The Chief Minister expressed that he had advised the All–Arunachal Pradesh Students Union (AAPSU) that their course of action was misguided and not in the best interest of the region.

In the past, the Arunachal government has appealed to the central government for a redistribution of the Chakma population, advocating against their permanent settlement. But tangible outcomes remained elusive. Complicating matters, the All-Assam Students Union and regional political figures have seized upon this public sentiment, attempting to ignite Assam-like protests. Distressingly, the

---

[154] *Letter D.O. No. Pol.236/72 dated May 3, 1982, of the Lieutenant Governor of Arunachal Pradesh to the Ministry of Home Affairs (MHA File No. 13024/5/73 AP Vol. III), National Archives of India*

Chief Minister noted that even influential members from his own party had misguided the students. He underscored the collaboration between AASU and AAPSU, combined with the backing of the People's Party of Arunachal (PPA) and the North Eastern Regional Students Union. This potent mix, he warned, has spurred AAPSU to announce further agitations slated for August 16th through 20th.[155]

On August 25, 1982, the Prime Minister's Office, through letter No. 25(261)/82-PM, forwarded a copy of a letter from the Secretary to the Chief Minister of Arunachal Pradesh to the Ministry of Home Affairs. This letter pertained to the demands of the All–Arunachal Pradesh Students Union.[156]

In response, on September 13, 1982, the Ministry of Home Affairs communicated back to the Prime Minister's Office under MHA UO No.13024/5/73-AP(Vol.III). The reply specifically addressed the students' demands and unequivocally stated......***there is no infiltration as such of foreigners in Arunachal Pradesh and the Chakmas were settled under definite schemes of rehabilitation of the Ministry of Rehabilitation. The Chakmas have stayed in Arunachal Pradesh for nearly 2 decades and the question of their removal from Arunachal Pradesh should not arise. The Arunachal Pradesh Government has taken steps to ensure, as far as possible, that these Chakmas do not come into socio-economic conflict with the local people. The Chief Minister, Arunachal Pradesh, in the course of discussion recently, suggested that the question of appointment of some Chakmas into paramilitary forces and Border Roads Organisations etc. might be considered and for such employment, they should be sent outside Arunachal Pradesh thereby not allowing the number of refugees to***

---

[155] *The Chief Minister, AP letter D.O. No. CM(AP)/9/82 to the Prime Minister on August 14, 1982 (MHA File No. 13024/5/73 AP Vol. III), National Archives of India*

[156] *PMO letter to CS, Govt. of AP vide letter No. 25(261)/82-PM on August 25, 1982 (MHA File No. 13024/5/73 AP Vol. III), National Archives of India*

grow. This aspect is being considered. Since the Chakmas from Arunachal Pradesh cannot be moved out, it is also desirable that the question of grant of citizenship to them is considered without much delay. However, in view of the present climate, the matter has been recommended to be deferred by the Government of Arunachal Pradesh. The Home Ministry also opined in the note that none of the demands of AAPSU should agitate students.[157]

(d) The Narrative is Woven against the Chakmas

Historical documents provide a lens into the central government's interactions with Arunachal Pradesh, underscoring a sustained effort since 1972 to address the question of Chakma citizenship in the state. This continuous dialogue signals the depth of concern surrounding the legal recognition and rights of the Chakma community within Arunachal Pradesh.

However, the landscape of these discussions witnessed a significant transformation in 1982. The Ministry of Home Affairs, the central authority responsible for citizenship matters, seemingly retracted from the dialogue. Instead of actively engaging with the Government of Arunachal Pradesh, it refrained from further discussions or consultations on bestowing citizenship upon the Chakma community. This shift in dynamics hints at a conscious decision by the central government to sideline the concerns and rights of the Chakma migrants.

In contrast, the Arunachal Pradesh government remained vocal and steadfast in its stance. It consistently relayed its unease concerning the Chakma populace to the Ministry of Home Affairs. Their communications were marked by a desire to relocate the Chakma community away from the state. Caught between these contrasting perspectives, the narrative presented by the state

---

[157] *MHA UO No.13024/5/73-AP(Vol.III) to PMO on September 13, 1982 (MHA File No. 13024/5/73 AP Vol. III), National Archives of India*

government of Arunachal Pradesh became increasingly influential, highlighting the complexities of the Chakma citizenship issue.

The discourse between the central and state governments underwent a significant shift over the Chakma issue. While the Central Government's momentum towards granting the Chakmas citizenship waned, the Arunachal Pradesh government remained resolute, advocating for the removal of the Chakmas from the state.

Illustrating this divergence, on July 31, 1984, the Arunachal Pradesh government, referencing No. POL. 236/72, formally approached the Ministry of Home Affairs, seeking the Central Government's stance on the Council of Ministers' proposal to relocate the Chakmas from the Union Territory.[158]

On April 10, 1986, correspondence between Chief Minister Gegong Apang of Arunachal Pradesh and the Home Minister of India took place. In his correspondence (DO No. CM/AP/15-86), Apang broached the subject of the Chakmas' relocation from the state. In response, the Home Minister on May 26, 1986 (DO. No. 8/2/86-AP) asserted that dispersing the Chakmas from Arunachal Pradesh, especially those settled for over two decades under a rehabilitation scheme, was neither feasible nor humane. However, he emphasised the importance of ensuring harmony between the Chakmas and the local tribal populace to avoid socio-economic conflict. The Home Minister categorically stated ***"the proposal to disperse Chakmas outside Arunachal Pradesh is not practicable. From the humanitarian angle also, it will be harsh to disperse them who have been settled for over two decades. They have been settled under a definite Scheme of Rehabilitation. However, care has to be taken that they do***

[158] *Arunachal Pradesh Government Letter No. POL. 236/72 on July 31, 1984, to MHA (MHA File No. 13024/5/73 AP Vol. III), National Archives of India*

not come into socio-economic conflict with the local tribal population". [159]

On October 7, 1986, the All–Arunachal Pradesh Chakma Students Association (AAPCSA) presented a memorandum to the Indian Prime Minister. This outlined the challenges the Chakmas faced in Arunachal Pradesh, including discrimination and neglect. The AAPCSA's charter covered demands such as Indian citizenship, employment opportunities in government services, development schemes, trade and business provisions, educational reservations, protections as an ethnic minority, and potentially a separate administrative region.

Responding to this, the PMO sought feedback from the Arunachal Pradesh government. They referenced D.O. No. 13024/5/73-AP (Vol.-III) and a prior teletext message (No. 15/13/86-AP from December 2, 1986) relating to a Lok Sabha question on the subject.

Subsequently, on July 8, 1987, the memorandum was forwarded to Arunachal's Chief Secretary, urging a detailed review of the Chakma situation. This included comments on AAPCSA's seven demands and reported past mistreatment of the Chakma community.

The same day, the PMO shared the memorandum, specifically highlighting the seven demands, with the Ministry of Home Affairs through D.O. No. 13024/5/73-AP (Vol.-III), seeking their input. Prominently, the first demand was about granting citizenship to the Chakmas, grounded in the Citizenship (Amendment) Bill passed in December 1985.

On July 31, 1987, referencing D.O. No. 26011/07/87-IC. I, the Ministry of Home Affairs responded to the PMO's letter concerning the AACSA's Charter of demands. Addressing the points raised in AAPCSA's memorandum, the MHA opined that ***"Chakmas who migrated to NEFA which was constitutionally part of Assam in 1964 and have***

---

[159] *Upgradation of Changlang Sub-Division into a full-fledged District, Ministry of Home Affairs, File No. 14/5/86-AP*

been resident of NEFA since then should be deemed to be citizens of India on the basis of the Citizenship (Amendment) Bill passed by the Parliament in 1985 conferring citizenship on all persons of Indian origin who came to Assam before 1.1.1966".

It further clarified that ***the Chakmas who migrated from erstwhile East Pakistan to Indian territories outside Assam are not covered by Section 6A of the Citizenship Act (Assam Accord). However, the children born in India to Chakmas on or after January, 1950 but before 1st July, 1987 have already become citizens of India by virtue of Section 3(1) of the Citizenship Act. However, the Children born after 1st July, 1987 cannot be treated as Indian citizens unless either of their parents is a citizen of India at the time of birth. And the Chakmas who fulfil the statutory requirements can be considered for grant of Indian citizenship under appropriate provisions of the Citizenship Act provided a policy decision is taken to grant citizenship to such category of persons.***[160]

On August 10, 1987, under reference No. 13024/5/73-AP (Vol.III) the Ministry of Home Affairs sought feedback from the Arunachal Pradesh Government on both the AACSA's seven-point demands and reported past mistreatment of the Chakma community.

In 1987, when Arunachal Pradesh achieved statehood from being a Union Territory, the political landscape underwent a noticeable shift. The state government began to frame and emphasise a narrative that cast the local Indigenous tribes as victims, overshadowed by the Chakma-Hajong settlement. They contended that the settlement of the Chakma-Hajong people was carried out without properly addressing the rights, customs, and traditions of the local tribes. In the eyes of the state, the Chakma-Hajong presence was perceived not just as a

---

[160] *MHA Letter D.O. No. 26011/07/87-IC.I. to PMO on July 31, 1987 (MHA File No. 13024/5/73 AP Vol. III), National Archives of India*

demographic shift, but as an encroachment upon the indigenous identity and heritage.

Previously, the central government had been making strides towards bestowing citizenship rights upon the Chakma-Hajong communities, recognizing their prolonged residency and predicaments. But with the state's renewed perspective, the trajectory took a stark turn. The aspiration to integrate the Chakma-Hajong people gave way to a burgeoning demand to evict them from the state entirely. This change in direction was in stark contrast to the earlier intentions of the central authorities.

The All–Arunachal Pradesh Students' Union (AAPSU), since 1979, played a pivotal role in shaping and reinforcing this narrative. Backed by the state's political machinery, the AAPSU spearheaded several vigorous protests and strikes. Starting in 1994, there was a surge in activities, particularly strikes, pushing for the deportation of the Chakma and Hajong communities. The AAPSU's relentless campaigns not only granted further legitimacy to the narrative against the Chakmas but also significantly shifted the discourse surrounding their original settlement. The balance tilted, with the historical context of the Chakmas' migration and their initial reasons for settlement becoming overshadowed by the state's evolving narrative.

The narrative that depicted the Chakmas as a menace to Arunachal Pradesh's socio-cultural fabric, initiated by the All–Arunachal Pradesh Students' Union (AAPSU), did not gain ground overnight. With sustained efforts, this perspective found firm footing, especially when it received patronage from influential sectors like the state government and political factions. Such endorsements from key stakeholders not only amplified the message but also lent it an air of authenticity and authority, enabling it to resonate more broadly within the populace.

Over time, as this narrative began to dominate the socio-political dialogue of Arunachal Pradesh, the nuances and historical complexities surrounding the Chakmas' migration and settlement were increasingly overshadowed.

The prevailing sentiment, influenced by these forces, began to view the Chakmas less as long-standing inhabitants with legitimate concerns and more as intruders, threatening the state's unique identity.

A turning point was reached when the AAPSU, harnessing this growing sentiment, decided to ramp up their efforts against the Chakma community. With renewed vigour and purpose, their campaigns and activities grew more intense, further solidifying the narrative against the Chakmas. The effects of this intensified movement were far-reaching, resulting in a complete recalibration of the state's discourse on the Chakmas. The initial reasons for their migration and the broader historical context of their settlement were relegated to the background, replaced by a narrative that saw them primarily as a challenge to Arunachal Pradesh's socio-cultural equilibrium.

(e) State's Strong Resistance to Central Govt.'s Intents on Chakma Rights

During the early 1990s, the All–Arunachal Pradesh Students' Union (AAPSU) championed a movement against the Chakma and Hajong communities in Arunachal Pradesh, asserting their deportation. This movement was not a standalone effort; there was tacit support from the state government, solidifying its influence and reach.

This matter grabbed national attention when, on August 5, 1992, Mr. Laeta Umbrey, an MP from Arunachal Pradesh, raised the Chakma issue in the Lok Sabha, India's House of Representatives. He emphasised the widespread sentiment in the state favouring the deportation of the Chakmas.

However, the Central Government offered a contrasting perspective. On September 23 of the same year, Mr. M.M. Jacob, holding the portfolio of Minister of State for Home and Parliamentary Affairs, responded to Umbrey's concerns. He underlined that the Chakma settlement in Arunachal Pradesh wasn't arbitrary but was a product of a well-considered plan executed in consultation with the

State Administration. Contrary to the claims of the state representatives, Jacob established that the Chakmas had been peaceful residents, with no significant anti-national activities or major disruptions to the state's law and order linked to them. He referred to a 1982 assessment by a Central Team that had visited the state, which suggested that granting citizenship rights to the Chakmas might encourage integration and responsible societal conduct. Jacob further emphasised that many Chakmas met the criteria for Indian citizenship, either because of their migration before 1971 or because they were born in India.[161]

Jacob's response was a clear call for understanding and compassion. He conveyed that deporting the Chakmas from Arunachal Pradesh was not just unwarranted but also unjust. The issue of Chakma rehabilitation was not a challenge for Arunachal alone, but a collective responsibility of the entire Indian nation.

Once again, on January 7, 1993, Mr. M.M. Jacob, the Minister of State for Home in the Government of India, responded to a letter dated March 26, 1992, from the Chief Minister of Arunachal Pradesh. The letter from the Chief Minister had addressed the matter of deporting the Chakmas from the state.

In his response, Mr. Jacob made it explicit that, from the perspective of the Central Government, the issue of deporting the Chakmas from the state was considered closed, and there was no perceived benefit in revisiting it. In fact, the Central Government strongly believed that the Chakmas of Arunachal Pradesh were entitled to citizenship under the Citizenship Act of 1955. Mr. Jacob urged the State Government to promptly confer citizenship upon the Chakmas so that they could enjoy all the rights associated with it.

---

[161] *White Paper on Chakma-Hajong Refugee Issue, Govt. of Arunachal Pradesh, 1996*

On June 27, 1994, the Chakma-Hajong issue in Arunachal Pradesh echoed in the Rajya Sabha, when Mr. Nyodak Yonggam, a parliamentarian representing the state, broached the topic of their repatriation.

Addressing the concerns raised, Mr. P.M. Sayeed, the Minister of State for Home Affairs, penned a detailed Direct Order (DO) letter on July 7, 1994. In his elucidation, he underscored the historical context of the Chakma-Hajong settlement in Arunachal Pradesh. He cited the pivotal Indira-Mujib Agreement of 1972 to shed light on the citizenship status of the Chakma-Hajongs. The agreement clearly stipulated that Chakma-Hajongs who had migrated to India from the former East Pakistan (present-day Bangladesh) prior to March 25, 1971, would be evaluated for Indian citizenship. This historical and diplomatic agreement, he implied, set a clear precedent for the consideration of their citizenship rights.

Despite the Central Government's move towards granting citizenship to the Chakma and Hajong communities in Arunachal Pradesh, the State Government remained unwavering in its opposition. This firm stance was accentuated by the All–Arunachal Pradesh Students' Union (AAPSU), which, bolstered by the tacit endorsement of the State Government, escalated its campaign against the Chakma and Hajong populations. In August 1994, AAPSU served a stark "Quit Arunachal Pradesh" notice to these communities. The union orchestrated extensive strikes and protests, rallying behind the powerful slogan "no deportation, no election". This slogan not only underscored their commitment to the cause but also sent a clear message: if the Central Government did not address the Chakma and Hajong issue to their satisfaction by January 1995, the protests would persist.

Reacting to the heightened tension and anticipating potential spill-over, the Government of Assam took stringent measures to fortify its borders against the influx of Chakmas. They enacted stringent policies, even going to the extent of authorising a "shoot-at-sight" directive for any Chakma individuals attempting to cross into Assam. The directive underscored the gravity of the situation and the lengths to which regional governments would go to enforce their stance.

In a bid to amplify their message and gain more traction against the Chakma and Hajong communities, the All–Arunachal Pradesh Students' Union (AAPSU) launched the "Jago Arunachal" campaign in August 1995. Through this initiative, they orchestrated a series of rallies across the state's diverse regions, targeting both the State and Central Governments. Their goal was clear: to compel the governments into evicting the Chakmas from Arunachal Pradesh.

In addition to the public demonstrations, AAPSU took a proactive stance in holding the state's political representatives accountable. They dispatched notices to both Members of Parliament (MPs) and Members of the Legislative Assembly (MLAs) from Arunachal Pradesh. In these notices, AAPSU voiced their concern and dissatisfaction over the perceived apathy of these elected officials, questioning their "silent and adamant attitude" towards the Chakma-Hajong conundrum. To ensure that their demands for accountability didn't go unnoticed, AAPSU established the "Massive Explanation-cum-Public Open Rally", setting its date for September 29, 1995. This platform was meant to facilitate direct communication between the public, the AAPSU, and their elected representatives.

Parallel to AAPSU's intensified campaign, political leaders recognized the need for dialogue and coordination. On August 5, 1995, an all-encompassing meeting of various stakeholders was convened in Itanagar. Led by the Chief Minister, this All-Party legislators' meeting brought together a diverse set of voices, ranging from political parties like AAPSU and the National Students' Union of India (NSUI) to grassroots leaders such as Panchayat representatives, village chiefs, and significant figures from the NGO sector. These discussions culminated in the decision to hold a collective rally on September 20, 1995. By including a vast array of participants, from student unions to prominent citizens, this event aimed to send a unified message about the state's stance on the Chakma-Hajong issue.[162]

On September 17, 1995, a delegation of ten members, led by the Chief Minister of Arunachal Pradesh, met with the Prime Minister and the Union Home Minister of India. Their primary objective was to urge the Union Government to instruct the relevant authorities to formulate a time-bound plan for the deportation of the Chakma and Hajong populations out of Arunachal Pradesh.

The culmination of these efforts came on September 20, 1995, with the staging of an All-Party Referendum Rally. This event witnessed the participation of the Chief Minister, all Ministers and Members of the Legislative Assembly, Members of Parliament from Arunachal Pradesh, members, and office bearers of the state units of all political parties, representatives of NGOs, and all student unions, including AAPSU. During this rally, a Six-point Resolution was passed, which, among other things, demanded that the Central Government remove the Chakmas and Hajongs from Arunachal Pradesh by December 31, 1995.

During the People's Referendum Rally on September 20, 1995, a notable resolution was passed, stating that members of all political parties in the state would be obliged to relinquish their primary party memberships if the Central Government did not facilitate the eviction of the Chakma and Hajong communities by the end of December 1995.

A significant event transpired on November 8, 1995, as Itanagar received a high-profile delegation. This team comprised Syed Sibtey Razi and Prof. Meijinlung Kamson, Union Ministers of State overseeing Home Affairs. Alongside them were other senior officials from the Ministry of Home Affairs. Their agenda in Itanagar was comprehensive: to engage in constructive dialogue with the

---

[162] *Student Movements in Arunachal Pradesh: S. Dutta (ISBN-81-86393-17-X)*

state's leadership, including the Chief Minister, cabinet ministers, and representatives of various political entities.

Moreover, their consultations were not limited to political corridors. They reached out to numerous stakeholders, such as prominent non-governmental organisations (NGOs), student union bodies like the All–Arunachal Pradesh Students' Union (AAPSU) and the National Students' Union of India (NSUI), and even key figures from the local commercial sectors.

Despite the depth and breadth of these discussions, the delegation did not provide a definitive commitment regarding the eviction of the Chakma and Hajong groups. However, they assured the state leadership that any decision regarding this issue would only be taken after comprehensive consultations with the State Government.

On December 20, 1995, Itanagar became the focal point of a pivotal gathering, comprising an array of influential figures: from the Chief Minister and his ministerial colleagues to legislative assembly members, student union leaders, and prominent NGO representatives. This assembly was convened to deliberate on the prevailing scenario, especially concerning the Central Government's viewpoint on the potential eviction of the Chakma and Hajong groups from Arunachal Pradesh. A significant part of the discourse was dedicated to gauging how effectively the resolutions from the People's Referendum Rally had been actualised.[163]

A prominent sentiment that emerged from the discussion was a collective discontentment towards the National Human Rights Commission (NHRC) for its decision to petition the Supreme Court, pointing to purported human rights transgressions committed by the All–Arunachal Pradesh Students' Union (AAPSU), believed to be backed, at least tacitly, by the State Government.

---

[163] *White Paper on Chakma-Hajong Refugee Issue, Govt. of Arunachal Pradesh, 1996*

The assembly culminated with the passing of a resolute declaration. It castigated the Ministry of Home Affairs for its endorsement of granting citizenship rights to the Chakma and Hajong groups, a move perceived as being at odds with the aspirations of Arunachal Pradesh's Indigenous inhabitants. Moreover, the Central Government drew criticism for its decision to deploy the Solicitor General of India, tasking him with countering the State Government's stance in the context of the NHRC's Supreme Court petition.

In addition, the assembly presented another significant directive. The consensus was that the Chief Minister of Arunachal Pradesh should engage in discussions at a meeting called by the union Home minister in Delhi. However, it was essential for the Chief Minister to tenaciously argue in favour of the immediate eviction of the Chakma and Hajong communities from the state. The conclave further urged the Indian Central Government to withhold citizenship rights for these communities as long as they inhabit Arunachal Pradesh. Central to the discussions was the demand for a formal declaration from the Union Government of India. The state representatives expected an unambiguous affirmation that the Central Government would take swift action to relocate the Chakma and Hajong populations from Arunachal Pradesh and that they would be denied Indian citizenship for the duration of their stay within the state's boundaries.

On December 29, 1995, a pivotal gathering occurred in Itanagar. This council united leaders from across the political spectrum, including the Chief Minister, cabinet ministers, Legislative Assembly members, student bodies, and diverse non-governmental entities (NGOs). The assembly achieved unanimity, endorsing three primary resolutions. These resolutions reiterated their longstanding stance on the Chakma-Hajong issue but introduced a notable modification: the earlier planned resignation of members from the core membership of national political entities was deferred. Instead, the spotlight was directed towards the High-Level Group, urging it to delve deeper and unearth a durable resolution to the Chakma-Hajong conundrum.

Coincidentally, that same day, with a nod from the Prime Minister, the Ministry of Home Affairs inaugurated a High-Level Group. Chaired by the union Home minister, its mission was to delve into the historical nuances of the Chakmas and Hajongs in Arunachal Pradesh and chalk out a strategic plan. The group's roster was illustrious, featuring Mr. S.B. Chavan, the Home Affairs Minister; Mr. Syed Sibtey Razi and Mr. H.R. Bharadwaj, Ministers of State for Home Affairs and Law, respectively; Mr. Gegong Apang, the Chief Minister of Arunachal Pradesh; and several senior officials from the Home Affairs and the Government of Arunachal Pradesh. The formation of this committee was seen as a concentrated effort to address the complexities of the issue.[164]

On January 5, 1996, under the stewardship of Mr. S.B. Chavan, the union Home minister, the High-Level Group held its inaugural meeting. In this assembly, the Group embarked on thorough discussions to carve out a strategic plan. The emphasis was on acquiring a holistic grasp of the Chakma-Hajong issue in Arunachal Pradesh, which meant tracing its historical roots, discerning the legal nuances, and understanding the contemporary scenario. To bolster their investigative efforts, the Group resolved to establish a sub-committee, which would integrate senior representatives from the Ministry of Home Affairs, the Ministry of Law, and the Arunachal Pradesh State Government.

Yet, the momentum garnered by the High-Level Group and its subsequent sub-committee was undercut by the Supreme Court's verdict on the NHRC's Writ Petition, delivered on January 9, 1996. The apex court's judgement, comprising specific directives for the State Government, effectively overshadowed the Group's initiatives. The directives were as follows:

---

[164] *White Paper on Chakma-Hajong Refugee Issue, Govt. of Arunachal Pradesh, 1996*

(i) Restricting the displacement of Chakmas unless it adheres to the due legal processes.

(ii) Ensuring that intimidations from the All–Arunachal Pradesh Students' Union (AAPSU) are dealt with strictly in line with legal protocols.

(iii) Directing that all citizenship pleas from Chakmas be sent to the Central Government for review.

(iv) Preventing the removal of any Chakma while their citizenship petition is being evaluated.

(v) Recommending the State Government to seek the deployment of Central Forces in response to any organised efforts aimed at the forceful eviction of Chakmas.

Upon examining the 1996 White Paper concerning the Chakmas and Hajongs in Arunachal Pradesh, released by the State Government, a clear contention becomes apparent. The Arunachal Pradesh Government believes that the favourable rulings from the Supreme Court for the Chakmas and Hajongs were influenced by the Central Government. They highlighted an affidavit presented by the Central Government in the Supreme Court, suggesting it provided a skewed representation, indirectly bolstering the Chakma and Hajong stance at the potential detriment of the native tribal community. This sentiment of perceived bias was noted as a cause of dismay for the indigenous tribes, as articulated in the White Paper.

Within the White Paper, the State Government took efforts to countermand any legal statutes or international accords which seemed to advocate for the Chakmas and Hajongs' citizenship rights, dismissing them as extraneous. The document culminated by underscoring the pronounced divergence in viewpoints between the State and Central Governments concerning the Chakma and Hajong settlements and affiliated issues in Arunachal Pradesh.

The State Government contended that the settlement of the Chakmas and Hajongs was intended to be temporary, whereas the Central Government regarded it as permanent. Furthermore, the Central Government emphasised the interests of the Chakmas and Hajongs, while the State

Government stressed the interests of the Indigenous tribal population. These conflicting "interests" created a significant divide.

Furthermore, the State Government expressed reservations regarding the decision-making process of the Central Government and the North-East Frontier Agency (NEFA) in accommodating the Chakmas and Hajongs within NEFA. The Central Government believed that settling these communities would make beneficial use of areas that were previously uninhabited, thus spurring regional development. From a strategic perspective, leaving lands along the border vacant was seen as a vulnerability. Previous crises highlighted the need to address this concern. Hence, populating these empty border territories was perceived to bolster frontier security and amplify defence preparedness.

14

IMPACT OF SETTLEMENT OF CHAKMAS ON THE DEMOGRAPHIC PROFILE OF THE STATE

The debate surrounding the settlement of Chakmas and Hajongs in Arunachal Pradesh hinges on the perceived threat to the indigenous fabric of the region. Both the state government and AAPSU voice concerns about the exponential growth of these communities, fearing the erosion of Indigenous cultures and the unsettling prospect of locals becoming minorities in their own homeland.

Looking back to the period preceding the Central Government's decision to settle Chakmas and Hajongs to NEFA, historical documents reveal a conscientious approach by the government. Preserving the unique demographic tribal makeup was a top priority at that time.

In the selection process for their resettlement into NEFA, the tribal identity of the Chakmas stood as a pivotal criterion. Vishnu Sahay, the Governor of Assam, in an April 10, 1964, correspondence to the Chief Minister, suggested settling these communities in the Tirap Division of NEFA, highlighting the availability of unoccupied land. He emphasised, ***"These Chakmas would be quite suitable people to get into Tirap Division of NEFA where there is easily found vacant land in the area about which you and I have often spoken".***[165]

In the context of the migration influx from East Pakistan, the Seventy-First Report of the Estimates Committee (1964-65) within the Ministry of Rehabilitation shed light on a crucial aspect. It underscored the necessity to carefully structure the rehabilitation plans for migrant tribal families,

---

[165] *White Paper on Chakma and Hajong Refugee Issue, Govt. of Arunachal Pradesh, 1996*

particularly the Chakmas, emphasising the importance of preserving their unique identity and cultural heritage.

The report advocated for a strategic approach, suggesting that efforts be directed towards settling these communities in compact areas. This deliberate approach aimed to afford them the space and environment conducive to retaining their distinct identity and cultural practices amidst the new setting.

The underlying sentiment was to ensure that the resettlement was not merely about geographical relocation but about safeguarding the essence of the Chakmas' way of life. It echoed a conscientious effort to provide them with a supportive framework that would enable the preservation of their traditions and culture even in the face of significant transitions and upheavals caused by migration.[166]

In the strategic endeavour of settling individuals from diverse backgrounds into NEFA, authorities were keenly mindful of the delicate balance required to protect tribal sentiments, rights, and cultural heritage. This was not merely relocation but a conscientious effort to ensure harmony between incoming communities and the existing tribal fabric.

Outlined in a letter marked No. RR. 17/64, dated April 21, 1965, written by P.N. Luthra, the Adviser to the Governor of Assam, were precise directives for administrators and political officers engaged in these settlement initiatives. These directives aimed to steer the process in a manner that respected tribal customs and culture. Some key instructions were:

- **Sensitivity to Tribal Dynamics:** Emphasising the need for a nuanced understanding of tribal

[166] *Report of Estimates Committee (1964-65) Seventy-First Report (Third Lok Sabha) Ministry of Rehabilitation (Reception, Dispersal and Rehabilitation of new Migrants arriving in India from East Pakistan since 1st January 1964)*

dynamics, the directives stressed respecting established tribal sentiments.

- **Cultural Preservation:** Plans were to preserve Indigenous cultures, actively protecting and promoting tribal heritage within NEFA.
- **Respect for Rights:** Upholding tribal rights was non-negotiable, ensuring that new settlers would not encroach upon or undermine them.
- **Customs and Traditions:** Administrators were tasked with safeguarding the traditional customs and practices of tribal communities, ensuring settlement schemes respected their uniqueness.

These directives were not formalities but reflected a sincere commitment to honour tribal identities while integrating new communities into NEFA's fabric. They stood as guiding pillars for responsible execution, fostering harmonious cohabitation while respecting the diversity of cultures within the region.

(i) Land should be voluntarily given by the people to whom an emotional approach has to be made. Such an approach should be made by the Political Officer himself and should consult the leaders in the areas to ensure that our resettlement proposal does not lead to misplaced agitation or misunderstandings.

(ii) Land should as per as possible not belong to any one and this point should be fully cleared herein its utilisation for settlement. There are areas where full rights are not likely to be affected by settlement of people in NEFA.

(iii) Land may be given to the settlers on lease for which term has to be prescribed along with the performas to be signed by the settlers.

(iv) Where land is given by the people voluntarily there ought to be written agreement about it on either side.

(v) Wherever any compensation is needed, it should be duly paid to the villagers and necessary documents prepared.

(vi) Only that much land which may be adequate to consolidate an economic holding should be allotted to each family coming from outside NEFA. As a rule, the ceiling for allotment of land for each family of settlers should be put up to this administration for approval.

(vii) The ground survey must precede any attempts at settlement.

(viii) Bearing in view the above points, the Political Officers are requested to send concrete proposals showing the land available in their areas for settlement. The proposal should specify the location of land, the number of families which can be settled having regard to the cultivability of the area and availability of water for irrigation.

According to the guidelines, comprehensive ground surveys, consultations with tribal leaders, selection of settlement lands unclaimed by tribal communities, and ensuring no infringement on tribal rights were strictly followed before initiating Chakma Settlement schemes in NEFA.

The resettlement of the Chakmas and Hajongs in the Noa-Dihing valley (now Diyun and Deban area) aligned with the settlement policy and involved thorough discussions with local leaders of that era.

Following the Indo-China conflict in 1962, NEFA's architects perceived its population density of 11 persons per square mile and demographic vacuum as a threat to the nation's defence and security against hostile neighbours.

The Noa-Dihing Valley, formerly abundant in dense forests, featured a canopy so thick that sunlight could not penetrate to the ground.

The villages established in the Noa-Dihing Valley, now inhabited by Chakmas, Hajongs, Deoris, and Ahoms, once belonged solely to wild animals and flora. It was an untouched wilderness devoid of modern human development, teeming with wild elephants, deer herds, monkeys, tigers, bears, and other creatures at every turn.

Initially, the area now known as "Diyun," predominantly inhabited by Chakmas, had no such designation. The name "Diyun" evolved from "Dihing," the river which was also known as Diyun prior to the settlement of Chakmas and Hajongs in 1964.

1. Demographic Analysis: 1961-2011 (Chakma Inhabited Areas)

(a) 1961 Census: Demographic Snapshot Preceding Chakma Resettlement

The demographic overview of Chakma-inhabited regions based on the 1961 Census reveals a significant transformation in Changlang District. In the current-day subdivisions of Diyun, Bordumsa, Kharsang, and Miao, spanning approximately 2156 square kilometres,[167] the Chakma settlement altered the demographic landscape drastically.

Before the Chakma settlement, the Census of 1961 reported a mere 1118 individuals across these four subdivisions. Among them, Indigenous groups accounted for just 843 people, comprising Singpho (610), Tikhak (195), and Khamti (38), while non-indigenous inhabitants numbered 275, including Mura (191) and Kachari (84). The population density was strikingly below half a person per square mile, depicting these vast lands as virtually uninhabited, hosting only 214 families before the Chakma settlement in 1964.

---

[167] *https://villageinfo.in/arunachal-pradesh/changlang.html*

Undoubtedly, the resettlement of approximately 2435 Chakma and Hajong families, totaling around 12,500 individuals, across the present-day areas of Miao, Diyun, Bordumsa, Kharsang, and Deban, induced a dramatic demographic shift. However, this settlement initiative was a deliberate government policy aimed at fulfilling specific objectives. The selection of these areas for settlement was influenced by the notably low population density, aligning with the government's strategic goals.

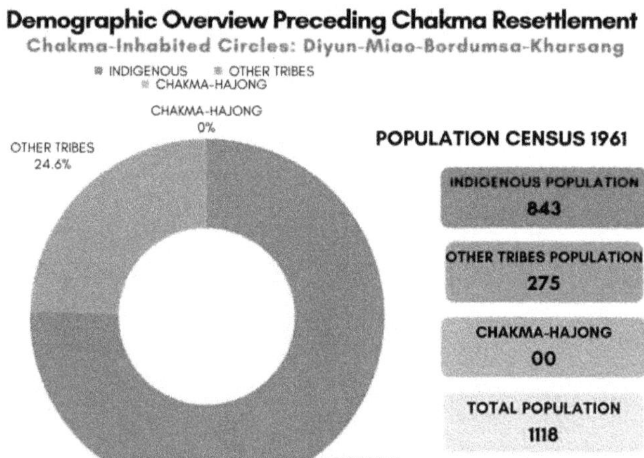

(b) 1971 Census: Demographic Overview Post Chakma Resettlement

According to the 1971 Census, these four sub-divisions had a combined population of 18,530 individuals, including 13883 Chakma and Hajongs, 2933 Indigenous people, and 1714 other tribes. Chakmas and Hajongs accounted for 74.9 percent of the population, Indigenous people were 15.8 percent, and other tribes' 9.2 percent.[168]

[168] *Census of India 1971, Series No. 24, Arunachal Pradesh, Part X, District Census Handbook Tirap District*

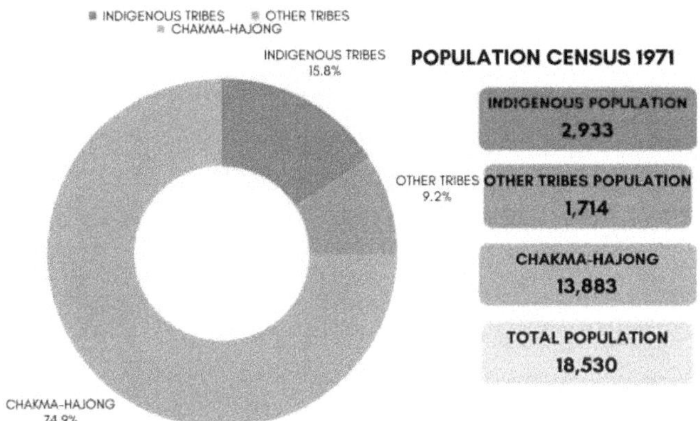

(c) 1981 Census: Demographic Overview

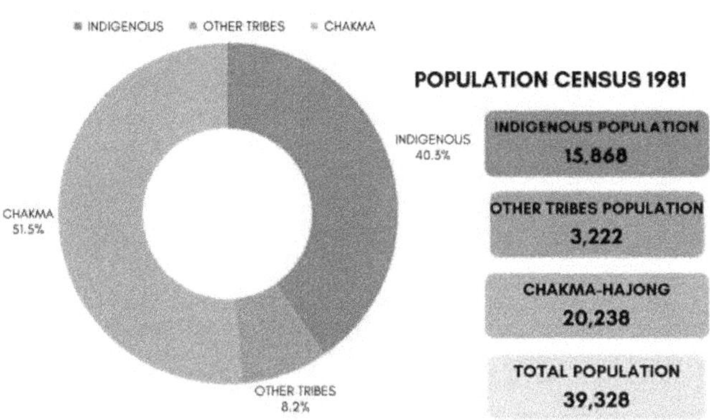

The percentage of Indigenous population made a rebound in the area as more Tangsas from the hilly areas of Changlang and Tirap settled in the Miao, Kharsang, Namphuk Forests and Bordumsa plains. This migration of

Tangsa and Nocte people from hilly areas to the plains was encouraged by the government for administrative reasons.

With this, the percentage of Indigenous population in the Chakma inhabited areas (Miao, Diyun, Bordumsa, Kharsang and Deban) increased from 15.8% in 1971 to 40.3 percent in 1981 and the population of Chakma and Hajong tribes declined from 74.9% in 1971 to 51.5 percent in 1981. The percentage of other tribes stayed at 8.2 percent. These four divisions had a total population of 39328 people of which Chakmas and Hajongs 20238, Indigenous 15868, and other tribes 3222. The Chakma and Hajong population was 11.2 percent higher than Indigenous population in the area.[169]

(d) 1991 Census: Demographic Overview

During this decade, the percentage of other tribes' population increased dramatically from 8.2 percent in 1981 to 22.9 percent in 1991, while Chakma and Hajong population share fell from 51.5 percent to 39.9 percent and Indigenous population share came down from 40.3 percent in 1981 to 37.2 percent in 1991.

According to the 1991 census, these four divisions had a total population of 63494 people: Chakmas and Hajongs 25348, Indigenous 23904, and other tribes 14242. Chakma and Hajong population was only 2.7 percent higher than Indigenous population which is only 1,444 persons more.[170]

---

[169] *Census of India 1981, Series No. 25, Arunachal Pradesh, Part xii A & B, District Census Handbook Tirap District*

[170] *Census of India 1991, Series - 3, Arunachal Pradesh, Part xii A & B, District Census Handbook Changlang District*

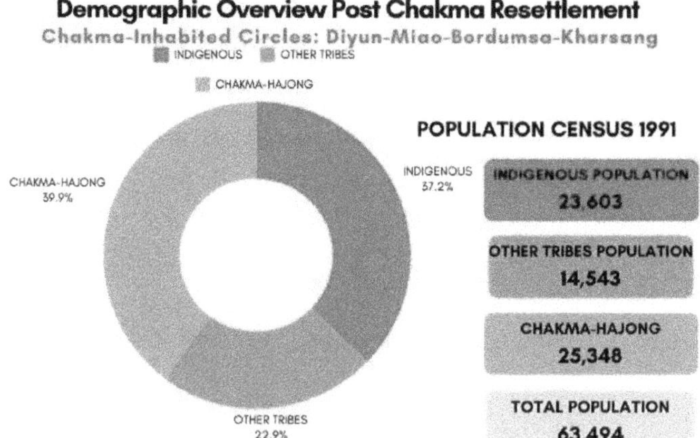

(e) 2001 Census: Demographic Overview

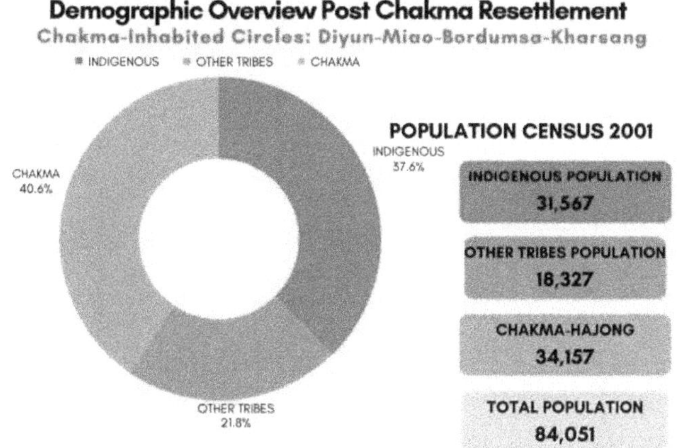

According to the census of 2001, the percentage of indigenous population in the area was 37.6 percent whereas the Chakma-Hajong population was 40.6 percent and the other tribes' share of the population was 21.8 percent.

The total population of these four subdivisions increased to 84,051 in 2001 from 63,494 in 1991. The Chakma and Hajong population was only 3 percent higher than Indigenous population which is only 2,590 persons.[171]

(f) 2011 Census: Demographic Overview Post Chakma Resettlement

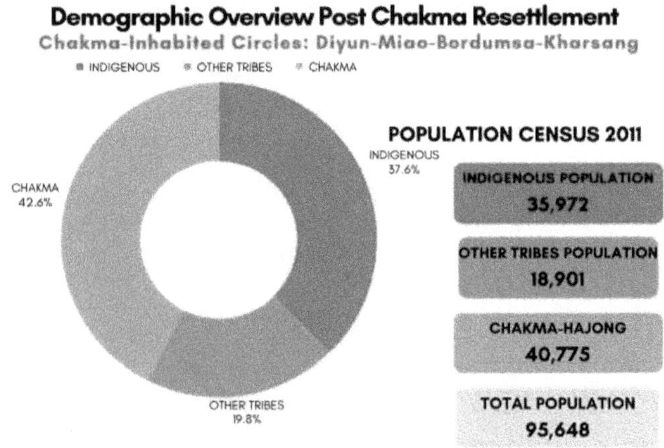

And as per 2011 census, the population of the whole area touched 95648, Chakmas and Hajongs' share was 40775 (42.6%), indigenous tribes' share was 35972 (37.6%) and other tribe's share was 18901 (19.8%)

The Chakma and Hajong population was now 5 percent higher than Indigenous population which is only 3,033 persons more.[172]

---

[171] *Census of India 2001, Series - 13, Arunachal Pradesh, Part A & B, District Census Handbook Changlang District*

[172] *Census of India 2011, Series - 13, Arunachal Pradesh, Part xii-A, District Census Handbook Changlang District*

2. Data Analysis (a) Census 1961 and (b) Census 1971 (Chakma Inhabited Areas)

Before Chakma Settlement (1961 Census):

- Total Population: 1118
- Total Area: 2156 square kilometres
- Population Density = 1118 / 2156 = 0.52 people per square kilometre
- Percentage of Indigenous Population = (843 / 1118) * 100 = 75.4%

After Chakma Settlement (1971 Census):

- Total Population: 18530
- Total Area: 2156 square kilometres
- Population Density = 18530 / 2156 = 8.59 people per square kilometre
- Percentage of Indigenous Population = (2933 / 18530) * 100 = 15.8%

Comparing the two sets of data, before the Chakma settlement, the population density was around 0.52 people per square kilometre, with approximately 75.4% of the population being indigenous tribes. After the settlement, the population density increased significantly to about 8.59 people per square kilometre, and the percentage of indigenous population decreased to approximately 15.8%.

3. Data Analysis (c) Census 1981 (d) 1991 (e) 2001 and (f) 2011 (Chakma Inhabited Areas)

1981 Census:

- Total Population: 39328
- Total Area: 2156 square kilometres
- Population Density = 39328 / 2156 =18.24 people per square kilometre

- Percentage of Indigenous Population = (15868 / 39328) * 100 = 40.34%

1991 Census:

- Total Population: 63494
- Total Area: 2156 square kilometres
- Population Density = 63494 / 2156 =29.44 people per square kilometre
- Percentage of Indigenous Population = (23603 / 63494) * 100 = 37.18%

2001 Census:

- Total Population: 84051
- Total Area: 2156 square kilometres
- Population Density = 84051 / 2156 = 38.98 people per square kilometre
- Percentage of Indigenous Population = (31567 / 84051) * 100 = 37.57%

2011 Census:

- Total Population: 95648
- Total Area: 2156 square kilometres
- Population Density = 95648 / 2156 = 44.36 people per square kilometre
- Percentage of Indigenous Population = (35972 / 95648) * 100 = 37.59%

4. Decadal Population Growth Rate and Compounded Annual Growth Rate (CAGR):

Let's calculate these rates for Indigenous Tribes and Chakma-Hajongs based on the provided data:

(a) Indigenous Tribes:

- Population in 1971: 2933
- Population in 1981: 15868
- Population in 1991: 23603
- Population in 2001: 31567
- Population in 2011: 35972

Decadal Growth Rates:

- Between 1971 and 1981: ((15868 - 2933) / 2933) * 100 = 441.74%
- Between 1981 and 1991: ((23603 - 15868) / 15868) * 100 = 48.70%
- Between 1991 and 2001: ((31567 - 23603) / 23603) * 100 = 33.80%
- Between 2001 and 2011: ((35972 - 31567) / 31567) * 100 = 13.96%

CAGR:

* Between 1971 and 2011: ((35972 / 2933) ^ (1/40)) - 1 = 10.57%

(b) Chakma-Hajongs:

- Population in 1971: 13883
- Population in 1981: 20238
- Population in 1991: 25348
- Population in 2001: 34157
- Population in 2011: 40775

Decadal Growth Rates:

- Between 1971 and 1981: ((20238 - 13883) / 13883) * 100 = 45.72%
- Between 1981 and 1991: ((25348 - 20238) / 20238) * 100 = 25.21%
- Between 1991 and 2001: ((34157 - 25348) / 25348) * 100 = 34.73%
- Between 2001 and 2011: ((40775 - 34157) / 34157) * 100 = 19.36%

CAGR:

Between 1971 and 2011: ((40775 / 13883) ^ (1/40)) - 1 = 7.88%

Indigenous Tribes: Decadal Population Growth Rate:

The Indigenous population exhibited varying growth rates over decades. Between 1971 and 1981, it experienced a remarkable growth of approximately 441.74%, indicating a rapid increase. Subsequent decades showed declining growth rates, with a shift from around 48.70% between 1981 and 1991 to about 13.96% between 2001 and 2011.

Compounded Annual Growth Rate (CAGR):

The overall compounded annual growth rate for Indigenous Tribes from 1971 to 2011 averaged around 10.57%, indicating a moderate growth trend despite fluctuations across decades.

Chakma-Hajongs: Decadal Population Growth Rate:

Chakma-Hajong population growth also fluctuated. The highest growth was witnessed between 1971 and 1981 at approximately 45.72%. Subsequently, the growth rates stabilised, hovering around 25-35% in the following decades, showing a gradual but moderated growth pattern.

Compounded Annual Growth Rate (CAGR):

The compounded annual growth rate for Chakma-Hajongs from 1971 to 2011 averaged around 7.88%, signifying a slower but sustained growth compared to the Indigenous population.

These growth rates indicate changing population dynamics for both Indigenous Tribes and Chakma-Hajongs over the decades, with the Indigenous population showing varying growth patterns while the Chakma-Hajong population exhibited a more consistent, albeit slower, growth trajectory.

5. Comparative Analysis: Chakma-Hajong Population in Changlang District - 2011 Census Snapshot

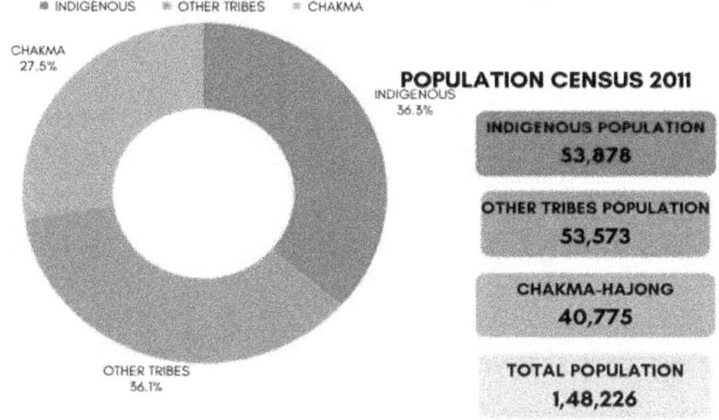

Comparative study of the total population of Changlang district as per 2011 census shows that the total population of the Indigenous people in the district has the highest percentage with 36.3 followed by other tribes at 36.1 percent and Chakma-Hajong population at 27.3 percent.

The population of the whole district was 148226, Chakmas and Hajongs' was 40775 (27.5%), indigenous tribes' was 53878 (36.3%) and other tribe's was 53573 (36.1%).[173]

Total Population in Changlang District - 2011 Census

- INDIGENOUS Tribes: 53,878 (36.30%)
- OTHERS: 53,573 (36.10%)
- CHAKMA-HAJONG: 40,775 (27.50%)

Observations:

- INDIGENOUS Tribes constitute the largest proportion at 36.30%.
- OTHERS represent a similar percentage, standing at 36.10%.

[173] *Census of India 2011, Series - 13, Arunachal Pradesh, Part xii-A, District Census Handbook Changlang District*

- CHAKMA-HAJONG accounts for 27.50% of the total population.

Insights:

- The Indigenous population and the category labelled as OTHERS are almost equal in numbers, each contributing around 36% to the total population.
- CHAKMA-HAJONG, while smaller in percentage compared to the other two segments, still represents a substantial population share, comprising over a quarter of the district's inhabitants.
- The data highlights a balanced distribution of population among these three segments within Changlang district.

6. Comparative Analysis: Chakma Population in Lohit District - 2011 Census Snapshot

In Lohit (now Namsai) District, the Chakma population was 4523 according to the 2011 census, constituting only 3.1% of the district's total population. In contrast, the Indigenous population numbered 47,410 (32.5%), while other tribes made up a significant 64.4% with 93,793 people. Thus, concerns about the exponential population growth of Chakmas affecting the district's demographic character are unfounded.[174]

---

[174] *Census of India 2011, Arunachal Pradesh Series-13 Part XII-A, District Census Handbook Lohit*

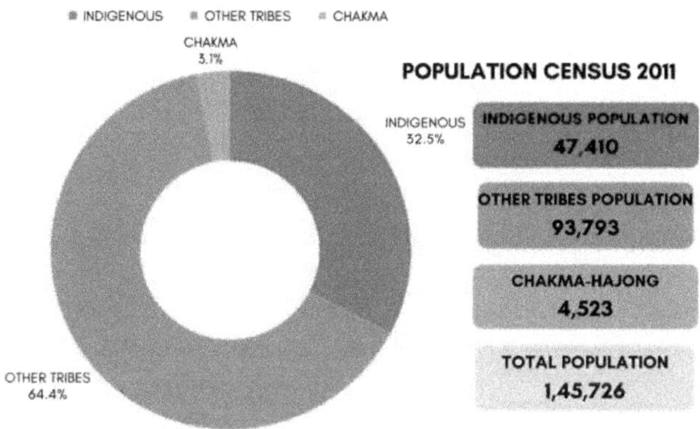

Total Population in Lohit District - 2011 Census

- INDIGENOUS Tribes: 47,410 (32.50%)
- OTHERS: 93,793 (64.40%)
- CHAKMA-HAJONG: 4,523 (3.10%)

Observations:

INDIGENOUS Tribes account for 32.50% of the total population.

OTHERS represent the majority, comprising 64.40%.

CHAKMA-HAJONG constitutes a smaller percentage, standing at 3.10%.

Insights:

- The Indigenous population constitutes a significant but minority portion, comprising around a third of the district's total inhabitants.
- The category labelled as OTHERS represents a substantial majority, constituting over half of the district's population.
- CHAKMA, while relatively smaller in percentage compared to the other segments, still contributes to the district's population, though it is the smallest among the three segments.

- The data signifies a considerable diversity in population composition within Lohit district, with the majority belonging to the category labelled as OTHERS, followed by the Indigenous population and CHAKMA-HAJONG forming a smaller proportion.

7. Comparative Analysis: Chakma Population in Papumpare District - 2011 Census Snapshot

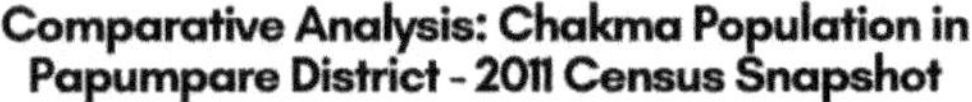

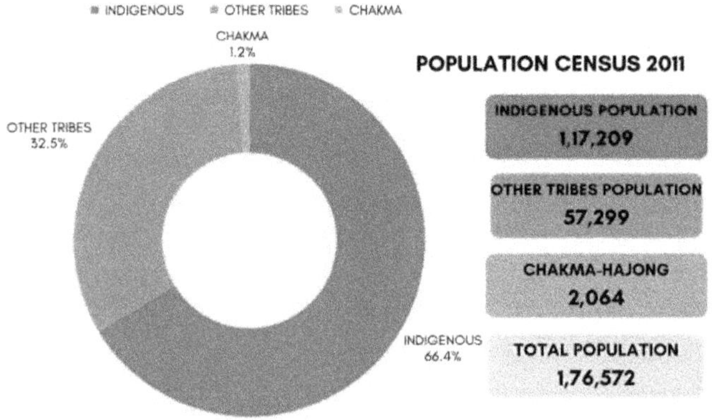

Given the negligible presence of the Chakma population in Papumpare district, concerns regarding exponential population growth and its influence on the demographic landscape are not significant. In Papumpare District, the Chakma community constitutes a mere 1.2%, accounting for just 2065 individuals. Comparatively, the Indigenous population stands at 117,209 (66.4%), while other tribal communities make up 57,299 (32.5%) of the district's populace. [175]

Total Population in Papumpare District - 2011 Census

[175] *Census of India 2011, Arunachal Pradesh Series-13 Part XII-A, District Census Handbook Papumpare*

- INDIGENOUS Tribes: 117,209 (66.40%)
- OTHERS: 57,299 (32.50%)
- CHAKMA-HAJONG: 2,064 (1.20%)

Observations:

INDIGENOUS Tribes constitute the largest proportion at 66.40%.

OTHERS represent a significant but smaller percentage, standing at 32.50%.

CHAKMA-HAJONG make up a smaller segment, comprising just 1.20% of the total population.

Insights:

- The Indigenous population significantly dominates the demographic landscape, constituting a substantial two-thirds of the district's total inhabitants.
- The category labelled as OTHERS, while not as prominent as the Indigenous population, still forms a significant minority, representing over a third of the population.
- CHAKMA-HAJONG, in contrast, accounts for a notably smaller portion, indicating a minimal presence compared to the Indigenous and OTHERS segments.
- The data showcases a clear majority of Indigenous population in Papumpare district, followed by a significant presence of OTHERS, and a very minimal representation of the CHAKMA-HAJONG community.

8. Dispelling the Myth of Chakma- Hajong Population Explosion in Arunachal Pradesh

One of the main arguments used against the Chakma and Hajong is the assumption that their population is rising exponentially in comparison to the indigenous population, and that this will alter the state's demographic character.

The Chakma Rights and Development Organisation (CRDO) team did thorough research to find out what is the truth based on government published reports, white papers and Census records.

As per official white paper published by the state government, a total of 2748 Chakma and Hajong families were finally rehabilitated in erstwhile NEFA, now Arunachal Pradesh by the Government of India under a definite plan of rehabilitation from the period 1964 to 1969 in Tirap (now, Changlang), Lohit (Namsai) and Subansiri (Papumpare) districts. Unlike the Tibetans who continue to remain as "honoured guests" and get Refugee benefits under the Tibetan Rehabilitation Policy (TRP) 2014, the Chakmas and Hajongs are living on their own in 46 proper villages across these 3 districts after their rehabilitation. They do not get any refugee benefits.

Based on the census survey data and the Chakma and Hajong population figures as recorded in the state government's published white paper, for the period from 1964 to 2011, the population has grown from 14,888 to 49,784 which is a net addition of 34,896 people during the said period. This translates to a growth of 234% in 47 years or 4.98% per year. Similarly, the first census done for NEFA was in 1961 and the population figures are available. For the 50-year period from 1961 to 2011 for Arunachal Pradesh, the population increased from 3.37 lakh to 13.84 lakh respectively. This translates to 311% growth for 50 years or 6.22% per year which is higher than that of Arunachal Chakma-Hajong rate of growth.

Population growth is non-linear and therefore using the same (1961-2011) data, the Compounded Annual Growth Rate (CAGR) for overall state population is 2.87% while for Chakma Hajong population from 1964 to 2011 during the 47-year period, it is 2.60% which is lower than the overall state population growth rate.

Now, in terms of the decadal growth rate for the most recent decade 2001 to 2011, for the overall state of Arunachal Pradesh, it is 26% while increase for Chakma and Hajong population, during the same decade stands at 17% which is significantly lower.

Finally, the Chakma Hajong population as a percentage of the overall Arunachal Pradesh population has declined from 4.3% in 1971 to 3.6% in 2011 which irrefutably allays the alleged fear of Chakmas-Hajong population explosion.[176]

Similar data is evident when conducting a comparative analysis in Arunachal Pradesh, showcasing comparable figures for the total population of Indigenous Tribes, Other Tribes, and the Chakma-Hajong community.

Total Population in Arunachal Pradesh - 2011 Census

- INDIGENOUS Tribes: 924,191 (66.80%)
- OTHERS: 410,917 (29.70%)
- CHAKMA-HAJONG: 48,619 (3.50%)

Observations:

INDIGENOUS Tribes constitute the largest proportion, accounting for 66.80% of the total population.

OTHERS represent a substantial but smaller share, making up 29.70%.

CHAKMA-HAJONG have a smaller presence, comprising 3.50% of the total population.

Insights:

- The Indigenous population significantly dominates Arunachal Pradesh's demographic landscape, constituting a substantial two-thirds of the state's total inhabitants.
- The category labelled as OTHERS, while considerable, remains a minority compared to the Indigenous population, representing almost a third of the population.
- CHAKMA-HAJONG, in contrast, forms a notably smaller segment, indicating a minimal presence in comparison to the Indigenous and OTHER segments.
- The data underscores the substantial majority of Indigenous population in Arunachal Pradesh, followed by a significant minority labelled as

[176] *https://crdo.chakma.in/issues/state-policy/2020/dispelling-the-myth-of-chakma-hajong-population-explosion-in-ap/*

OTHERS, and a very minor representation of the CHAKMA-HAJONG community.

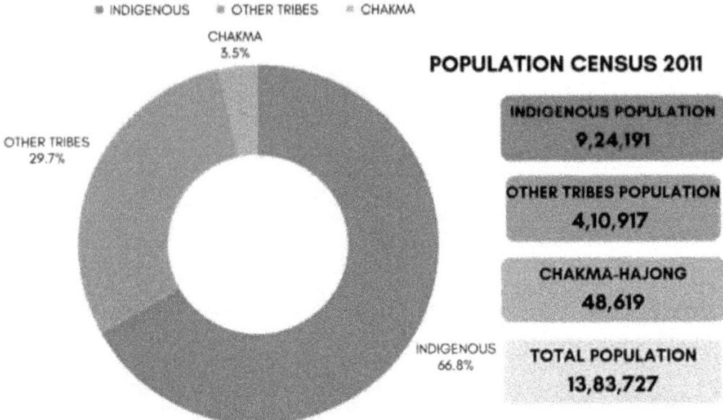

15

THE STATE'S POLICY OF NON - RECOGNITION OF CHAKMAS AS CITIZENS

Today, the Chakma and Hajong communities in Arunachal Pradesh find themselves in a unique and challenging position. While approximately 90% of them are legally Indian citizens by birth under Section 3 of the Citizenship Act of 1955, their experience at the hands of the State Government tells a different tale. This dichotomy sees a legal framework endorsing their citizenship on one end, contrasted starkly with a state policy that vacillates between hesitant acknowledgment and outright denial.

Nevertheless, the State Government persists in its refusal to acknowledge their rightful citizenship status. Alarmingly, this denial of recognition to the descendants of the original Chakma migrants born in Arunachal Pradesh post-1964 seems to be the state's enduring policy.

It is important to add nuance to this argument. Suggesting that the Chakmas and Hajongs are universally treated as non-citizens, foreigners, or refugees by the state is an oversimplification. 9,401 Chakmas and Hajongs participated in the electoral process in 2024, casting votes in both state assembly and parliamentary elections. This number was 1,947 in 2004 when they first voted.

Additionally, numerous central government schemes – a privilege not extended to refugees in the country are extended to the Chakmas and Hajongs. The challenge arises when discussing their access to state-sponsored schemes and specific central government programs. While Chakmas benefit from a number of schemes sponsored by the central government, they are conspicuously sidelined when it comes to state-sponsored schemes and some of the central government schemes as well.

A consistent pattern emerges where the Chakmas face exclusion, especially when central government welfare schemes are rolled out via the Panchayati Raj Institutions (PRIs). Given that these PRIs are closely tethered to the data infrastructure and operational protocols of their state counterparts, the gap in benefit allocation becomes more evident. This trend suggests that the structural and functional dynamics of these local governance bodies might be fostering a systemic bias against the Chakmas.

This mixed policy approach from the state provides a limited set of rights and benefits to the Chakmas, preventing a narrative of absolute deprivation. It brings forth a conundrum: On one hand, there is a legal mandate that supports their citizenship, while on the other, a persistent state policy that selectively recognizes their rights.

The state's treatment of the Chakmas and Hajongs reflects a complex duality: a policy of 'Outright Non-Recognition as Citizens' contrasted with a 'Selective Recognition Policy.' The former cruelly denies them all rights, while the latter, though providing some privileges, fails to grant full acknowledgment of their legal status and citizenship. This ambivalent stance perpetuates a troubling limbo for these communities, where they grapple with restricted privileges amid enduring challenges, caught in a perpetual struggle for their rightful place within the legal and social framework.

Upon closer evaluation, it becomes evident that the non-recognition policy plays a more dominant role in shaping the Chakmas' lived experiences.

1. Impact of State's Non-Recognition and Selective Recognition policy Policy Towards Chakmas

The State's non-recognition and selective recognition policy of the Chakma-Hajong communities in Arunachal Pradesh as citizens by the state government has had several profound impacts on these communities including denial of basic rights. Without official recognition, they are systematically excluded from the matrix of civil, political, and socio-economic rights.

(a) Legal Recognition: While the vast majority (over 90%) of the Chakma and Hajong populations are born citizens, their recognition as such by the Arunachal Pradesh state government remains elusive. Due to this lack of legal recognition as citizens by the state government, the Chakma and Hajong communities in Arunachal Pradesh grapple with a significant challenge.This absence of official recognition creates a myriad of obstacles, denying them access to basic rights and privileges inherently associated with citizenship.

The repercussions of this non-recognition are profound. Without formal recognition of their status as citizens, these communities face severe limitations in exercising their rights. They encounter barriers in owning property, participating in democratic processes, accessing government services and various schemes, and enjoying the full spectrum of civil liberties available to recognized citizens. This systemic exclusion perpetuates a cycle of disparity and marginalisation, deeply ingrained within the fabric of society.

The implications are far-reaching, impacting fundamental aspects of civic life. It restricts their ability to engage fully in democratic processes, leaving them sidelined from decision-making that affects their lives. Moreover, the inability to own property undermines their economic stability and hampers their prospects for socio-economic advancement.

The perpetual limbo caused by this lack of recognition perpetuates a sense of alienation within their own homeland. It breeds a feeling of disconnection and marginalisation, creating barriers to their integration within broader society. This persistent state of uncertainty and exclusion hinders community development, stifles opportunities for growth, and perpetuates a cycle of socio-economic disadvantage.

Recognizing their citizenship is not just about legal documentation; it's about affirming their place in society, empowering them to participate fully, and fostering inclusivity within the diverse fabric of Arunachal Pradesh.

(b) Access to Identity and Domicile Documentation: Access to crucial identity and domicile documents remains a formidable challenge for the Chakma and Hajong communities in Arunachal Pradesh, significantly impacting their eligibility for various entitlements and schemes in the state. Their struggle to obtain official documents like birth certificates, trade licences, residential proof certificates, passports, and land documents creates barriers that hinder their access to essential services, employment and educational opportunities and rights.

The absence of these fundamental identity documents exacerbates their situation. The denial of domicile documentation, such as residence certificates, further complicates matters, rendering them ineligible for employment opportunities in central services. Moreover, the imposition of a blanket ban on state service employment adds to their limited options for career prospects.

This chronic lack of access to identity and domicile documents has a cascading effect, rendering many of them ineligible for inclusion in the electoral roll and excluding them from accessing a plethora of schemes spanning financing, skill development, education, sports, agriculture, rural self-employment, and healthcare. This deprivation amplifies their social, economic, and political exclusion, intensifying their struggle for recognition and access to basic rights.

The denial of these foundational documents serves as the root cause of various interconnected deprivations faced by the Chakma and Hajong communities. It acts as a barrier to their integration within the societal framework, perpetuating a cycle of marginalisation and limiting their opportunities for progress and inclusion in various spheres of life. Addressing this issue necessitates urgent reforms to ensure equitable access to essential documentation, fostering the integration and empowerment of these communities within the state.

(c) Political Marginalisation: The Chakma-Hajong communities grapple with political marginalisation as a direct consequence of not being recognized legally by the state government, which in turn results in the disenfranchisement of a substantial portion of their population. While a portion—approximately 9,401 individuals—have been included in Arunachal Pradesh's voter lists, acknowledging their status as citizens, a significant number remain unable to exercise their voting rights.

Annually, thousands of Chakma and Hajong residents come of age and seek to register to vote, only to face rejections often based on tenuous reasons. Despite this, there is a silver lining as a steady number, particularly youth between the ages of 18 to 25, manage to secure their spot on the electoral roll.

Observing the voter trends in the 49 Bordumsa-Diyun Assembly Constituency reveals a promising increase in voter registration among these communities, indicating a gradual move towards greater inclusion:

- In 2004, the number of Chakma and Hajong voters was recorded at 1,168.
- This number saw a slight decrease in 2009, coming down to 1,089.

- The 2014 elections marked an increase, with 1,381 voters registered.
- A significant surge was seen in 2019 with the number climbing to 3,305.
- Continuing this upward trend, 2024 witnessed a registration of 6,396 voters.

Summary of Voter Increment Percentages (after every 5 years):

- From 2004 to 2009: There was a decrease of about 6.76%.
- From 2009 to 2014: There was an increase of about 26.81%.
- From 2014 to 2019: There was a significant increase of about 139.32%.
- From 2019 to 2024: There was an increase of about 93.6%.

Annual Average of Voter Increment:

Annual Increment 2004 to 2009 = -15.8 (Voters)

Annual Increment 2009 to 2014 = 58.4 (Voters)

Annual Increment 2014 to 2019 = 384.8 (Voters)

Annual Increment 2019 to 2024 = 618.2 (Voters)

This data indicates that, despite a slight initial decrease in voter numbers between 2004 and 2009, there has been a notable overall upward trend in voter registration among the Chakma and Hajong communities, with a particularly significant leap observed between 2014 and 2019.

The Disparity in Electoral Inclusion: In the realm of electoral dynamics, a disconcerting incongruity persists, notably in the context of the Chakma and Hajong communities. It is imperative to underscore that despite a substantial demographic of over 25 thousand eligible

Chakma and Hajong voters, the stark reality reveals a rather dismal scenario. Annually, a commendable 5000 individuals from these communities seek inclusion in the electoral roll, signalling a robust democratic engagement. However, the disheartening truth remains that, as of today, a mere fraction of that number, specifically 5000, has been successfully incorporated into the electoral roll.

This glaring discrepancy cannot be divorced from the pernicious influence of the State's Non-Recognition Policy towards the Chakma community. The contours of this policy cast a long shadow over the democratic aspirations of a sizable portion of the population. It operates as a formidable barrier, impeding the seamless integration of Chakma and Hajong individuals into the electoral process.

The deleterious effects of the Non-Recognition Policy are multifaceted. Firstly, it acts as a deterrent to the rightful inclusion of eligible voters, creating a disheartening dissonance between the aspirations of the Chakma and Hajong communities and the practicalities of electoral representation. Secondly, the policy engenders a sense of disenfranchisement, where the civic participation of a sizable demographic is stifled, undermining the very essence of a participatory democracy.

Moreover, the underrepresentation of Chakma and Hajong voters in the electoral roll not only skews the political landscape but also perpetuates a cycle of marginalisation. It perpetuates a narrative where certain communities are systematically excluded from the democratic process, fostering an environment where their concerns and perspectives remain sidelined.

(d) Systematic Exclusion of Chakmas and Hajongs from Panchayati Raj System: In Arunachal Pradesh, the Chakmas and Hajongs find themselves in the grip of a disconcerting exclusionary narrative, particularly concerning the Panchayati Raj Institution (PRI) – a cornerstone of rural self-governance in India. This exclusion not only denies them a voice in local affairs but also severs their ties to crucial processes of economic development and social justice.

The deliberate exclusion of Chakmas and Hajongs from the electoral rolls of Panchayati Raj has far-reaching implications. The very essence of democratic governance, epitomised by PRI, hinges on the direct participation of local populations in electing representatives who shape the trajectory of local development. However, the systemic omission of these communities from this democratic process effectively disenfranchises them, leaving them bereft of a say in decisions that significantly impact their lives.

As PRI assumes the responsibility of formulating plans for economic development and social justice at various levels, the exclusion of Chakmas and Hajongs reverberates in the denial of these communities from the fruits of such endeavours. The result is a stark absence of their perspectives and needs in the blueprints for progress, perpetuating a cycle of marginalisation.

Furthermore, the exclusion has broader implications, extending to the jurisdiction of the District Planning Committee. Chakma-Hajong areas find themselves sidelined from the consolidation of plans prepared by Panchayats, hindering their access to budgetary allocations, revenue shares, and grants from state and central governments. This omission creates a palpable void in the distribution of resources essential for fostering development and addressing pressing issues in these communities.

The ramifications of this exclusion are acutely felt in the sphere of village-level governance. Panchayati Raj, with its village local government structures, plays a pivotal role in the development of rural areas, encompassing crucial aspects like primary education, healthcare, agriculture, and women and child welfare. The sidelining of Chakmas and Hajongs not only deprives them of these developmental initiatives but also stifles their participation in shaping the future of their communities.

(e) Exclusion from Food Security: Food security is a fundamental aspect of a community's well-being, ensuring access to adequate and nutritious food for all individuals. In the context of the Chakma and Hajong communities in Arunachal Pradesh, the National Food Security Act's Ration Cards hold immense potential to uplift the marginalised sections by providing essential food items through the Public Distribution System (PDS).

However, the exclusion of Chakmas from the PDS system significantly impacts their access to this crucial support mechanism. Without inclusion in the PDS, these communities are deprived of the benefits offered by the National Food Security Act. This exclusion exacerbates their vulnerability, hindering their ability to secure essential food supplies and undermining their food security.

The absence of access to subsidised food grains and essential commodities through the PDS not only affects the nutritional needs of these communities but also deepens socio-economic disparities. It perpetuates a cycle of deprivation, amplifying the challenges faced by already marginalised populations.

The denial of Ration Cards under the National Food Security Act to the Chakma community represents a systemic failure in ensuring equitable access to basic necessities. It highlights the urgent need for inclusive policies that encompass all sections of society, irrespective of ethnicity or background.

(f) Exclusion from Scholarship: Accessing scholarships presents a persistent challenge for students hailing from the Chakma-Hajong communities, who encounter barriers in tapping into crucial educational opportunities offered by schemes like the Pre-Matric Scholarships Scheme for Minorities, Post-Matric Scholarships Scheme for Minorities, and the Merit Cum Means Scholarship for Professional and Technical Courses.

Despite these scholarships being a Central Sector Scheme with full funding provided by the Ministry of Minority Affairs, the roadblocks arise when students from these communities apply through the online portal of the ministry. Unfortunately, their applications face rejection at the state government's authorization level, which oversees the implementation of the scheme.

This discrepancy between the central scheme's intentions and the state administration's implementation creates a significant hurdle for deserving students. The rejection of their applications stifles their access to crucial financial aid meant to support their educational pursuits. This denial not only undermines the students' aspirations for higher education but also perpetuates a cycle of limited opportunities for these minority communities.

The extent of deprivation and discrimination can be seen in the following incident. In 2021, local MLA Somlung Mossang aimed to support two meritorious Chakma students, along with others from the constituency, using MLALAD funds through the district administration. As a result, Deputy Commissioner Mr. Devansh Yadav issued a notification (No. C/DPU/MLALADS/SCHOLARSHIP/BSA/20-21) on August 20, 2021. However, under pressure from the All Changlang District Students' Union (ACDSU), an affiliate of AAPSU, the scholarships for these deserving Chakma students were unjustly cancelled. This discriminatory act further highlights the systemic victimisation faced by the Chakma community.[177]

The situation highlights a crucial disconnect between the central scheme's objectives and the local execution, depriving students from marginalised communities of the intended benefits.

(g) Exclusion from Healthcare Schemes: Accessing public healthcare schemes remains a formidable challenge

[177] *https://arunachaltimes.in/index.php/2021/08/25/union-against-scholarship-to-chakma-students/*

for the Chakma and Hajong communities due to their lack of recognition as citizens by the state government, which bars them from easily accessing crucial government healthcare benefits essential for their well-being.

The Pradhan Mantri Jan Arogya Yojana (AB PM-JAY) and Chief Minister Arogya Arunachal Yojana (CMAAY), initiated by the Central and State Governments respectively, aim to provide quality and cashless healthcare. This vision endeavours to achieve Universal Health Care for all by 2030. However, despite these noble objectives, the Chakma and Hajong communities find themselves excluded from these flagship health care programs.

The exclusion stems from their ineligibility due to lacking the necessary documentation, which is not provided by the state administration. Essential documents like residential certificates, which render individuals eligible for these schemes, are not issued to the Chakma and Hajong communities by the local administration, rendering them unable to access the benefits.

This exclusion denies these marginalised communities their rightful access to essential healthcare services, perpetuating disparities and neglecting their fundamental health needs. The inability to obtain necessary documentation due to bureaucratic hurdles exacerbates their vulnerability and perpetuates a cycle of systemic neglect within the healthcare system.

(h) Exclusion from Schemes implemented through PRI and State Government and lack of documentation: The Government of India administers numerous social welfare programs spanning diverse sectors to cater to the needs of various demographic segments. These initiatives encompass domains like education, healthcare, employment, poverty alleviation, women's empowerment, rural development, and more.

While Chakmas do receive certain benefits from various schemes, particularly those sponsored by the central government, a discernible trend emerges in the unequal distribution of welfare advantages. Notably, there is a distinct pattern whereby Chakmas are excluded from accessing many social welfare schemes.

The discrepancy in the allocation of benefits becomes apparent when examining the specific sets of social welfare schemes that Chakmas are denied access to. This denial is particularly pronounced in the case of schemes that are closely aligned with the data and operational framework of the Panchayati Raj Institutions of the state. This suggests a systemic bias that could potentially stem from the structure and functioning of these local governance bodies.

The intricate connection between the denial of access to social welfare schemes and the utilisation of Panchayati Raj data hints at a complex interplay of factors. The data-driven nature of these schemes implies that Chakmas are excluded due to a lack of representation or recognition within the local governance structures. This exclusion further underscores the broader challenges faced by the Chakma community in fully integrating into the decision-making processes and benefit allocation mechanisms at the grassroots level.

This is a compilation of significant central schemes that are implemented by the PRI and State Government, systematically excluding the Chakma and Hajong communities from their benefits:

Sl.	Schemes	Lead Ministry	Sector
1	Mahatma Gandhi National Rural Employment Guarantee Act	MoRD	Rural Wage Employment
2	PM Awas Yojana-(Gramin)	MoRD	Rural Housing

3	PM Fasal Bima Yojana	Ministry of Agriculture and Farmers Welfare	Multiple Agriculture
4	PM Jan Vikas Karyakaram	MoMA	Development
5	PM Kaushal Vikas Yojana	MoSD&E	Skill Development
6	PM Kisan Samman Nidhi	MoF	Agriculture
7	PM Kisan Urja Suraksha Evam Utthan Mahabhiyan	MoNRE	Agriculture
8	Rashtriya Gram Swaraj Abhiyan	MoPR	Rural development
9	Svamitva Yojana	MoPR	Rural development
10	Pre-Matric Scholarships Scheme for Minorities	MoMA	Education
11	Post Matric Scholarships Scheme for Minorities	MoMA	Education
12	Merit Cum Means Scholarship for Professional and Technical Courses	MoMA	Education

13	Agnipath Scheme	Ministry of Defence	Defense
14	Antyodaya Anna Yojana	MoCAFPD	Hunger
15	Ayushman Bharat Yojana (AB PM-JAY	MoHFW	Health
16	Deendayal Antyodaya Yojana	MoRD	Skill Development
17	Deendayal Upadhyaya Grameen Kaushalya Yojana (DDU-GKY)	MoRD	Skill Development
18	Eklavya Model Residential School	MoTA	Education
19	Kasturba Gandhi Balika Vidyalaya	MoHRD	Education
20	Khelo India	MoYAS	Sports
21	National Social Assistance Scheme	MoRD	Pension
22	PM Fasal Bima Yojana	Multiple	Agriculture
23	PM Mudra Yojana	MoF	Financing

The following compilation includes significant state government schemes that specifically exclude the Chakma and Hajong communities:

Sl.	Schemes	Lead Department	Sector
1	Arunachal Pradesh UPSC Combined Civil Services Coaching Scheme	Dept. of Higher & Technical Education	Education
2	Arunachal Pradesh State Stipend Scheme	Dept. of Higher & Technical Education	Education
3	Chief Minister Arogya Arunachal Yojna	Department of Health and Family Welfare	Health
4	Arunachal Pradesh Chief Minister Yuva Kaushal Yojna	Department of Health and Family Welfare	Dept. of Skill Development & Entrepreneurship
5	Arunachal Pradesh Chief Minister Krishi Rinn Yojna	Department of Agriculture	Agriculture
6	Arunachal Pradesh Chief Minister Shasakt Kisan Yojna	Department of Agriculture	Agriculture
7	Arunachal Pradesh Chief Minister Vidya Scheme	Department of School Education	Education

8	Arunachal Pradesh Deen Dayal Upadhyaya Swavalamban Yojana	Department of Finance, Planning and Investment	Entrepreneurial
9	Arunachal Pradesh Chief Minister's White Revolution Scheme	Dept. of Animal Husbandry, Veterinary & Dairy Development	Animal Husbandry, Veterinary & Dairy
10	Arunachal Pradesh Chief Minister Krishi Samuh Yojana	Department of Agriculture	Agriculture
11	Arunachal Pradesh Chief Minister Agriculture Mechanisation Scheme	Department of Agriculture	Agriculture
12	Arunachal Pradesh Chief Minister Free Cancer Chemotherapy Scheme	Department of Health and Family Welfare	Health
13	Arunachal Pradesh Atma Nirbhar Bagwani Yojana	Department of Horticulture	Horticulture

14	Arunachal Pradesh Atma Nirbhar Krishi Yojana	Department of Agriculture	Agriculture
15	Arunachal Pradesh Atma Nirbhar Plantation Yojana	Department of Agriculture	Agriculture
16	Arunachal Pradesh Atma Nirbhar Pashu Palan Yojana	Dept. of Animal Husbandry, Veterinary & Dairy Development.	Agriculture
17	Arunachal Pradesh Atma Nirbhar Matsya Palan Yojana	Department of Fisheries	Fisheries
18	Deen Dayal Upadhyaya Bunkar Yojana	Dept. of Textile & Handicraft	Employment
19	Deen Dayal Swavalamban Yojana	Dept. of Finance, Planning & Investment	Entrepreneurship

(i) Limited Economic Opportunities: The economic prospects for Chakmas and Hajongs in the state are notably restricted, severely limiting their ability to engage in business operations and access various economic opportunities. This constraint creates a cycle wherein poverty becomes entrenched, perpetuating a reliance on limited resources and opportunities.

Setting up a business or launching entrepreneurial ventures necessitates obtaining necessary documentation and approvals from relevant departments. However, the accessibility of such essential documentation from the administration remains a rarity for the Chakma community. This lack of access to required paperwork poses significant challenges, hindering their ability to initiate businesses and engage in economic activities. Consequently, this becomes a fundamental factor contributing to their socio-economic disadvantage within the region.

This lack of access to essential documentation and streamlining of administrative processes is pivotal in depriving the Chakma and Hajong communities from participating more actively in economic endeavours. Unable to facilitate easier access to necessary paperwork and approvals, these communities cannot overcome barriers, fostering entrepreneurship and broader economic engagement. This, in turn, fosters the cycle of dependence, offering no avenues for self-sustainability and economic growth within these communities leading to socio economic backwardness.

(j) Withdrawal of Residence Certificates & Deprivation of Employment in Government Services: The employment scenario for the Chakma and Hajong communities in government services has been marred by systematic exclusion. A state policy dating back to September 29, 1980 (Order No. Pol-21/81) from the State Government officially barred their employment in state government services, closing off any opportunities and access to such employment prospects entirely. While there was a window available for employment in Central Services for the Chakmas and Hajongs, it was contingent upon obtaining a basic domicile certificate in the form of a Residence Certificate (RC). This RC was pivotal, rendering them eligible for employment not just in government services but also in defence and other sectors.

However, in a recent development, a notification dated November 4, 2022 (No. POL/CH-2/2022-23/100) issued by Shri Rajeev Takuk, Joint Secretary (Political), Government of Arunachal Pradesh, brought a seismic shift. This notification revoked all Residence Proof Certificates (RPCs) previously issued to the Chakma and Hajong people residing in Changlang District, Arunachal Pradesh. Subsequently, on November 14, 2022, the Residence Certificates issued to these communities were officially cancelled through an order (No. CHG/JS/GUARD-01/2022) by the Deputy Commissioner of Changlang District.

This revocation of essential documentation has dealt a severe blow to the employment prospects of the Chakma and Hajong communities. It further exacerbates their exclusion from not only state government services but also from opportunitics in various other sectors. Such policy shifts disrupt the socio-economic fabric of these communities, closing off avenues for employment and progress, and intensifying their struggles for integration and livelihood opportunities within the state.

The critical withdrawal of essential documentation unfolded in response to the AAPSU's demand from the State Government on July 18, 2022, urging the cancellation of Residence Proof Certificates (RPC) issued to the Chakmas and Hajongs within a 15-day span. This call precipitated a consequential high-level meeting on July 29, 2022, convened in the CS Conference Hall, chaired by Mr. Kaling Tayeng, IAS, Commissioner (Political), specifically addressing the RPC issue.

During this meeting, a pivotal decision emerged to form a committee tasked with investigating the Residential Proof Certificate matter in Changlang District. Simultaneously, a directive was issued for the immediate suspension of the RC. Consequently, on July 31, 2023, the Commissioner (Political) took a definitive step by suspending the issuance of new RPCs to the Chakmas and Hajongs through order No. POL/CH-2/2022-23.

Impact of Cancellation of Residence Certificate: This action proved to be a decisive blow for the prospects of Chakmas and Hajongs seeking employment in central services. The withdrawal of these crucial certificates severely curtailed their eligibility, effectively closing off avenues for employment in central services, further exacerbating their struggle for inclusion and livelihood opportunities.

The abrupt revocation of Residence Certificates for the Chakmas and Hajongs resulted in their immediate disqualification from seeking employment in coveted central services, notably including within the Indian Army, Central Armed Police Forces (CAPF), and other defence establishments. This sudden policy change dealt a severe blow to their aspirations for crucial roles in national defence and security sectors, significantly limiting their career opportunities and aspirations in these esteemed services.

The cancellation of Residence Certificates, beyond impacting government employment prospects, has had far-reaching implications across crucial spheres:

- **Education:** These certificates serve as prerequisites for admission to educational institutions and are vital for accessing specific educational schemes and scholarships, severely limiting educational opportunities for the affected individuals.
- **Access to Government Services:** The revocation has hindered access to a myriad of government services, welfare programs, and subsidies intended for residents, further exacerbating the exclusion of these communities from essential services.

- **Legal Standing:** Residence Certificates function as evidence of residency in legal matters, property transactions, and are essential for acquiring licences and permits. Their cancellation disrupts legal proceedings and essential transactions for these individuals.

- **Government Benefits:** The loss of these certificates impedes access to various social welfare schemes, healthcare benefits, and government programs, depriving the affected individuals of critical support designed for residents.

The importance of Residence Certificates extends beyond employment—they play a pivotal role in accessing education, services, legal entitlements, and essential benefits, serving as a cornerstone in facilitating access to a broad spectrum of governmental and social provisions.

2. The selective recognition policy policy towards Chakmas

The ongoing plight of the Chakma and Hajong communities represents a complex interplay between national citizenship laws and local political resistance in Arunachal Pradesh. When examining the state's approach towards the Chakma community, two distinct policies emerge: the non-recognition policy and the selective recognition policy. The non-recognition policy represents a blanket refusal by the state to acknowledge the rightful citizenship status of the Chakmas, whereas the selective recognition policy hints at a more conditional, sporadic acknowledgment of their status, often driven by specific circumstances or necessities.

The extension of various central and state government schemes to the Chakmas and Hajongs marks a significant acknowledgment of their status as recognized citizens within the system. These schemes, typically inaccessible to refugees, illegal migrants, or foreigners, signify a recognition of the Chakma and Hajong communities' legitimate presence as integral members of the nation.

By being eligible for these schemes, the Chakmas and Hajongs are accorded a distinct recognition that sets them apart from individuals falling under the category of refugees, illegal migrants, or foreigners. This acknowledgment underscores their lawful residency and inclusion within the country's citizenry, allowing them access to governmental benefits and initiatives designed for Indian citizens.

The provision of these benefits acknowledges the Chakma and Hajong communities' rightful place as legitimate residents and citizens, granting them access to essential resources and opportunities meant for Indian citizens. It also reflects a step towards their integration into the socio-economic fabric of the nation, distinguishing their status from other categories of individuals within the broader context of citizenship and residency.

Here is a compilation of important central schemes that offer benefits to the Chakmas and Hajongs residing in Arunachal Pradesh.

Sl. No.	Schemes	Lead Ministry	Sector
1	PM-POSHAN	MoWCD	Health, Education
2	Samagra Shiksha Abhiyan	MoE	Education
3	Jal Jeevan Mission	MoJS	Rural Development
4	PM Shram Yogi Mandhan	MoLE	Financial security
5	PM Matritva Vandana Yojana	MoWCD	Mother Care
6	PM Ujjwala Yojana	MoP&NG	Energy, Health, Poverty
7	PM Mudra Yojana	MoF	Financing
8	Digital India	MeitY, MoF	IT

9	Sukanya Samridhi Yojana	MoWCD	Girl child
10	Deendayal Upadhyaya Gram Jyoti Yojana	MoP	Rural Electrification
11	PM Jan Dhan Yojana	MoF	Financial inclusion
12	Janani Suraksha Yojana	MoHFW	Mother Care
13	National Health Mission	MoHFW	Health
14	PM Gram Sadak Yojana	MoRD	Rural Development
15	Integrated Child Development Services	MoWCD	Child, Mother care
16	Pradhan Mantri Garib Kalyan Anna Yojana	Ministry of Consumer Affairs & Food and Public Distribution	Food Security
17	Saubhagya-Pradhan Mantri Sahaj Bijli Har Ghar Yojana	Ministry of Power	Rural Electrification
18	NERCORMP	Ministry of DoNER	Livelihood, Rural Development

Here is a compilation of important state schemes that offer benefits to the Chakmas and Hajongs residing in Arunachal Pradesh.

Sl. No.	Schemes	Lead Dept.	Sector
1	Arunachal Pradesh Girl Students Health & Hygiene Scheme	Department of Education	Girl Child
2	Arunachal Pradesh Chief Minister Vidya Scheme	Department of Education	Girl's Education
3	Arunachal Pradesh Dulari Kanya Scheme	Department of Health and Family Welfare	Girl Child
4	Arunachal Pradesh Free School Uniform Scheme	Department of Education	Education

Conclusion: The Chakma and Hajong communities in Arunachal Pradesh face a complex scenario where, despite being legally Indian citizens under the Citizenship Act of 1955, the State Government's stance presents a contradiction. While the law endorses their citizenship, the state policy oscillates between reluctant acknowledgment and outright denial. This refusal to recognize the descendants of Chakma migrants born post-1964 remains a persistent state policy. Yet, it is crucial to note that while not universally labelled as non-citizens, around 5,000 Chakmas and Hajongs have engaged in the electoral process since 2004. Moreover, they benefit from certain central government schemes, although they often face exclusion from state-sponsored programs and some central schemes. Particularly, the local governance bodies seem to perpetuate bias, affecting the allocation of benefits, indicating a systemic issue. This inconsistent state approach leads to a 'Selective Recognition Policy,' offering limited rights yet falling short of full integration, leaving the community in a limbo of restricted privileges and enduring challenges. This dual policy framework reveals a dominant non-recognition policy overshadowing sporadic acknowledgments, significantly shaping the Chakmas'

***Legal Citizenship vs. State Stance:** The Chakma and Hajong communities in Arunachal Pradesh, although legally recognized as Indian citizens under the Citizenship Act of 1955, face a conflicting reality. While the law affirms their citizenship, the state's position presents a contradiction. The dichotomy lies in the state policy, which vacillates between hesitant acknowledgment and outright denial of their status.

***Persistent Denial of Recognition:** Despite legal provisions, the state persists in denying recognition to the descendants of Chakma migrants born in Arunachal Pradesh post-1964. This denial remains an enduring aspect of the state's policy towards these communities.

***Varied Treatment - Political Participation and Central Schemes:** Not universally labelled as non-citizens, approximately 9,500 Chakmas and Hajongs are currently participating in the electoral process since 2004. Furthermore, they benefit from certain central government schemes, indicating a more nuanced approach compared to outright exclusion.

***Disparity in State and Central Welfare Schemes:** Although they benefit from select central government schemes, they face exclusion from several state-sponsored programs and specific central schemes. This disparity is especially evident when these welfare programs are implemented through local governance bodies, highlighting a systemic bias against the Chakmas.

***Structural Bias in Local Governance:** The functioning dynamics of local governance bodies, particularly the Panchayati Raj Institutions (PRIs), contribute significantly to the exclusionary patterns faced by the Chakmas. These bodies' operational protocols and data infrastructure accentuate the gap in benefit allocation, exacerbating the community's challenges.

***Limited Rights vs. Persistent Challenges:** This mixed policy approach offers a limited set of rights and benefits to the Chakmas, preventing a narrative of absolute deprivation. However, it creates a conundrum wherein their citizenship is legally mandated, yet persistent state policies selectively recognize their rights, leaving them in a perpetual state of limbo.

***Selective Recognition Policy:** This stance by the state can be categorised as a 'Selective Recognition Policy.' While it doesn't entirely strip away their rights, it falls short of complete acknowledgment and integration, leading to a continuous balancing act between limited privileges and enduring challenges.

***Non-Recognition vs. Selective Recognition Policies:** Examining the state's approach reveals two distinct policies towards the Chakma community. The non-recognition policy represents a categorical refusal to acknowledge their citizenship, while the selective recognition policy hints at conditional acknowledgment, often driven by specific circumstances.

***Dominance of Non-Recognition Policy:** Despite occasional acknowledgments, the non-recognition policy significantly shapes the Chakmas' experiences, playing a more dominant role in determining their lived reality. This prevailing policy casts a considerable shadow over sporadic acknowledgments, profoundly impacting the community's integration and experiences within the state.

16

ENDLESS STRUGGLES OF THE CHAKMAS: RELOCATION BIDS AND THE SEARCH FOR ENDURING SOLUTIONS

In today's world, the Chakmas living in Arunachal Pradesh face many challenges because of the state's exclusionary policies. The State Government does not recognize them as citizens and excludes them from the demographic fabric of Arunachal Pradesh, which leads to systemic marginalisation. This policy deliberately sidelines the Chakmas, preventing them from participating in government and hindering their comprehensive development.

As a result, the Chakma community faces numerous challenges, as discussed earlier. These include being excluded from essential services like access to identity and domicile documents, meaningful political participation, integration into the Panchayati Raj system, and eligibility for various government schemes related to food security, education, welfare, and poverty alleviation. These numerous obstacles make it exceedingly difficult for the Chakmas to secure their fundamental rights and well-being.

Amidst the myriad challenges faced by the Chakma and Hajong communities, there are contemporary issues rooted in historical contexts and consequences of prolonged deprivation, alienation, and marginalisation.

When we discuss enduring solutions to the Chakma-Hajong issue, it is essential to address these contemporary challenges as well.

However, the perspectives on finding a lasting solution are vastly different between the parties involved. The Chakma-Hajongs seek a resolution based on acceptance and recognition as citizens of the state. In contrast, the state government and the AAPSU view relocation of the Chakma-Hajongs from the state as the solution, a stance that is unacceptable to the Chakma-Hajongs.

Before delving into contemporary challenges and proposed solutions to the long-standing Chakma-Hajong issue, it is important to explore the concept of "relocation" and its origins as a proposed resolution.

Part-I (RELOCATION)

(1) The Rise of Deportation/Relocation Demand: A Chronology

Prior to 1979, there was no demand for the relocation or deportation of the Chakma and Hajong people from Arunachal Pradesh. Concerns about these communities primarily revolved around regulating their activities, particularly to prevent potential forest encroachments and the unregulated induction of refugees or other non-Arunachalis into the Union Territory.

The stance of the people of Arunachal Pradesh changed after the anti-foreigner agitation in Assam spilled over into the state in 1979. This regional event shifted the focus, leading to demands for the deportation or relocation of the Chakma and Hajong communities.

Let us also examine the historical record of Central government responses to the state government's demands for the relocation or deportation of the Chakma and Hajong communities.

(A) 1979: Anti-Foreigner Movement Spreads and Identities Blur: The anti-foreigner agitation spearheaded by the All-Assam Students' Union (AASU) in Assam had ripple effects in Arunachal Pradesh. As the unrest spread, the All–Arunachal Pradesh Students' Union (AAPSU) rose to prominence. They championed a movement aimed at identifying and deporting foreigners from the state.

In this process, a crucial mistake was made. The Buddhist Chakma community and the smaller Hajong Hindu tribal group, who had resided in Arunachal Pradesh for decades, were mistakenly branded as "foreigners" and "illegal migrants."

(B) April 22, 1980: The growing tensions were further documented in a letter dated April 22, 1980 (ref D.O. No. CM/AP/R/80) from Mr. Gegong Apang, the then Chief Minister of Arunachal Pradesh, to the Home Minister of India. The letter conveyed how the "intensification of the agitation concerning foreigners in Assam" had led to a similar movement by the AAPSU. A key demand of this movement was the expulsion of Chakma and Tibetan refugees from Arunachal Pradesh.

This official communication highlights how the unrest in Assam directly influenced the rise of relocation demands for the Chakma and Hajong communities in Arunachal Pradesh.

> RESPONSE: ***In response to a letter from the CM, the union Home minister replied on July 19, 1980 (No. 13024/5/73-AP. II), explaining the historical context of Chakma settlements in the state. The decision to settle Chakma migrants in Arunachal Pradesh aimed to reduce the refugee burden in certain North-Eastern states, with Arunachal Pradesh agreeing to help rehabilitate these refugees. This decision was made through consultations with the Government of India, the Arunachal Pradesh Administration, and the local population to identify suitable settlement sites.***
>
> ***The Home Minister noted the practical difficulties of relocating the Chakma population elsewhere in the country at this point. Therefore, the letter emphasised the importance of convincing the people of Arunachal Pradesh to support the Chakma settlements, highlighting the need for local***

understanding and cooperation to resolve the issue effectively.

(C) February 16, 1982: A meeting took place at the Residential Office of Chief Minister Gegong Apang with a central team comprising members from the Ministry of Home Affairs and the Ministry of Rehabilitation. During the meeting, the Chief Minister opposed granting citizenship to the Chakmas and suggested that the only solution was to relocate them out of the state.

RESPONSE 1: ***Mr. R.N. Hota, Joint Secretary, Ministry of Rehabilitation noted that the Chakmas were brought to Arunachal Pradesh in 1964-65 by the Government of India and were not infiltrators. Unlike post-1971 Bangladeshi infiltrators, these refugees were recognized and settled by the government. He emphasised that their needs should be met either through the Arunachal Pradesh budget or by special sanction from the Ministry of Rehabilitation. Regarding the policy for the Chakmas, Mr.Hota stated that after 17 years of having settled them in Arunachal Pradesh there would be no case for throwing them out.***

RESPONSE 2: ***Shri B.P. Mishra, Deputy Secretary of the Ministry of Home Affairs, highlighted the distinction between Assam infiltrators and the settled Chakmas in Arunachal Pradesh, who were registered refugees brought in 1964. He pointed out that even Assam's leaders accepted registered refugees settled by the government. He stressed that removing the Chakmas was not feasible due to potential repercussions across the country, especially in Assam. Mishra reiterated that refugees who arrived before March 25, 1971, could not be deported due to government policies and international commitments.***

(D) On August 14, 1982, in reference to D.O. No. CM(AP)/9/82, the Chief Minister of Arunachal Pradesh addressed the Prime Minister. He highlighted that the Arunachal government had previously appealed to the central government for the redistribution of the Chakma population, arguing against their permanent settlement in the state.

> RESPONSE: ***On August 25, 1982, the Prime Minister's Office forwarded the Chief Minister's letter to the Ministry of Home Affairs, referenced as letter No. 25(261)/82-PM. In response, on September 13, 1982, the Ministry of Home Affairs replied to the Prime Minister's Office under MHA UO No.13024/ 5/73-AP(Vol.III). The reply clearly stated that there was no infiltration of foreigners in Arunachal Pradesh and that the Chakmas were settled there under specific rehabilitation schemes by the Ministry of Rehabilitation. Given that the Chakmas had resided in Arunachal Pradesh for nearly two decades, the question of their removal should not arise.***

(E) On July 31, 1984, the Arunachal Pradesh government, in reference to No. POL. 236/72, wrote to the Ministry of Home Affairs seeking the Central Government's position on the State's Council of Ministers' proposal to relocate the Chakmas from the state.

(F) On April 10, 1986, Chief Minister, Mr. Gegong Apang of Arunachal Pradesh, via DO No. CM/AP/15-86, raised the issue of relocating the Chakmas with the Home Minister of India.

> RESPONSE: ***In Reply, on May 26, 1986, the Home Minister, via DO. No. 8/2/86-AP, stated that relocating the Chakmas, especially those settled for over two decades under a rehabilitation scheme, was neither feasible nor humane. He stressed the importance of ensuring harmony between the Chakmas and the local tribal population to prevent socio-economic conflicts.***

The Home Minister categorically stated, "The proposal to disperse Chakmas outside Arunachal Pradesh is not practicable. From a humanitarian angle, it will be harsh to disperse those who have been settled for over two decades. They have been settled under a definite Scheme of Rehabilitation. However, care must be taken to ensure they do not come into socio-economic conflict with the local tribal population."

(G) On August 5th, 1992, Arunachal Pradesh MP, Mr. Laeta Umbrey, brought the issue of the Chakmas to the Lok Sabha. He highlighted a strong desire within the state for the Chakmas to be deported.

RESPONSE: ***On September 23rd, 1992, in response, Mr. M.M. Jacob, Minister of State for Home and Parliamentary Affairs, addressed Mr. Umbrey's concerns. He clarified that the Chakmas' settlement in Arunachal Pradesh was meticulously planned and implemented in cooperation with the state government.***

He also emphasised understanding and empathy. He argued that deporting the Chakmas from Arunachal Pradesh was not only unwarranted but also unjust. He emphasised that the rehabilitation of the Chakmas was not just an issue for Arunachal Pradesh but a collective responsibility of the entire Indian nation.

(H) On March 26, 1992, the Chief Minister of Arunachal Pradesh wrote to the Ministry of Home Affairs (MHA) regarding the deportation of the Chakmas from the state.

RESPONSE: ***On January 7, 1993, in response, Mr. M.M. Jacob, the Minister of State for Home, replied that the Central Government considered the issue of deporting the Chakmas closed and saw no benefit in revisiting it. He emphasised that the Central Government strongly believed the Chakmas in Arunachal Pradesh were entitled to citizenship***

under the Citizenship Act of 1955. Mr. Jacob urged the State Government to promptly grant citizenship to the Chakmas so they could enjoy all associated rights.

(I) On June 27, 1994, the issue of the Chakmas and Hajongs in Arunachal Pradesh came up again in the Rajya Sabha. Mr. Nyodak Yonggam, a member of parliament from the state, raised the question of their deportation.

RESPONSE: ***On July 7th, 1994, Mr. P.M. Sayeed, Minister of State for Home Affairs, responded with a Direct Order (DO) letter. He explained why the Chakmas and Hajongs were settled in Arunachal Pradesh in the first place, mentioning a historical agreement called the Indira-Mujib Agreement of 1972.***

This agreement, according to Mr. Sayeed, was important because it allowed certain Chakmas and Hajongs who came to India before 1971 to be considered for Indian citizenship. He said that this agreement established an apparent reason why they should be considered for citizenship. Therefore, the question of their deportation does not arise.

(J) In August 1994, tensions flared as the All–Arunachal Pradesh Students' Union (AAPSU) issued an ultimatum to the Chakma and Hajong communities demanding they leave Arunachal Pradesh. This was accompanied by widespread strikes and protests organised by AAPSU. Their rallying cry became "no deportation, no election," pressuring the central government to act.

AAPSU set a strict deadline of January 1995, demanding the deportation of the Chakmas and Hajongs from the state.

(K) In August 1995, tensions over the Chakmas and Hajongs escalated. The All–Arunachal Pradesh Students' Union (AAPSU) launched the "Jago Arunachal" (Awaken Arunachal) campaign. This campaign involved rallies across the state, targeting both the state and central governments.

Their goal was clear: to pressure both governments into deporting or relocating the Chakmas from Arunachal Pradesh.

(L) On August 5th, 1995, to amplify their message, an all-party legislators' meeting led by the Chief Minister was held in Itanagar. This meeting brought together a wide range of participants, from political parties like AAPSU and the National Students' Union of India (NSUI) to local leaders like Panchayat representatives, village chiefs, and NGOs.

These discussions resulted in a unified front. A massive rally was planned for September 20th, 1995. By including everyone from students to prominent citizens, the goal was to send a strong, unified message to the central government about the state's stance on deporting the Chakmas and Hajongs.

(M) On September 17th, 1995, in a significant move a delegation led by Arunachal Pradesh's Chief Minister met with the Prime Minister and Home Minister of India. They urged for a time-bound plan from the central government for deporting the Chakma and Hajong communities from the state.

(N) On September 20th, 1995, a massive show of unity unfolded in the form of an All-Party Referendum Rally. This rally brought together a wide range of participants: the Chief Minister, all government officials, state and national parliamentarians, representatives from political parties, NGOs, and student unions, including AAPSU.

The rally culminated in a powerful statement: a Six-Point Resolution. This resolution demanded, among other things, the removal of the Chakmas and Hajongs from Arunachal Pradesh by the end of 1995 (December 31st).

Furthermore, the resolution included a significant consequence. If the central government failed to act by the deadline, members of all state political parties would be forced to resign their party memberships.

(O) On September 29th, 1995, AAPSU organised a "Massive Explanation-cum-Public Open Rally." This rally aimed to further pressure the state's political representatives to actively support their demand for the deportation or relocation of the Chakmas and Hajongs.

(P) On November 8th, 1995, a high-level delegation from the central government arrived in Itanagar for talks with Arunachal Pradesh's leadership. The delegation included Syed Sibtey Razi and Prof. Meijinlung Kamson, Ministers of State for Home Affairs, along with senior officials.

The meeting brought together the Chief Minister, cabinet ministers, representatives of various political parties, prominent NGOs, and student bodies. All parties involved had strongly advocated for the relocation of the Chakmas and Hajongs from the state.

> RESPONSE: ***However, despite these voices, the central government delegation did not offer a concrete commitment regarding the relocation.***

(Q) On December 20th, 1995, key figures in Arunachal Pradesh convened a high-profile meeting. The Chief Minister, cabinet ministers, legislators, student union leaders, and prominent NGO representatives all gathered to discuss the ongoing situation.

The central focus of the meeting was the central government's position on the potential relocation of the Chakma and Hajong communities from the state.

> RESPONSE: ***Supreme Court Judgement: On January 9, 1996, the Supreme Court delivered a landmark judgement that effectively halted all efforts to relocate the Chakmas and Hajongs from Arunachal Pradesh. The judgement clearly directed that the state government could not displace these communities without following proper legal procedures.***

(2) Revival of Relocation Demand: A Chronology

Following the Supreme Court's ruling against the eviction or relocation of Chakma and Hajong communities, the intensity of the AAPSU's anti-Chakma movement significantly waned. While the court's decision provided much-needed relief and security to these communities, the relocation demand never entirely disappeared from the AAPSU's agenda.

However, a notable shift occurred in 2021. The discourse surrounding the relocation of Chakmas resurfaced, this time primarily driven by Arunachal Pradesh Chief Minister Pema Khandu and Union Minister Kiren Rijiju, rather than the AAPSU.

This marked a notable change in the trajectory of the relocation issue, with high-level political figures now at the forefront of the debate.

A. On February 20, 2020, Hon'ble Home Minister Shri Amit Shah invited representatives of the Chakma and Hajong communities to a meeting in Itanagar to discuss their issues. The meeting was attended by Hon'ble CM of Arunachal Pradesh, Shri Pema Khandu; Deputy CM Shri Chowna Mein; Shri Himanta Biswa Sarma, then NEDA Chairman and now CM of Assam; Shri Kiren Rijiju, then Minister of Sports (now Minister for Law and Justice); and Shri Jitendra Singh, Hon'ble Minister of State for DONER. During the meeting, the Hon'ble Home Minister assured the delegation that the issue would be resolved before Diwali 2020 and unequivocally stated that the Chakmas and Hajongs would not be relocated and would continue to permanently reside within Arunachal Pradesh.

B. On August 15, 2021, during his Independence Day speech, Hon'ble Chief Minister of Arunachal Pradesh, Mr. Pema Khandu, announced that "illegal" Chakma and Hajong migrants would be relocated to other states with honour. Subsequently, Shri Kiren Rijiju, Hon'ble Minister of Law and Justice, during his "Jan Ashirwad Yatra" held from

August 19 to 21, reiterated that the Chakmas and Hajongs could not remain in the state because Arunachal Pradesh is a tribal state. He emphasised that the protection provided by the Citizenship Amendment Act, 2019, and the Bengal Eastern Frontier Regulation, 1873, to the state's tribal population could not be diluted, and thus, the Chakmas and Hajongs must be relocated outside the state.[178]

Subsequently, on **August 25, 2021**, the AAPSU expressed its support for Chief Minister Pema Khandu's statement regarding the relocation of Chakmas and Hajongs from the state. They also praised Union Law Minister Kiren Rijiju's statement that Chakmas and Hajongs could not remain in Arunachal Pradesh due to its status as a tribal state.[179]

Following the August 15, 2021, Independence Day speech by Mr. Pema Khandu, Chief Minister of Arunachal Pradesh, where he revealed the relocation plan for the Chakma and Hajong communities, both he and Union Minister Mr. Kiren Rijiju have made similar statements on several occasions.

On **January 6, 2022**, Kiren Rijiju addressed the Chakma-Hajong issue, stating that the Chakma and Hajong people had already been asked to seek alternative living arrangements. He also mentioned that Union Home Minister Amit Shah had proposed a plan to settle the issue, expressing hope that all stakeholders would cooperate.[180]

Again, on **April 11, 2023,** Rijiju informed reporters that talks were ongoing to amicably resolve the matter by

---

[178] *https://arunachaltimes.in/index.php/2021/08/17/arunachal-union-govt-to-resolve-chakma-hajong-issue-cm/*
[179] *https://www.sentinelassam.com/north-east-india-news/arunachal-news/aapsu-welcomes-cm-pema-khandus-statement-on-relocation-of-chakma-hajong-551907*
[180] *https://northeastlivetv.com/topnews/chakma-hajong-arunachal-pradesh/*

resettling the Chakma and Hajong communities elsewhere in the country.[181]

Kiren Rijiju once again brought up the Chakma-Hajong issue ahead of the 2024 polls in Arunachal Pradesh. On March 25, 2024, and on several other occasions, he stated that efforts are ongoing to decide on a place for the resettlement of the Chakma and Hajong people outside Arunachal Pradesh.[182]

On **April 22, 2024**, Rijiju told journalists that talks had been initiated with Union Home Minister Amit Shah and Assam Chief Minister Dr. Himanta Biswa Sarma regarding the relocation of the Chakma-Hajongs to Assam. This statement triggered protests in Assam. The following day, Chief Minister Himanta Biswa Sarma clarified that the central government had not discussed anything about relocating the Chakma and Hajong refugees to Assam.[183]

(3) Chakma-Hajongs' Stand on Relocation

The resurgence of relocation discussions in 2021 ignited a fierce and unwavering resistance from Chakma and Hajong NGOs and CBOs. These communities have vehemently opposed the relocation proposal through multiple channels, including formal memoranda to the Prime Minister's Office, Home Ministry, Chief Minister's Office, and other government departments.

---

[181] https://www.sentinelassam.com/north-east-india-news/arunachal-news/chakma-and-hajong-refugees-cant-settle-permanently-in-arunachal-pradesh-says-union-minister-kiren-rijiju-645258

[182] https://www.deccanherald.com/india/arunachal-pradesh/bjp-rakes-up-chakma-hajong-issue-ahead-of-polls-in-arunachal-pradesh-slammed-by-group-2953037

[183] https://www.business-standard.com/india-news/no-talks-with-centre-on-relocating-chakma-hajong-refugees-in-state-cm-124042300535_1.html

Publicly, they have been equally resolute, declaring in national media that relocation is a non-starter. Such a move, they argue, would not only fail to resolve the issue but would also precipitate a humanitarian crisis, effectively reversing decades of progress. The sentiment is clear: relocation is tantamount to uprooting an entire community.

The Chakma-Hajongs have made it clear that if the government decides to relocate them to another state after nearly 60 years of settlement, they will only leave as dead bodies, not as living people. Such is the strength of their sentiment against relocation.

(4) Is Relocation of Chakma-Hajongs to Other States Practicable?

The proposition of relocating the Chakma and Hajong communities to another state is fraught with challenges and appears to be a highly impractical solution.

(i) Precedence and Feasibility:

- **Lack of Historical Precedent:** There is no historical precedent in independent India for the relocation of a settled community from one state to another. Such a move would set a dangerous precedent.
- **State Acceptance:** It is highly unlikely that any other state would willingly accept a population of around fifty thousand people, given the strain it would place on resources and infrastructure.
- **Humanitarian Crisis:** Forcibly relocating a community would inevitably lead to a humanitarian crisis. The psychological, social, and economic impacts would be devastating.

(ii) Relocation: Political Manoeuvring or Genuine Solution?

The recent statements by Union Minister Kiren Rijiju and Arunachal Pradesh Chief Minister Pema Khandu regarding the potential relocation of Chakma and Hajong communities to Assam have sparked controversy and confusion.

- **Contradictory Statements:** The subsequent denial by Assam Chief Minister Himanta Biswa Sarma casts doubt on the sincerity of the relocation proposal.
- **Political Gain:** It is plausible that the relocation discourse is being used as a political tool to garner support or divert attention from other issues.
- **Lack of Consultation:** Crucially, the Chakma and Hajong communities have not been consulted about any relocation plans and have categorically rejected the idea.

(iii) Other Implications:

- **Legal Implications:** Relocating a protected tribal community could have serious legal implications, potentially violating constitutional safeguards.
- **Economic Impact:** The economic cost of relocating such a large population would be immense, including expenses for resettlement, rehabilitation, and infrastructure development.
- **Social and Cultural Disruption:** Uprooting a community from its ancestral homeland would have profound social and cultural consequences.

In conclusion, the relocation of Chakma and Hajong communities is not only impractical but also unethical and counterproductive. It is essential to seek long-term solutions that address the root causes of the issues faced by these communities, rather than resorting to forced displacement.

Part-II
(CHAKMA CONTEMPORARY CHALLENGES)

In the preceding chapters, we delved into the historical roots of the Chakmas' challenges, attributing much of their present predicaments to the longstanding issue of landlessness since their settlement in Arunachal Pradesh. This persistent problem has served as the genesis for a multitude of difficulties faced by the Chakmas today. Compounding these challenges, the community grapples with the ongoing repercussions of soil erosion along the flood-prone Noa-Dihing River. Additionally, the contemporary adversities confronting the Chakma community in Arunachal Pradesh are intricately linked to the exclusionary policies of the state, further accentuating their struggles and impeding their integration into the Arunachal Pradesh' societal framework.

1. Landlessness and Annual Flood-Induced Soil Erosion:

In the initial phase of the Chakma community's settlement in Arunachal Pradesh, the envisioned plan entailed allocating each family a parcel of 5 acres of land. Accompanying this allocation were rehabilitation measures, including financial aid, cattle, tools, and potential employment opportunities within the government sector, all aimed at fostering self-reliance. Unfortunately, the implementation fell short, leaving hundreds of families bereft of the promised land, leading to persistent landlessness.

As time unfolded, the predicament of land scarcity intensified due to the recurrent floods along the Noa-Dihing River. These annual inundations not only obstructed the government's capacity to fulfil its land allocation commitments but also exacerbated the pre-existing challenge of landlessness. The convergence of failed resettlement plans, and the escalating impact of perennial floods has resulted in a complex interplay of factors contributing to the enduring issue of landlessness among the Chakma community in Arunachal Pradesh.

1.1. Uprooted by Water: The Devastating Impact of OIL diverting water from Burhi-Dihing to Noa-Dihing on the Chakmas

The Dihing River originates at the lofty heights of the Eastern Himalayas, at an elevation of 2,375 metres (7,792 ft) above sea level, from the Patkai Hills. As this river meanders through its journey, it undergoes a significant transformation near downstream Miao, giving rise to two distinct streams – Burhi-Dihing (Old Dihing) and Noa-Dihing (New-Dihing).

The Burhi-Dihing has long been the primary conduit for the river's flow, carrying more than 95% of the Dihing's water volume. In contrast, the modest Noa-Dihing, with an average width of merely 3-5 metres, shares a smaller portion, emphasising its unassuming nature.

In 1964-69, the government granted the Chakmas a settlement in the tranquil valley of the Noa-Dihing. Little did they know this seemingly gentle stream would soon take a tragic turn.

In 1971-72, Oil India Limited (OIL) initiated Petroleum Mining Operations at Manabhum near Diyun. To facilitate transport of heavy machinery, they partially blocked the Burhi-Dihing, diverting water to the Noa-Dihing. This intervention significantly altered the river's natural flow, reducing the once-dominant Burhi-Dihing to a shadow of its former self.

The once-gentle Noa-Dihing, transformed into an unruly beast, reshaped not only the landscape but also the lives of the Chakmas. Its relentless expansion and increased water volume uprooted settlements, rendering hundreds of families landless.

Burdened with excess water, the Noa-Dihing became a capricious giant, its course shifting unpredictably. This unleashed unimaginable hardships on the inhabitants, as the once-stable river carved new paths, disrupting settlements and shattering livelihoods.

Thus, the Noa-Dihing, initially a mere a gentle stream, became a symbol of both hope and heartbreak, its story forever intertwined with the displaced Chakma people and their ongoing struggle for a secure future.

1.2. Quantum of Land Loss: From Tributary to Torrent, Eroding Land and Lives

The once tranquil Noa-Dihing stream, now a symbol of sorrow for many, has inflicted devastating losses on the Chakma settlements along its banks. Recurring floods, fueled by soil erosion, have ripped away approximately 1,800 hectares of land from their settlements, impacting villages like Moitripur, Gautampur, Shantipur, Jyotipur, Dumpani, Udaipur, Mudoidweep and Bijoypur. This translates to a staggering loss of around 4,500 acres, rendering an estimated 900 families landless (according to Survey and Analysis conducted by Chakma Rights and Development Organisation (CRDO), a representative community-based body working for the rights and development of the beleaguered and marginalised Chakma people of Arunachal Pradesh.

The river's transformation is stark: its average width has ballooned from a mere 3-5 metres to a formidable 1 kilometre, relentlessly devouring the Chakmas' homes and livelihoods. While the exact figures need further verification, the impact is undeniable.

1.3. A Stark Monument to Erosion: The Tale of the Ring Well

See the Ring Well in the picture below, standing tall and proud, its purpose is to offer life-giving water to a village. Built in the mid-1980s as a source of drinking water in the middle of Maitripur village beside a community sports field and a school.

Now, that same well, not amidst a bustling community, but stranded in the middle of a raging river, over 800 metres from the village land. This is the haunting reality of the ring well in Maitripur village, a silent witness to the relentless erosion unleashed by the Noa-Dihing.

The well now serves as a poignant reminder of what was lost. Once surrounded by homes and laughter, it now stands isolated, a stark testament to the quantum of land swallowed by the river's fury.

This is not just a well; it's a story etched in concrete and steel. It speaks of families displaced, lives uprooted, and a community battling the elements. Every crack in its aged surface narrates a tale of struggle, resilience, and the yearning for a permanent home.

The well's plight isn't an isolated incident. It's a microcosm of the larger story unfolding across the Chakma settlements. It compels us to acknowledge the gravity of the situation, seek solutions, and stand in solidarity with those battling the river's wrath.

(2) The Grim Reality of Unrecognized Chakma Villages: Trapped in Disparity

For the Chakma community, displacement due to floods and land scarcity has presented a harsh reality from the early years of settlement. In response to the dire circumstances of landlessness caused by a lack of government land allotment and the recurring threat of floods, the affected Chakma population resorted to encroaching upon nearby forests. This encroachment, a natural and immediate reaction, stemmed from their desperate need for survival and sustenance, as no alternative means were available. The villages thus established in the early years of Chakma settlement in Arunachal Pradesh, including Dharmapur, Milanpur, Gulokpur, and Ratnapur in Miao and Namphuk Forests, while Jyotsnapur, Rajnagar and Kamakhyapur emerged through this encroachment of forest land into Diyun Reserved Forest.

While these villages were eventually recognized and regularised, others remain in limbo, denied access to crucial government support and basic necessities. This is the story of Modakka Nalah, Aranyapur, and Shillong Pahar - villages established by landless flood victims after 1975 that continue to struggle for recognition.

The lack of recognition translates to a life devoid of crucial government assistance. These villages grapple with higher poverty rates, limited access to education, and a host of unresolved issues like child labour, social control challenges, inadequate support from administration and inadequate infrastructure. Their plight remains unseen and unheard, their needs unmet.

Stuck in a cycle of neglect, the unrecognised Chakma villages of Modakka Nalah, Aranyapur, and Shillong Pahar face a grim reality. Denied their rightful place within the community, these families are locked in a web of disparities, unable to access basic necessities and opportunities that could transform their lives.

Here is the stark picture:

- **Living in the dark:** No access to electricity plunges these villages into darkness, hindering education, economic opportunities, and basic comfort.
- **Thirsting for progress:** Clean drinking water remains a distant dream, jeopardising health and hygiene.
- **Sick and unseen:** Lack of healthcare services leaves residents vulnerable to illness, with little hope for medical attention.
- **Excluded from progress:** Government schemes meant to uplift communities bypass these forgotten villages, widening the gap in development.

This absence of recognition has crippled the overall well-being of these communities. Poverty casts a long shadow, education remains elusive, and the potential for a brighter future seems to fade with each passing day.

(3) Challenges of Small Land Holdings amongst the Chakmas

During the period of rehabilitation, spanning several decades, the government allocated land to the 2,899 Chakma and Hajong families, constituting a population of 14,888 individuals. Each family, comprising three adults and two minors, received an allotment of 5 acres on average, a crucial provision intended for their self-sustainability. However, reflecting on the present scenario, six decades later, reveals a significant demographic shift.

The population has surged to an estimated 65,000 individuals, distributed across 12,670 families, marking an astonishing increase of approximately 430 percent. This statistical revelation indicates that what was once a single family has now transformed into four families over time. Unfortunately, this population growth has not been paralleled by a corresponding increase in land holdings.

The consequence of this demographic expansion has exerted immense pressure on the existing land, amplifying the challenges associated with small land holdings. Despite the notable increase in families, the land allocated per family during the rehabilitation era has remained static. As a result, the once self-sustaining landholdings have become increasingly insufficient to meet the needs of the growing community.

Over time, this sustained pressure has led to the fragmentation of families, resulting in a natural progression towards landlessness. Many of these displaced families, now without sufficient land for sustenance, have turned to a precarious existence as dependents on land owned by local tribesmen. In a bid to secure their livelihoods, they have resorted to sharecropping arrangements, navigating the complexities of land dependency.

Consequences:

- **Landlessness and Dependency:** Due to population increase exceeding land allocation, many families have become landless, relying on sharecropping or support from local tribes, creating insecurity and dependence.
- **Poverty and Food Insecurity:** Fragmentation of existing land reduces agricultural productivity, contributing to poverty and difficulty meeting basic needs.
- **Environmental Degradation:** Intensive use of smaller landholdings can lead to overgrazing, deforestation, and soil erosion, further impacting livelihoods and the environment.
- **Social Tensions:** Competition for scarce resources and land disputes can create social tensions within and between communities.

(4) Employment Discrimination Against Chakma-Hajong Communities

Since September 29, 1980, Chakma-Hajongs have been prohibited from obtaining employment in state government services as per order No. Pol-21/81. This systematic denial of access to government jobs has severely limited their opportunities for economic advancement and hindered their overall progression.

The exclusion of Chakma-Hajongs from state government employment has not only marginalised this community but also perpetuated socioeconomic disparities. Denying them government jobs has deprived them of stable income sources and social mobility, exacerbating their vulnerability and reinforcing a cycle of poverty. Such policies undermine the principles of equality and justice, violating their fundamental rights and stifling their potential contributions to the state's development.

(5) Educational Disparity: A Barrier to Chakma-Hajong Advancement

Education serves as the foundation for any society's progress. However, years of systemic neglect have significantly impacted the educational attainment of the Chakma and Hajong communities.

This lack of access to higher and technical education support from the government hinders overall community development. The underrepresentation in prestigious professions like IPS, IAS, doctors, engineers, professors etc. serves as a stark illustration of this disparity. Notably, the absence of Chakma-Hajong students in the top ranks of state board exams (class X and XII) further highlights the educational gap.

(6) Denial of Trade Permits and Licences to Chakma-Hajongs

Trade licences granted to Chakma-Hajongs were revoked under the pretence of renewal, obstructing their economic activities since the 1990s. Earlier, granting trade licences proved to be a successful strategy. It fostered an entrepreneurial spirit among the Chakma-Hajongs, enabling them to generate income and contribute meaningfully to the local economy.

Beyond financial gain, these licences fostered a sense of autonomy, self-worth, and dignity. Freely pursuing chosen professions empowered the Chakma-Hajongs to transition from passive recipients of aid to active contributors to their own well-being and society as a whole.

(7) Revoking Residence Certificates Deepens Socio Economic Marginalisation of Chakmas and Hajongs in Arunachal Pradesh

On September 29, 1980, the State Government issued Order No. Pol-21/81, effectively barring Chakmas and Hajongs from employment in state government services. This policy completely shut off any employment prospects in state-run sectors for these communities, leading to significant socio-economic marginalisation. Over four decades, this order reinforced their exclusion, severely limiting their opportunities for stable and formal employment within the state government.

The situation worsened on November 4, 2022, when the Government of Arunachal Pradesh, through order No. POL/CH-2/2022-23/100, revoked the Residence Certificates (RC) for Chakmas and Hajongs. Issued by Joint Secretary (Political) Shri Rajeev Takuk, this revocation barred these communities from central government employment, including prestigious roles in the Indian Army, CAPF, and other defence services. This decisive action critically hindered their career prospects and further entrenched their socio-economic challenges, stripping them of the opportunity to contribute to national defence and security.

Beyond employment, the cancellation of Residence Certificates has profound implications. These certificates are essential for admission to educational institutions, access to educational schemes, and various scholarships. Their revocation also limits access to government services, welfare programs, and legal benefits, significantly disrupting the lives of affected individuals. The loss of these certificates means exclusion from social welfare schemes, healthcare benefits, and essential government programs, depriving these communities of crucial support and reinforcing their marginalisation in multiple spheres of life.

(8) Limited Opportunities, Forced Migration: A Challenge for Chakma Livelihoods in Arunachal Pradesh

Due to the scarcity of livelihood opportunities in Arunachal Pradesh, many Chakma youths are compelled to migrate to industrial cities in search of employment. Major industrial cities like Noida, Gurgaon, Bengaluru, Tiruppur, Chennai, New Delhi, and Surat have become prime destinations for these young job seekers.

However, the lack of adequate skills and qualifications among these migrants limits their employment options predominantly to unskilled labour in factories. Those with minimal qualifications and decent communication skills manage to find jobs in the service industry, including sectors such as retail and hospitality.

This migration trend underscores the urgent need for skill development and educational programs tailored to the Chakma youth, enabling them to secure better employment opportunities and improve their socio-economic status. Investing in such initiatives can significantly enhance their employability and reduce the necessity for migration.

Sintu Chakma, in his paper published on September 15, 2017, in the Tribal Intellectual Collective India Journal titled "Chakma Society at the Crossroads: Unravelling Realities of Chakma Youths from Arunachal Pradesh," writes, "The youths, mostly boys, are migrating for survival as livelihood options back at home are very few and limited. In cities, most of them are engaged in factories and plants as daily wage labourers. Those few who can speak English are fortunate enough to get jobs in BPOs and shopping malls and are paid a moderate salary. This phenomenon of forced migration is impacting negatively on the youths and on their respective families as well. The livelihood crisis and its subsequent large-scale migration of Chakma youths is a direct consequence of the extremely vulnerable situation of the Chakmas of Arunachal Pradesh."[184]

(9) Domestic Child Labourers of Chakma Children in Arunachal Pradesh

Extreme poverty and lack of education in Arunachal Pradesh's Changlang district, particularly in remote and unrecognised Chakma settlements, have created fertile ground for child trafficking networks and agents to supply domestic child labourers.

Predatory recruiters, often known to the community, exploit these vulnerabilities. They lure parents with false promises of better opportunities in Itanagar and distant areas for their children.

These agents function as a well-oiled machine, fulfilling the demand for domestic help in affluent households across Arunachal Pradesh. An estimated 90% of child domestic workers are supplied through these middlemen.

While official data is scarce, estimates suggest that roughly 1,000 Chakma minors are currently working as domestic help throughout the state. Tragically, some are reported "dead, missing, or untraceable."

The most affected villages, including unrecognised settlements like Modakka Nalah and Aranyapur, alongside remote villages like Mudoidweep, Udaipur, Dharmapur, and the Deban area.

Economic desperation is undeniably the primary factor driving child labour and trafficking within the Chakma community. Urgent action is needed to address poverty and provide alternative opportunities for these families.

---

[184] *https://www.ticijournals.org/chakma-society-at-the-crossroads-unravelling-realities-of-chakma-youths-from-arunachal-pradesh/*

Abuse of these domestic child labourers is rarely reported officially, but many such crimes come to light when these child labourers return home.

As reported by Maitreyee Boruah, a reporter from the Journalism Centre on Global Trafficking on 12 Oct 2023: "Eight years ago, Purudhan Chakma (50) and his wife Liduvi Chakma (45) from Aranyapur village sent their eldest son, then 12 years old, to work in a home in Diyun. They were paid Rs 12,000 by the employer. "Later, the employer took my son to Itanagar. Since then, he has been missing. We have tried to file a case against the employer, but the police dissuaded us. We have lost all contact with the employer. The last time we spoke over the phone, he told us our son was not with him anymore," alleged the mother. [185]

"Phaneswar Chakma (58) is a widow from Aranyapur village. In 2021, she sent her daughter to work in Pasighat, the headquarters of East Siang district in Arunachal Pradesh. Her daughter, then 15 years old, died by suicide at her employer's place within a month of her joining. "I went to Pasighat and brought back her body. I was told in Pasighat that a post-mortem was done on her, which confirmed suicide. Before her funeral here, we realised the post-mortem was not done. I doubt foul play behind her death. She would never have died by suicide," Chakma said. The 58-year-old wants justice for her daughter. "But I am a poor widow and have no means to pursue a case against the employer."

[185] *https://thefederal.com/category/the-eighth-column/bhonti-culture-how-minor-girls-from-assam-are-sold-into-slavery-in-arunachal-pradesh-98342?infinitescroll=1*

Part-III (PERMANENT RESOLUTION OF THE CHAKMA - HAJONG ISSUE)

As explored in previous chapters, the Chakma-Hajong community in Arunachal Pradesh faces a persistent struggle for "acceptance". Shifting narratives have unfortunately hindered their integration into the state's social fabric.

However, it is crucial to acknowledge the contrasting experiences of migrant resettlement across India. During the same period, over 8.5 lakh Hindu, Christian, and Buddhist refugees from East Pakistan were successfully integrated into various states. West Bengal, Meghalaya, Assam, Bihar, Uttar Pradesh, Delhi, Madhya Pradesh, Maharashtra, the Andaman & Nicobar Islands, and others embraced these communities, fostering seamless societal inclusion.

In stark contrast, Arunachal Pradesh has yet to extend similar acceptance and recognition to the Chakma-Hajong population. This disparity stands out when compared to the successful integration efforts in other parts of the country.

Moving forward, a permanent resolution hinges on Arunachal Pradesh embracing historical realities. By upholding India's constitutional values of unity and diversity, the state can acknowledge the Chakma-Hajong community as an integral part of its society. Recognizing their citizenship and restoring their rights would be a crucial step towards reconciliation and a more inclusive future.

The Joint Action Committee (JAC) of Chakma & Hajong Community-Based Organizations (CBOs) and NGOs have proposed a permanent solution to the Chakma-Hajong issue through various representations to the Prime Minister, Home Minister, State's Chief Minister, and other relevant ministers. Their proposal is based on two key principles: Assimilation/Integration and Separation/Autonomy.

1. Assimilation/Integration-Based Approach:

"One of the best ways to resolve the issue once and for all is to accept the reality of history and build on the Indian constitutional ethos of unity and diversity. A fact-based approach, it is based on assimilation and cultural/political integration of Chakmas and Hajongs to Indian mainstream as part of historical evolutionary process. In fact, the foreigner issue in the parent state of Assam was resolved using the dimension of 'time' - 25 March 1971 being used as the cut-off date to determine whether one is accepted as a citizen or not. A similar guiding principle can be formulated in Arunachal Pradesh too. However, for this to happen, restoration of all rights is imperative as it will lead to empowerment and integration of the Chakma-Hajongs and allow them to flourish."

This approach advocates for the full integration of the Chakma and Hajong communities into the socio-political fabric of Arunachal Pradesh, emphasising the restoration of their rights as a crucial step towards their empowerment and seamless inclusion in the mainstream.

2. **Separation/Autonomy-Based Approach:**

If the Assimilation/Integration-based approach is not feasible, the JAC suggests providing autonomy to the Chakma and Hajong communities as an alternative solution. This proposal includes:

2.1. **Creation of an Autonomous or Regional Council:**

"Provide for a separate territorial area in the form of an Autonomous Council for the Chakmas in Arunachal Pradesh and have it directly administered/governed by the Union Government in the existing settlement areas under the 6th schedule of the Indian Constitution. It is a win-win solution for it will remove the so-called 'burden of Chakma refugees' on the state government on the one hand and will also not take away the jobs/facilities of other Arunachalese on the other as the Council so created can be directly funded and administered by the Union government. In fact, Autonomous Councils have proven to be very useful creative instruments within the framework of the Indian Constitution which could be replicated, with minor modifications, as required."

2.2. **Consideration of a Union Territory:**

"In case provision of an Autonomous Council is not feasible in Arunachal Pradesh as the state is still not covered under the 6th Schedule, then alternatively a Union Territory can be considered comprising the existing Chakma settlement areas directly administered/funded by the Centre. (This proposal is being placed so that the Government of India devises an overall development package for Chakmas and Hajongs of Arunachal Pradesh keeping in mind the rights of local people is not jeopardised or diluted, otherwise Chakmas and Hajongs are ready to live together with other tribes/communities in peaceful co-existence as referred to above.)"

The JAC's proposals aim to find a balanced and sustainable resolution to the Chakma-Hajong issue, ensuring that their rights and well-being are safeguarded while maintaining harmony with the local communities in Arunachal Pradesh.

In line with JAC's proposed solution, Prof. Nani Bath, a renowned political scientist from the Department of Political Science at Rajiv Gandhi University, Itanagar, has suggested the "Creation of a Chakma Regional Council to be directly controlled by the Government of India" in his book From India to India. He presents this as a democratic solution to the ongoing Chakma-Hajong issue in Arunachal Pradesh.

3. **Special Impetus & Reservations for the Upliftment of the Chakma-Hajong Community**

The Chakma and Hajong communities of Arunachal Pradesh have faced decades of deprivation and marginalisation. To address these historical injustices and promote their upliftment, it is essential to implement a multi-faceted approach that includes both a permanent resolution for their acceptance and special impetus from the Central Government.

A permanent resolution regarding the status of the Chakma and Hajong communities is crucial. This resolution would pave the way for their gradual acceptance within the fabric of Arunachal Pradesh, fostering assimilation and integration. Such acceptance is not just a matter of legal recognition but also of social inclusion, which can help reduce the prejudice and discrimination these communities have historically faced.

3.1. Special Impetus from the Central Government

To rectify the injustices and backwardness resulting from prolonged deprivation, there must be a significant and targeted effort from the Central Government. This special impetus should include:

(a) Educational Support:

- Establishing educational institutions and scholarship programs specifically for Chakma and Hajong students to ensure they have access to quality education.
- Vocational training centres to enhance employability and skill development.
- Allocate a certain percentage of seats in educational institutions.
- Targeted Scholarship Programs: Allocation of scholarships under various government schemes should be specifically designated for Chakma-Hajong students pursuing higher and technical education. Currently, these students are often deprived of scholarships or have their applications denied when applying through the national scholarship portal.

(b) Healthcare Initiatives:

- Setting up advanced healthcare facilities in regions predominantly inhabited by these communities.

- Extending the benefit of the government's flagship health insurance/ assurance schemes like PMJAY/CMAAY etc.

(c) Economic Development Programs:

- Launching initiatives to promote entrepreneurship and self-employment within these communities.
- Providing financial assistance and micro-credit schemes to support small businesses and agricultural activities.
- Reinstating a system for granting trade licences to the Chakma-Hajong communities would empower them economically and build a more self-reliant future. It would rejuvenate the Chakma community with a business-oriented mindset, allowing them to generate income and actively contribute to the local economy.

3.2. Reservation and Quota to address Socioeconomic Needs of Chakma and Hajong Communities in Arunachal Pradesh

To ensure adequate representation of the Chakma and Hajong communities in both state and central services, a separate reservation or quota system needs to be established.

(a) Granting Scheduled Tribe (ST) Status

- The Chakmas share recognition as an ST with their counterparts in other Indian states. The 105th Rajya Sabha Petition Committee's recommendation in 1997 strengthens their case for ST status in Arunachal Pradesh.
- To ensure a smooth transition and protect the rights of existing Indigenous tribes, a separate quota system for ST (Plains) and ST (Hills) could be established based on well-defined criteria.

(b) Inclusion in Economically Weaker Section (EWS) Category

- Recognizing the potentially lengthy constitutional process for granting ST status, the Chakma and Hajong communities can be included in the EWS category in the interim.
- This will provide them with immediate access to reservation benefits, promoting their economic well-being.

(c) Quota in State Government Employment

- Currently, the Arunachal Pradesh Public Service Commission allocates 80% of government jobs to Arunachal Pradesh Scheduled Tribes (APST) and 20% to unreserved candidates.
- To compensate for past disadvantages and offer fair employment opportunities, 10% of the existing unreserved quota (20%) can be earmarked for Chakma and Hajong candidates.
- This targeted allocation will foster their economic advancement and contribute to their overall development while maintaining a significant share of government jobs for APST candidates.

(d) Empowering Chakma Youth Through Special Recruitment Drives

- Initiate a special recruitment drive in the Indian Army and Paramilitary Forces to channel the energies of loyal Chakma youth, enabling them to serve their country with pride and fervour.
- This initiative will not only provide meaningful employment opportunities but also foster a sense of national pride and belonging among Chakma individuals, contributing to their personal growth and the nation's security.

These measures would ensure equal representation and promote the advancement of the Chakma-Hajong communities. By creating a fair and equal platform, they would enable Chakma and Hajong individuals to compete and succeed, thereby elevating their socio-economic status.

This comprehensive approach would foster their overall development and integration into society.

4. **Cultural Preservation:**
    - Promoting and preserving the unique cultural heritage of the Chakma and Hajong communities through cultural festivals, documentation, and educational programs.
    - Encouraging inter-community cultural exchange to foster mutual respect and understanding.

5. **Infrastructure Development:**
    - Improving infrastructure in Chakma and Hajong inhabited areas, including roads, housing, and public utilities.
    - Ensuring access to clean water and sanitation facilities.

6. **Landlessness and Annual Flood-Induced Soil Erosion among the Chakma Community**

The Chakma community in Arunachal Pradesh has endured a protracted struggle with landlessness, exacerbated by recurrent flooding along the Noa-Dihing River. Inconsistent government policies have resulted in hundreds of families lacking permanent land ownership. Moreover, annual inundations have not only hindered the government's land allocation efforts but have also intensified the existing land scarcity crisis.

A comprehensive approach is imperative to address this multifaceted issue. To mitigate the impact of flooding and soil erosion, measures such as riverbank stabilization, embankment construction, and sustainable land management practices are crucial. Simultaneously, the government must prioritize the rehabilitation and resettlement of landless Chakma families by identifying suitable land for their permanent habitation. By providing these families with secure and stable living conditions, the government can contribute to their long-term well-being and economic independence.

Furthermore, exploring alternative livelihood opportunities can empower the affected community to build resilience and reduce dependency on land-based resources.

CONCLUSION: Upliftment is the Solution

The upliftment of the Chakma-Hajong community stands as the pivotal solution to the long-pending Chakma-Hajong issue. To address this matter effectively, a comprehensive and sustained effort from both the Central and State Governments is imperative.

Firstly, implementing a permanent resolution for their acceptance within Arunachal Pradesh is crucial. This involves legal recognition and protection of their rights, ensuring that they are acknowledged as integral members of the state's diverse community. Such recognition would rectify historical injustices and provide a solid foundation for their future.

Secondly, a special impetus for their development is necessary. This can be achieved through targeted socio-economic programs that focus on education, healthcare, employment, and infrastructure development. By enhancing their access to quality education and healthcare, creating job opportunities, and improving living conditions, we can significantly uplift their standard of living. This will not only benefit the Chakma-Hajong community but also contribute to the overall progress of Arunachal Pradesh.

Furthermore, ensuring adequate representation through reservations in educational institutions, government jobs, and political bodies is essential. This affirmative action will empower the Chakma and Hajong communities, giving them a voice in decision-making processes and enabling them to participate actively in the state's governance and development.

A comprehensive approach that includes these measures will help integrate the Chakma and Hajong communities into the socio-economic fabric of Arunachal Pradesh. This integration is not merely about coexistence but about building a society where diversity is celebrated, and every community contributes to the state's prosperity.

In the long run, such initiatives will pave the way for a more inclusive and equitable society. This holistic development is in the best interest of the Chakma-Hajong communities, the people of Arunachal Pradesh, and the state as a whole. By addressing the root causes of their marginalization and promoting their advancement, we can foster a harmonious and prosperous Arunachal Pradesh where every individual, regardless of their background, has the opportunity to thrive.

BIBLIOGRAPHY

1. Chittagong Hill Tracts and Boundary Commission Award (National Archives of India)
2. Chakma Resistance to British Domination 1772-1798 by Suniti Bhushan Qanungo, Professor, Department of History at Chittagong University
3. Land Rights of the Indigenous Peoples of the
4. Chittagong Hill Tracts, Bangladesh, IWGIA Document No. 99, Copenhagen 2000 by Rajkumari Chandra Kalindi Roy (ISBN: 87-90730-29-1)
5. Press Information Bureau, Government of India, Feature "Foodgrains Airdropped for Buddhist Migrants, Evacuation Posing Big Problem", May 10, 1964
6. Note of B.N. Rau submitted to Jawaharlal Nehru on August 14, 1947, on Chittagong Hill Tracts and Boundary Commission Award (National Archives of India)
7. Rehabilitation of refugees and others in Assam including hill districts and North East Frontier Agency (MHA File No. 15/12/64(SR)-A, National Archives of India
8. MHA File No. P-II/125/2/68, Minstry of External Affairs, Starred Question No. 48 by Shri Babu Rao Patel on 14.2.68 Racial on Genocide in Pakistan (National Archives of India)
9. 1947 - The story of Rehabilitation, U. Bhaskar Rao ISBN-9789354091858
10. Report of Estimates Committee (1959-60) Ninety-Sixth Report (Second Lok Sabha), Ministry of Rehabilitation, Govt. of India [Eastern Zone]
11. Report of Estimates Committee (1964-65) Seventy-First Report (Third Lok Sabha) Ministry of Rehabilitation (Reception, Dispersal and Rehabilitation of new Migrants arriving in India from East Pakistan since 1st January 1964)
12. Rehabilitation of Displaced Persons and Repatriates, Facts and Figures at a Glance, 1967,

Committee of Review of Rehabilitation Work in West Bengal, Ministry of Labour, Employment and Rehabilitation, New Delhi

13. Assam Archive File: Land for rehabilitation of refugees in Cachar District, Assam 1964
14. Assam Archive File: General Administration Reports on Relief and Rehabilitation activities for the year 1965-66.
15. The Indian Frontier Administrative Service: Romanticism and Hostile Borders by Claude Apri https://claudearpi.blogspot.com/2014/12/romanticism-and-hostile-borders.html
16. NEFA-An Introduction: R.N. Haldipur
17. MHA File No. 210(11)/63-NI (Agricultural Settlement in NEFA Model Schemes for settlement corresponding regarding Vijaynagar/Preetnagar Settlements) National Archives of India
18. Public Accounts Committee (1977-78) Sixth Lok Sabha, Twenty-First Report on Resettlement of Ex-Servicemen Near Seijosa, Ministry of Home Affairs
19. Report of the Committee to study Refugee Settlements in Arunachal Pradesh constituted by the Govt. of Arunachal Pradesh vide Memo No. POL.236/72, dated 08.12.1976
20. Press India Bureau, Weekly Digest of News, Vol.IX. No. 15 dated April 11, 1965
21. MHA File No. 210(11)/63-NI (Agricultural Settlement in NEFA Model Schemes for settlement corresponding regarding Vijaynagar/Preetnagar Settlements) National Archives of India
22. White Paper on Chakma and Hajong Refugee Issue, Govt. of Arunachal Pradesh, 1996
23. Rehabilitation of refugees and others in Assam including hill districts and North East Frontier Agency. MHA File No. 15/12/64-SR/R-A (National Archives of India)
24. The Seventy-First Report of the Estimates Committee (Third Lok Sabha)

25. https://archive.pib.gov.in/archive/ArchiveSecondPhase/EXTERNAL%20AFFAIRS/1965-APRIL-MAY-VOL-2-EXTERNAL-AFFAIRS/PDF/EXT-1965-04-04_036.pdf
26. Tour Note of Mr. L.J Johnson, ICS, Additional Secretary, Ministry of Rehabilitation, Govt. of India on his visit to Assam between 08.06.65 and 13.06.65
27. Record note of discussion by Minister of Rehabilitation, Government of India, with the Rehabilitation Minister, Assam, Chief Secretary, Assam, Rehabilitation Secretary, Assam and other officers of the State Government dated 22.06.1965
28. Tour Note of H.S Butalia, Liaison Officer, Ministry of Rehabilitation, Govt. of India vide No. 13(23)/65-RH.I dated 19th July, 1965 regarding his visit to Goalpara and Garo Hills District and Tripura
29. Development & Resettlement of of ex-services Sectors of the Indo Pakistan border and NEFA (217/16/65-NEFA) National Archives of India
30. Influx/Removal of Tibetan refugees in NEFA (File No. File No. NI/102/1/65) Extract from Secy (UT)'s Note dated 8.1.1966 on his tour to NEFA from 14.12.1965 to 22.12.1965 (National Archives of India)
31. Assam Archive File: Movement of Second Group of Chakma Refugees from Cachar & Mizo District to NEFA (File No. RHMC-6/66)
32. Development Resettlement of of ex-services Sectors of the Indo Pakistan border and NEFA (217/16/65-NEFA) National Archives of India
33. Committee of Review of Rehabilitation Work in West Bengal, Ministry of Labour Employment and Rehabilitation, New Delhi dated 22nd February 1967. Legislation, Survey Reports and Statistics/Compilation No. I (Fact and Figures at a Glance)
34. Assam Archive File: General Administration Reports File No. RHE.35/66

35. Estimates Committee, 8th Report, Fourth Lok Sabha, Ministry of Employment & Rehabilitation, 1967-68
36. Letter of Mr. P.N. Luthra, Adviser to the Governor of Assam vide No. D.O.R.R.14/69 dated 10th April 1969 to M.R. Yardi, Additional Secretary, Ministry of Home Affairs, New Delhi
37. Letter of P.B Kar, Director of Forests, NEFA to Liaison Officer, Ministry of Rehabilitation, Shillong vide No. FOR/RR/128/66/10380 dated July 22, 1966
38. Letter of Camp Commandant, Saranarthipur Migrants Camp, Monacherra to SDO, Hailandi vide No. SCE9/66/1033 dated 29.07.1966.
39. Letter of Under Secretary, Govt. of Assam to the R&R Commissioner, Assam, Shillong dated August 30, 1966
40. Letter of Camp Commandant, Silcoorie New Migrants Camp, Cachar to CO, Miao, Tirap vide No. RR/SC-B/23/65/125 dated October 7, 1966
41. A Comprehensive Note on Chakma Settlers in Changlang District by Mr. Arun Goyal, IAS, Deputy Commissioner, Changlang enclosed in his letter No. CA-108/89 dated Changlang the 8th September, 1990 to the Home Secretary, Govt. of Arunachal Pradesh.
42. Archive of India, File No. 13024/5/73AP (Settlement of Chakma Refugees in Arunachal Pradesh)
43. Internal Displacement, Migration, and Policy in Northeastern India Author(s): Uddipana Goswami East-West Center (2007) http://www.jstor.com/stable/resrep06479
44. Recommendation of Estimates Committee Seventy-First Report (Third Lok Sabha) Ministry of Rehabilitation (Reception, Dispersal, and Rehabilitation of new migrants arriving in India from East Pakistan since 1st January 1964)

45. Chittagong Hills Tract and the Boundary Commission's Award, File No. 7/6/6, Ministry of Home Affairs
46. Scheme for settlement of ex-servicemen families in Seijosa and another scheme for settlement of ex-servicemen families in Namdapha region of Miao-Vijaynagar. File No. 11(9)/1969 NEFA
47. Public Accounts Committee Report 1977-78, Sixth Lok Sabha, 21st Report, RESETTLEMENT OF EX-SERVICEMEN NEAR SEIJOSA
48. Settlement of ex-servicemen in Amboliang area of Noa-Dihing valley in Tirap District. File No. 11/31/70-NEFA, Ministry of Home Affairs
49. Special Development incentives for sparsely populated Border Areas and settlement of ex-servicemen-Settlement along the Indo-Bhutan-Tibet Border-Ref from Cabinet Sectt. MHA, NOTES/CORRESPONDENCE File No. 1/5/87-AP
50. Land for rehabilitation of refugees in Cachar District, Assam 1964, File No. RHH/35/1964
51. Visit of Members of Parliament to NEFA in May 1966 (File No. NI/463/2/66) National Archives of India
52. MHA File No. 13024/5/73-AP. II (Development and Regulatory Measures, Security Matters - Settlement of Chakma Refugees in Arunachal Pradesh) - National Archives of India
53. Number of Families inducted into Noa Dihing Valley under Scheme II
54. Census of India 1971, Series No. 24, Arunachal Pradesh, Part X, District Census Handbook Tirap District
55. Report of the Committee about Resettlement in Miao Sub-Division, 1979 (J.M Syiem Committee, Deputy Commissioner, Changlang District)
56. CENSUS OF INDIA 1971, ARUNACHAL PRADESH
57. A Comprehensive Note on Chakma Settlers in Changlang District by Mr. Arun Goyal, IAS, Deputy Commissioner, Changlang enclosed in his letter No. CA-108/89 dated Changlang the 8th September,

1990 to the Home Secretary, Govt. of Arunachal Pradesh.

58. A Note on Chakma Refugees in Arunachal Pradesh, MHA File No. 13024/5/73 AP-II (Archive of India)
59. Development and Regulatory Measures-Settlement of Chakma Refugees in Arunachal Pradesh (MHA File No. 13024/5/73 APII), National Archives of India
60. Development and Regulatory Measures-Settlement of Chakma Refugees in Arunachal Pradesh (MHA File No. 13024/5/73 APII), National Archives of India
61. 1994 Sup (1) Supreme Court Cases 615 STATE OF ARUNACHAL PRADESH Versus KHUDIRAM CHAKMA (Civil Appeal No. 2182 of 1993)
62. https://www.ssb.gov.in/index1.aspx?lsid=39&cid=0&lev=2&lid=11&langid=1
63. https://web.archive.org/web/20090410004725/http://arunachalpradesh.nic.in/rural/html/glance.htm
64. https://namsai.nic.in/history/
65. Recommendations of the Inaugural Session of Pradesh Council of Arunachal Pradesh held at Shillong from 2nd to 6th Oct' 72
66. Development and Regulatory Measures-Settlement of Chakma Refugees in Arunachal Pradesh (MHA File No. 13024/5/73 AP Vol. III), National Archives of India
67. MHA File No. 9/12/82-AP Lok Sabha Starred Question No. 541 for 6.10.82 by Shri Amar Roy Pradhan regarding proposal to remove Tibetans and Chakmas from Arunachal Pradesh. (National Archives of India)
68. Ministry of Home Affairs, Govt. of India, Departments of Internal Security, States and Home (Annual Report 1995-96)
69. ALL ARUNACHAL PRADESH STUDENTS' UNION: A STUDY OF ITS HISTORY AND LEADERSHIP (IJRSSH) 2017, Vol. No. 7, Issue No. I

70. Student Movements in Arunachal Pradesh: S. Dutta (ISBN-81-86393-17-X)
71. MHA File No. 9/12/82-AP Lok Sabha Starred Question No. 541 for 6.10.82 by Shri Amar Roy Pradhan regarding proposal to remove Tibetans and Chakmas from Arunachal Pradesh. (National Archives of India)
72. File Name: Fortnightly Confidential Report from Government of Arunachal Pradesh. MHA File No. 7/14/89-AP (National Archives of India)
73. https://nhrc.nic.in/press-release/archives-human-rights-cases
74. National Human Rights Commission vs State Of Arunachal Pradesh & Anr on 9 January 1996 Equivalent citations: 1996 AIR 1234, 1996 SCC (1) 742
75. https://ccrchap.wordpress.com/
76. Landmark Judgements on Election Law (A compilation of Important Judgements pronounced by the Supreme Court of India, High Courts and Election Commission of India) Volume - V by Election Commission of India
77. Order of Member Secretary, Arunachal Pradesh State Legal Services Authority, Itanagar in SC Case-Writ Petition (Civil) No. 510/2007
78. MHA Letter No. 4/366/63-IC dated June 16, 1965, to the State Government of Assam, West Bengal, Tripura, Manipur and Nagaland.
79. Ministry of Rehabilitation letter No. 16(10)/66-RH. II dated November 30, 1966, to the Chief Secretaries of Assam, West Bengal/Nagaland, Tripura, Manipur
80. Note for the Secretaries' Committee on Internal Affairs" vide No. 13024/5/73-AP dated November 4, 1975 (National Archives of India)
81. Intelligence Bureau Report No. D.I.B. UO No. 17/Tribe(Q)/72/(13) dated 03/04/1973 (National Archives of India)
82. Arunachal Pradesh Administration Letter D.O. No. POL.236/72 dated June 22, 1973 (National Archives of India)

83. Ministry of Home Affairs letter to Intelligence Bureau vide U.O No. U-13024/5/73-AP on October 4, 1973
84. Intelligence Bureau Report dated the 5th March, 1974 vide U.O. No. 18/Tribe(Q)/73(8) (National Archives of India)
85. Ministry of Rehabilitation letter No. 16(10)/66-RH.II dated November 30, 1966 to the Chief Secretaries of Assam, West Bengal/Nagaland, Tripura, Manipur (National Archives of India)
86. Note vide No.13024/5/73-AP dated November 4, 1975, from MHA to Committee of Secretaries of Internal Affairs (National Archives of India)
87. Minutes of the Meeting of Secretaries Committee on Internal Affairs held on 16 December 1975. Doc No. CD-1255/75 (National Archives of India)
88. MHA letter No. U-13024/5/73-AP to the Government of Arunachal Pradesh on January 12, 1976, (National Archives of India)
89. MHA letter to Government of Arunachal Pradesh vide No. U-13024/5/73-AP dated November 9, 1976 (National Archives of India)
90. MHA letter No. U.13024/5/73-AP to the Secretary of the Lt. Governor, Government of Arunachal Pradesh on July 15, 1977 (National Archives of India)
91. MHA letter No. U.13024/5/73-AP to the Secretary of the Lt. Governor, Government of Arunachal Pradesh on July 15, 1977 (National Archives of India)
92. MHA letter to Govt. of Arunachal Pradesh vide No. 13024/5/73-AP on various dates. National Archives of India
93. MHA Letters to Chief Secretary, Govt. of AP vide Do. No. 13024/5/73-AP on various dates. National Archives of India
94. Letter of the Chief Minister of Arunachal Pradesh to the Home Minister of India vide D.O. No. CM/AP/R/80 on April 22, 1980 (MHA File No. 13024/5/73 AP Vol. III), National Archives of India

95. Home Minister's letter D.O. No. 13024/5/73-AP.II on July 19, 1980 to the Chief Minister of Arunachal Pradesh (MHA File No. 13024/5/73 AP Vol. III), National Archives of India
96. Director of Rehabilitation, AP letter No. DRS/SSSA/36/80 on August 19, 1980, to Ministry of Supply and Rehabilitation (MHA File No. 13024/5/73 AP Vol. III), National Archives of India
97. MHA letter D.O No. 12/1/80-Desk.IV dated October 24, 1980 to Govt. of Arunachal Pradesh
98. MHA letter D.O. No.13024/5/73-AP on November 24, 1980, to the Ministry of Rehabilitation
99. Private Member's Resolution of Arunachal Pradesh Legislative Assembly on September 23, 1980
100. Ministry of Rehabilitation Letter No. 12/1/80-Desk.IV dated February 12, 1981 to the Govt. of Arunachal Pradesh (MHA File No. 13024/5/73 AP Vol. III), National Archives of India
101. Director of Rehabilitation, AP letter to Ministry of Supply and Rehabilitation & MHA vide No. DRS/SSSA/36/80 dated February 25, 1981 (MHA File No. 13024/5/73 AP Vol. III), National Archives of India
102. IB's opinion on the matter of grant of citizenship vide Letter No. 34/0/80(20)-823 dated March 7, 1981, to MHA (MHA File No. 13024/5/73 AP Vol. III), National Archives of India
103. MHA Letter No. 13024/5/83-AP the to Lt. Governor of Arunachal Pradesh on 15.10.1981 (MHA File No. 13024/5/73 AP Vol. III), National Archives of India
104. Ministry of Rehabilitation Letter D.O. No. 12/1/80-Desk IV dated January 16, 1982 (MHA File No. 13024/5/73 AP Vol. III), National Archives of India
105. Minutes of the Meeting held in the Residential Office of the CM, Arunachal Pradesh on 16.02.1982 (MHA File No. 13024/5/73 AP Vol. III), National Archives of India

106. Letter D.O. No. Pol.236/72 dated May 3, 1982 of the Lieutenant Governor of Arunachal Pradesh to the Ministry of Home Affairs (MHA File No. 13024/5/73 AP Vol. III), National Archives of India
107. The Chief Minister, AP letter D.O. No. CM(AP)/9/82 to the Prime Minister on August 14, 1982 (MHA File No. 13024/5/73 AP Vol. III), National Archives of India
108. PMO letter to CS, Govt. of AP vide letter No. 25(261)/82-PM on August 25, 1982 (MHA File No. 13024/5/73 AP Vol. III), National Archives of India
109. MHA UO No.13024/5/73-AP(Vol.III) to PMO on September 13, 1982 (MHA File No. 13024/5/73 AP Vol. III), National Archives of India
110. Arunachal Pradesh Government Letter No. POL. 236/72 on July 31, 1984, to MHA (MHA File No. 13024/5/73 AP Vol. III), National Archives of India
111. Upgradation of Changlang Sub-Division into a full-fledged District, Ministry of Home Affairs, File No. 14/5/86-AP
112. MHA Letter D.O. No. 26011/07/87-IC.I. to PMO on July 31, 1987 (MHA File No. 13024/5/73 AP Vol. III), National Archives of India
113. Student Movements in Arunachal Pradesh: S. Dutta (ISBN-81-86393-17-X)
114. https://villageinfo.in/arunachal-pradesh/changlang.html
115. Census of India 1971, Series No. 24, Arunachal Pradesh, Part X, District Census Handbook Tirap District
116. Census of India 1981, Series No. 25, Arunachal Pradesh, Part xii A & B, District Census Handbook Tirap District
117. Census of India 1991, Series - 3, Arunachal Pradesh, Part xii A & B, District Census Handbook Changlang District

118. Census of India 2001, Series - 13, Arunachal Pradesh, Part A & B, District Census Handbook Changlang District

119. Census of India 2011, Series - 13, Arunachal Pradesh, Part xii-A, District Census Handbook Changlang District

120. Census of India 2011, Arunachal Pradesh Series-13 Part XII-A, District Census Handbook Lohit

121. Census of India 2011, Arunachal Pradesh Series-13 Part XII-A, District Census Handbook Papumpare

122. https://crdo.chakma.in/issues/state-policy/2020/dispelling-thc-myth-of-chakma-hajong-population-explosion-in-ap/

123. https://arunachaltimes.in/index.php/2021/08/25/union-against-scholarship-to-chakma-students/

124. https://appsc.gov.in/Index/institute_home/ins/RECINS001

125. https://www.ticijournals.org/chakma-society-at-the-crossroads-unravelling-realities-of-chakma-youths-from-arunachal-pradesh/

126. https://thefederal.com/category/the-eighth-column/bhonti-culture-how-minor-girls-from-assam-are-sold-into-slavery-in-arunachal-pradesh-98342?infinitescroll=1

127. Letter from the JAC of Chakma & Hajong CBOs/NGOs to the Prime Minister of India dated January 3, 2022

128. From India to India by Prof. Nani Bath, ISBN: 978-93-5741-776-1

129. https://arunachaltimes.in/index.php/2021/08/17/arunachal-union-govt-to-resolve-chakma-hajong-issue-cm/

130. https://www.sentinelassam.com/north-east-india-news/arunachal-news/aapsu-welcomes-cm-pema-khandus-statement-on-relocation-of-chakma-hajong-551907

131. https://northeastlivetv.com/topnews/chakma-hajong-arunachal-pradesh/
132. https://www.sentinelassam.com/north-east-india-news/arunachal-news/chakma-and-hajong-refugees-cant-settle-permanently-in-arunachal-pradesh-says-union-minister-kiren-rijiju-645258
133. https://www.deccanherald.com/india/arunachal-pradesh/bjp-rakes-up-chakma-hajong-issue-ahead-of-polls-in-arunachal-pradesh-slammed-by-group-2953037
134. https://www.business-standard.com/india-news/no-talks-with-centre-on-relocating-chakma-hajong-refugees-in-state-cm-124042300535_1.html

ABOUT THE AUTHOR

Arunjit Kambey Chakma is a passionate social activist dedicated to championing the rights of the Chakma people in Arunachal Pradesh. Hailing from Diyun, Arunachal Pradesh, he holds a master's degree in English.

A seasoned advocate for rights, Arunjit has been at the forefront of the Chakma community's struggle for justice, serving in leadership roles within organizations such as the Arunachal Pradesh Chakma Students Union (APCSU), Chakma National Council of India (CNCI-AP), and Chakma Rights and Development Organization (CRDO).

In a bold step towards making a tangible impact, Arunjit relinquished a promising corporate career in Delhi in 2013. Driven by a deep-rooted commitment to his community, he returned to his roots to work tirelessly for the welfare of the Chakma people. His inspiring journey serves as a beacon for young, talented individuals, encouraging them to contribute to societal change from the grassroots.

www.ingramcontent.com/pod-product-compliance
Lightning Source LLC
LaVergne TN
LVHW021146160826
845679LV00024B/2069

* 9 7 9 8 8 9 5 1 9 3 8 1 5 *